JOSHUA TO CHRONICLES

JOSHUA TO CHRONICLES:
AN INTRODUCTION

Antony F. Campbell, SJ

Westminster John Knox Press
LOUISVILLE • LONDON

Book design by Sharon Adams
Cover design by Mark Abrams

First edition
Published by Westminster John Knox Press
Louisville, Kentucky

This book is printed on acid-free paper that meets the American National Standards Institute Z39.48 standard. ∞

PRINTED IN THE UNITED STATES OF AMERICA

04 05 06 07 08 09 10 11 12 13 — 10 9 8 7 6 5 4 3 2 1

Library of Congress Cataloging-in-Publication Data

Campbell, Antony F.
    Joshua to Chronicles : an introduction / Antony F. Campbell.
        p. cm.
    Includes bibliographical references and index.
    ISBN 0-664-25751-8 (alk. paper)
    1. Bible. O.T. Joshua—Criticism, interpretation, etc. 2. Bible. O.T. Judges—Criticism, interpretation, etc. 3. Bible. O.T. Ruth—Criticism, interpretation, etc. 4. Bible. O.T. Samuel—Criticism, interpretation, etc. 5. Bible. O.T. Kings—Criticism, interpretation, etc. 6. Bible. D. T. Chronicles—Criticism, interpretation, etc. I. Title.

    BS1295.52C36 2004
    222'.061—dc22

                                                        2003061154

For the faith
that offers meaning
and withholds certainty

Contents

Abbreviations

AASF(B)	Annales Academiae Scientiarum Fennicae, Series B
AB	Anchor Bible
ABD	*Anchor Bible Dictionary*. Edited by D. N. Freedman. 6 vols. New York, 1992
AnBib	Analecta biblica
ANET	*Ancient Near Eastern Texts Relating to the Old Testament*. Edited by J. B. Pritchard. 3d ed. Princeton, 1969
BBB	Bonner biblische Beiträge
BBET	Beiträge zur biblischen Exegese und Theologie
Bib	*Biblica*
BibInt	*Biblical Interpretation*
BJS	Brown Judaic Studies
BKAT	Biblischer Kommentar, Altes Testament. Edited by M. Noth and H. W. Wolff
CBC	Cambridge Bible Commentary
CBQMS	Catholic Biblical Quarterly Monograph Series
Comm.	Commentary
FOTL	Forms of the Old Testament Literature
FRLANT	Forschungen zur Religion und Literatur des Alten und Neuen Testaments
HAT	Handbuch zum Alten Testament
HSM	Harvard Semitic Monographs
ICC	International Critical Commentary

JBL	*Journal of Biblical Literature*
JHNES	Johns Hopkins Near Eastern Studies
JPSV	Jewish Publication Society Version (1955)
JSOT	*Journal for the Study of the Old Testament*
JSOTSup	Journal for the Study of the Old Testament: Supplement Series
KAT	Kommentar zum Alten Testament
LXX	Septuagint (Greek)
MT	Masoretic Text (Hebrew)
NCB	New Century Bible
NJPS	New Jewish Publication Society Version (1985)
NRSV	New Revised Standard Version
OBO	Orbis biblicus et orientalis
OBT	Overtures to Biblical Theology
OG	Old Greek
OTG	Old Testament Guides
OTL	Old Testament Library
OTS	Old Testament Studies
RB	*Revue biblique*
SBLDS	Society of Biblical Literature Dissertation Series
SBT	Studies in Biblical Theology
SOTSMS	Society for Old Testament Studies Monograph Series
VT	*Vetus Testamentum*
WBC	Word Biblical Commentary
WMANT	Wissenschaftliche Monographien zum Alten und Neuen Testament
ZAW	*Zeitschrift für die alttestamentliche Wissenschaft*

Introduction

THE NEED FOR INTERPRETATION

Interpreting Scripture has a lot in common with getting to know family. We can think we know people who are close family members quite well, then we discover that our knowledge is limited to a much smaller area than we thought—even for close family. Where more distant family members are concerned, we may be aware that we know only a little and with delight we come to discover how much more there is to know and how remarkably and surprisingly rich their lives are—or that they are perhaps even worse than we might have feared. The Scriptures can be like that. What is close to us we may think we know well, but there is so much more to discover; what is more distant we can be delighted to know better, or in all honesty prefer to have left unknown.

When we come to learn the art of interpretation, there are a number of tasks that challenge us. It would be easy enough to talk about the various disciplines traditionally involved (such as text criticism, source criticism, form criticism, tradition criticism, redaction criticism, and so on). It would be easy enough to talk about the need for knowledge of archaeology and geography and ancient history and ancient languages and all that. More recently, new approaches would need to be taken into account—for example, canonical, feminist, historical, literary, narrative, poststructuralist, reader-response, rhetorical, social-scientific, socioeconomic, structural, and so forth. Important as all these are—and they all have their role to play—there are things that are more important if our interpretation of the Scriptures is going to have full meaning for us.

1

Just as we may need to get to know members of the family from the inside, so we need to get to know the Scriptures from the inside. It is important to have a sense of where people are coming from—origins, birthplaces, grandparents, the determining emotional experiences. It is vital to have a sense of where the Scriptures are coming from, whether from above or from below, or from some sort of mix of both. For some, the Scriptures are like the new Jerusalem, "coming down out of heaven from God" (Rev 21:2). For others, the Scriptures grow up from within the community like the mustard seed that "becomes the greatest of all shrubs" (Mark 4:32). For others again, there is a subtle mixture of "above" and "below" that is not easily identified. No decision is more important for an interpreter of the Scriptures. No one can make this decision for another; each interpreter must read the Scriptures, within their tradition, and reach that decision from their encounter with the Scriptures themselves. Empirical observation suggests that believers operate within the parameters of their traditions and their churches; an individual decision is not a retreat into individualism but an individual's appropriation and integration of that faith to which they commit themselves.

For members of the Jewish and Christian families, the Bible is at the foundation of their faith. Decisions about it are not to be taken lightly. Without knowing anything more than the place of dignity which a member holds in the family, one can accept such a family member's authority. Without ever exhausting the mystery of a person, one can be admitted to an intimacy of knowledge from which acceptance of authority flows. So it is with the Scriptures. Where faith is robust, owned from "the inside," sacred texts can be explored with respect and without timidity; where faith is more fragile, outer directed and not owned, sacred texts are more likely to be treated with respect and awe—but are not to be explored.

Generation gaps exist within families, and reaching out across such gaps can demand an enormous amount of effort and energy. The "generation gap" between ourselves and the Scriptures is a yawning chasm, but it cries out to be crossed. We live in a world of widespread education, modern medicine, engines of all sorts and electricity in all shapes, transistors and travel, and above all immediate and mass communications. How does a traveler from New Zealand answer an urchin in Palestine who asks, "From what village are you?" This one answered, "My village is very far away." The gap between us was not crossed. In the world of the Scriptures, education was the privilege of a few, medicine was minimal, energy came from body or beast, travel was no faster than a camel, and most communication was the responsibility of royal emissaries or centered on the marketplace and the trade routes. An enormous leap of imagination is required of today's reader to realize how utterly other was the world of the Scriptures.

Such a leap is required to enter so different a world and discover whether it was primitive by comparison with ours, or very different but just as deep. Anthropologists can tell us "primitive" is an inappropriate word to use of cultures that are deeply different from our own. It is only when fuller awareness has led to intimacy that we can experience the truth of what those anthropologists mean. Most students and readers today, while they may regard the Scriptures as sacred, harbor the conviction that they come from a culture that was primitive by comparison with ours.

Only when we encounter in the Scriptures the thoughtful writing of men and women facing the same problems we in our deeper moments face do we realize that across the yawning gap between our cultures there extends a shared humanity that can surprise us. Opinion has it that unbelief—or better, belief in a world without God—was less common in ancient Israel than in much of modern society. Perhaps. Deep cynicism and skepticism were certainly around in ancient Israel. The prophet spoke, and doubters scoffed, "Let him make haste, let him speed his work that we may see it; let the plan of the Holy One of Israel hasten to fulfillment, that we may know it!" (Isa 5:19). It shows little respect for the prophet or for God. The quest for meaning in life was acute. For Abraham and Israel, a destiny: to be source of blessing "for all the families of the earth" (Gen 12:3; also 26:4 and 28:14). For Qohelet, a question: "What do people gain from all the toil at which they toil under the sun?" (Qoh 1:3). For Job, a complaint: "Why is light given to one in misery, and life to the bitter in soul?" (Job 3:20). For the psalmist, wonderment:

> When I look at your heavens, the work of your fingers,
>   the moon and the stars that you have established;
> what are human beings that you are mindful of them,
>   mortals that you care for them?
>
> (Ps 8:3–4)

Calculated injustice in society was something Israel experienced all too often; it was roundly condemned by Israel's prophets:

> Alas for those who devise wickedness
>   and evil deeds on their beds!
> When the morning dawns, they perform it,
>   because it is in their power.
> They covet fields, and seize them;

> houses, and take them away;
> they oppress householder and house,
> people and their inheritance.
> (Mic 2:1–2)

The potential for disillusion among those who based their lives on faith
was present in Israel, and the mystery of God's presence was equally
part of Israel's experience. Both were remembered in relation to one of
Israel's archetypal prophetic figures:

> Then he [Elijah] was afraid; he got up and fled for his life. . . . He asked
> that he might die: "It is enough; now, O LORD, take away my life, for
> I am no better than my ancestors." (1 Kgs 19:3–4)

> But the LORD was not in the wind; and after the wind an earthquake,
> but the LORD was not in the earthquake; and after the earthquake a
> fire, but the LORD was not in the fire; and after the fire a sound of
> sheer silence. When Elijah heard it, he wrapped his face in his mantle
> and went out and stood at the entrance of the cave. (1 Kgs 19:11–13)

The mystery of human sinfulness and divine forbearance puzzled Israel
often. "I will never again curse the ground because of humankind, for
the inclination of the human heart is evil from youth" (Gen 8:21; cf.
Exod 32:7–14 and Num 14:11–25).

The fundamental struggle to come to grips with the experience of
life in relationship with God is on almost every page of the Older Testament. Almost every question that can be raised is raised. Almost every
answer that can be given is given—and some of those answers then are
as naive and unsatisfactory as are some of those offered today. Those
who want assurance and comfort will find them. Those who want questions and challenges will find them. Far from having little in common
with a society that is utterly other than our own, we find the shared
issues of human existence demanding thought and reflection then as
now. It is never easy to put words on the great issues and questions of
faith. It is folly to think that the generations of ancient Israel did not
grapple with these issues as deeply as we are invited to.

We have texts available to us on bookshelves, in libraries, on computers. They did not. Texts were almost certainly accessible to a few at
the temple; probably to equally few at royal courts; possibly also in the
libraries of establishment families (e.g., the house of Shaphan in Jerusalem). We use concordances and computers. They did not. We may
indulge in hermeneutical sophistication. They did not use such language. They had time to think and think deeply. Often we do not, for
we live in pressured times.

For one last time, we may look again at the analogy of encounter with another person. Some of us are content to know most people on a surface level. We take them at face value, as they present themselves or as they are presented to us. We do not ask questions, we do not explore motivation. What we see is what we get. For many, this is how they approach the Scriptures. They take the Scriptures at face value, as they have been presented to them. They find in their Scriptures much that is affirming of their faith and nourishing for their lives.

Some of us with some people need to go beyond the surface that is presented and get under the skin, get in closer touch with the inner person. Whether for ourselves or for others, we need to know what makes a person tick, what past influences shape their present, what emotions or needs drive or draw them, what motivations are at work in what they do. For some of us, this is how we approach the Scriptures. We notice details of language and behavior and we wonder what is going on. We need to explore what past experiences may have left their trace in the shape of the Scriptures. We try to get under the skin of the Scriptures and run the risk of being fascinated or repelled by what we find.

If we are wise, we extend a tolerance to each other in society; it takes all sorts. If we are wise, we extend an equal tolerance to each other in faith communities; there too it takes all sorts. A community of faith that gives away its foundations will lose its core. A community of faith that is afraid to explore its core runs the risk of discovering one day that its foundations have been irreparably eroded.

INTERPRETING JOSHUA TO KINGS

There is no doubt that Israel is portrayed as a migrant people: "A wandering Aramean [i.e., Jacob] was my ancestor" (Deut 26:5). Israel's ancestors were portrayed coming originally from the great civilizations of the Mesopotamian river valleys. Famine forced them into Egypt, the civilization of the Nile valley. In Egypt they claimed to have become a people (Exod 1:7–9). The movement from Egypt to the Jordan valley is the work of one generation, the Mosaic generation. Moses is born at the start of Exodus; he dies at the end of Deuteronomy, within sight of the promised land, but outside it.

These first five books of Israel's Scriptures (Genesis, Exodus, Leviticus, Numbers, and Deuteronomy) form the Pentateuch, the revered Torah. Alas, despite all the reverence that may be evinced, for many they are "boring old books." Except for the utterly dedicated, most

Bible readers I know have not followed Exodus past chapter 25, find Leviticus off-putting, and have been prevented by the beginning and end of Numbers from ever looking at the middle. For some, Genesis to Deuteronomy is the epic of Israel's origins, supplemented with priestly laws and lore. An ancient epic of origins hardly does justice to these traditions. True, they contain stories of Israel's forebears—Abraham and Sarah, Isaac and Rebekah, Jacob with Leah and Rachel, even Joseph. True, the Mosaic generation is there, from Egypt to the desert edge. But an epic of Israel's origins the Pentateuch is not.

Another description sounds unlikely, but may be closer to the mark: The Pentateuch is a collection of the traditions, laws, and lore of Israel that constitute and define its identity. Israel is the people of Abraham, the descendants of Jacob/Israel, their ancestors. Israel is the people brought out of Egypt under Moses' leadership, who met with God at Sinai, who under Moses' leadership was brought to the edge of the land they believed theirs, by the promise of God to their forebears. Almost nothing of major significance in the life or theological thought of later Israel has not somehow been explored in this Pentateuchal collection. The Pentateuch may be thought of as the originating myth of ancient Israel—where an originating myth is the account that myth makers caused to be believed as to what constituted it as a people, giving them identity and destiny, their place and role in the world.

In the Christian version of the biblical canon, Joshua, Judges, Samuel, and Kings are referred to as the historical books; in the Jewish version, they are referred to as the former prophets. Neither term is really right. Prophets loom large in Samuel and Kings, but not in Joshua and Judges; history is a background to these books, but they are more theological than historical. In our lives, we realize that experience needs interpretation—meaning to be made and words found to express it. Experience of God often needs theological interpretation. It is true that "historians write because they have convictions about the past and present and want to communicate their beliefs" (Nelson 1998, 21); it is also true that not all that is written about the past is to be termed "history." Memoirs, for example, may be a source for historians, but many do not qualify as history. Potential sources for history must not be confused with the history written from them. The so-called historical books may "fall short of our standards for history writing" (Nelson 1998, 27); it may be that their aim is not the writing of history. Mills speaks of "two ways of evaluating the text, as history and as theology" (Mills 1999, 2). Much reflection is needed, and no simple answer should satisfy.

The books of Joshua through Kings deal with the period from

Israel's occupation of Canaan to Israel's final exile from that land in the early sixth century B.C.E., covering a period of some seven centuries. They do not present a history of those centuries; there are too many gaps and too much contradiction within the books for that. What these books enshrine in historical sequence are the texts in which thinkers within Israel sought to interpret the people's experience. Israel moved into a land. Israel tried living in the land without central government. Israel had the experience of the emergence of central government (kingship). Israel had the grim experience of being overwhelmed by more powerful nations, with an Assyrian exile putting an end to the northern kingdom and a Babylonian exile ending the southern kingdom. These are major experiences for any people. For a people who believed themselves chosen by God, these experiences demanded interpretation. The texts of Joshua–Kings preserve some of the interpretations. As reading will reveal, these are not the official interpretations authorized by ancient Israel; for many experiences, there is more than one interpretation and they are not always compatible. What the books offer us are the texts that Israel in due course recognized as its canonical Scriptures and the interpretations of experience to be found in those texts.

The movement of any migrant group is from danger to safety, from insecurity to security, from landlessness to ownership and belonging—in Israel's case from Tent to Temple. A migrant family looks for property to possess; a migrant people looks for land to occupy as their own, promising opportunity for their children. Migrants must determine how they will live, what weight they will give to the customs of the old country and what they must observe within the new (or, if one subscribes to the theory that Israel emerged from within Canaan: for "old country" and "new," read "old situation" and "new"). A migrant people in a new land or a people newly established in a new situation must determine what political and social structures will best enable them to defend themselves and prosper.

These are the issues for Israel addressed in the books of Joshua, Judges, Samuel, and Kings. As migrants newly arrived in Palestine, returning to the land of their forebears' sojourning, they sought to stake out the territory as their own. So the book of Joshua.

They struggled to find behaviors that enabled them to keep the old ways and find new prosperity in this new land—and they failed. The book of Judges places a pattern on their behavior, on their experience of God, and allows the pattern to dissolve into the ultimate deterioration of social order within the people.

With the books of Samuel and Kings a new phenomenon emerges. Prophets establish the monarchy as a unifying force to give the nation defensive capability and political unity. Under David, it works. Under Solomon, it survives. The task of Israel's thinkers and writers is to show how, despite this start, the nation fails to survive. With Solomon, the seeds of destruction are sown. Builder of the temple, Solomon is given God's promise but also an ominous warning (1 Kgs 9:1–9). With Solomon's apostasy, all the weight of this warning will fall on his son's generation (11:1–13). Solomon's kingdom is divided between Rehoboam, his son who reigns over Judah and maybe Benjamin, and Jeroboam, designated by God's prophet to be king over ten tribes (1 Kgs 11:26–40). No sooner is Jeroboam in power than he acts in ways that seal the fate of the northern kingdom (1 Kgs 12:25–33). No sooner have strong rulers been established in power in united Israel than the trajectory leading to the end of Israel as an independent nation-state is in view.

The task that the biblical text sets itself in bringing together the traditions of Joshua through Kings is to catalogue much of the factual background to the disaster, to trace the patterns that are discernible, to look for understanding in the faith of Israel, and to place before Israel the theological dilemma of its being a people that began with such high hopes and ended with those hopes dashed so swiftly and shatteringly. The hopes had every reason to be high—Israel's destiny was from God, its promises were sworn by God, its guidance came from God. Its end was to be swallowed up by the imperial powers of Assyria and Babylon—whose aggression Israel's theologians named as the action of Israel's God.

This is the task the biblical text has set itself. The task that we undertake here as its interpreters is to seek out the understanding of the text and its message (as in the previous paragraph), to explore how the text contains this message, how it communicates it, and what is offered as its validation. A further task I undertake here, in relation to Samuel–Kings, is to provide a comparison with Chronicles. All too often, 1–2 Chronicles are treated as a parallel and pious version of Samuel–Kings. In my judgment, that is not the case. Chronicles, beginning at creation and concluding at the end of the exile with Cyrus's decree for the rebuilding of the temple in Jerusalem, is, I believe, best understood as a story of the temple. Comparison with Samuel and Kings will show this.

As students of the Bible today we need to explore its nature, our need for it, and our use of it. For people of Judeo-Christian faith, it is "the word of God." What precisely that means and how precisely God speaks in this word has to be discovered by exploring this Scripture. That is how we discover its nature. The nature of the word speaks to us about the nature of the speaker. We have a need for the word. Like the rest of our needs, if we do not understand this need, we will remain unaware of it and it will influence our thinking and our behavior. The use we make of the word has to respect its nature and also has to honestly meet our need. Exploration and interpretation are no small tasks.

Use will involve recognition of several centuries of historical-critical study. The importance of such study is not so much to recover Israel's history, whether the history of the people, or the history of their literature, their religion, or their social institutions. Rather, historical-critical study is of immense importance for its revelation of the nature of the biblical text. So important is this task, we need to repeat it for ourselves in each generation. At the same time, we recognize biblical literature as great literature, part of the Judeo-Christian world's literary heritage. One of the tasks that lies before each generation is to broker some form of successful marriage between these two realms of study: the historical-critical and the literary. Where honesty is absent, the marriage will fail. Given the evident correctness at the core of both approaches, critical work will be obliged to disqualify its own results if they prove to be incompatible with literary study. Equally, a literary approach cannot advocate results that are incompatible with the achievements of critical study. Neither can be dismissive of the other.

Many studies of these so-called historical books are devoted to identifying traces of "possible," or "probable," or—usually worse still—"doubtless" historical value that is "genuine," "authentic," or "certainly old." Robert Boling writes of "our passion for dating" (Boling, comm., 224). It is a passion that I do not share here. Nor is this book concerned to back up faith with facts. The Bible does not witness to such a concern. The Bible affirms faith and calls for faith; it seldom appeals to facts to turn faith into knowledge. The Bible gathers together too many tensions to be involved with backing up faith by fact. It amalgamates traditions; it seldom adjudicates between them. These biblical texts have evolved from Israel's struggle to articulate its destiny, its faith, and the meaning of its life as a people of God. The purpose of this book is to scrutinize that articulation, to seek to understand it, to be open to learning from it.

It would be neither honest nor wise to ignore the human effort that has gone into producing the Scriptures. The traces of that human effort are present in the text, and biblical scholarship for a century or two has placed those traces under intense scrutiny. The human effort at the origins of the Scriptures is evident and should not be denied. It would be neither honest nor wise to ignore the human need for the Scriptures in some of today's great communities of faith. The need in church, synagogue, and beyond is there and demands to be met. The challenge we face today is to meet today's need with an honesty and integrity that does not directly or indirectly deny the nature of Scripture and that does not cripple Scripture's capacity to meet today's needs.

At the origins of the Scriptures, faith is entitled to claim the presence and activity of the spirit of God, bringing about awareness and self-revelation. What faith will not encounter in the Scriptures is the evident and unmediated revelation of God. God is not demonstrated or proved without need for faith; biblically, God is discerned within faith.

Such central themes as creation and salvation offer good examples of what I mean. The Scriptures witness strongly to faith that God created the world; they provide such different and manifold portrayals of creation that it is evident the Scriptures cannot claim to know how God created the world (e.g., Gen 1:1–2:4a; Gen 2:4b–25; Job 26 and 38; Pss 74 and 104; Prov 8:22–31; Isa 51:9–10). Faith believes that God is creator; faith does not know, nor need to know, how God created.

Israel's deliverance from the armed force of Egypt at the Sea of Reeds is a celebrated instance of God's saving power. In the biblical text rehearsing this deliverance (Exod 13:17–14:31), traditions are combined that do not allow us to know what happened; they allow us only to believe that God delivered. According to one tradition, in this text, the Israelites were told to stay still, to allow God to fight for them, and they did not cross the Sea—probably because they were already on the other side of it. "The LORD will fight for you, and you have only to keep still" (Exod 14:14). According to another tradition, Israel was told to go into the sea on dry land, with the waters forming a wall for them on their right and on their left. "Stretch out your hand over the sea and divide it, that the Israelites may go into the sea on dry ground" (Exod 14:16). Both traditions are combined in a single text to proclaim faith in God's deliverance of Israel. "The people feared the LORD and believed in the LORD and in his servant Moses" (Exod 14:31; for fuller details, see Campbell and O'Brien 1993, 238–54). The combined text does not allow us to know how that deliverance was achieved. Faith believes that God delivered Israel; faith does not know, and knows it does not know, how God achieved that deliverance.

These two examples are paradigms of much that is in Scripture. Faith discerns the presence and activity of God—sometimes rightly, sometimes not. Faith is not given access to evident and unmediated knowledge of God.

This need to discern the presence and activity of God calls for a deeply reflective approach. This book does not attempt to recover from its texts the history of the period. The biblical books from Joshua through Kings may come to us under the guise of history; they appear to give an account of their people's past. On closer inspection, I believe they are better understood as a reflection on their people's experience. Israel found itself in the land (Joshua); there was a period before kings came on the scene (Judges); there was the emergence of kingship (Samuel); there was the ultimate failure of the monarchy to survive (Kings). The texts are attempts at the interpretation of these experiences. They invite reflection. This book is written in the belief that it does not do honor to God to "call evil good and good evil" (Isa 5:20). Job's "Will you speak falsely for God, and speak deceitfully for him?" (Job 13:7) should not be a charge leveled against interpreters of Joshua through Kings. Reflection is called for. There is much that I believe cannot be called good in Joshua and in Judges. The gap between the expression of God's will and its realization in human affairs is one of the elements inviting reflection in Samuel and Kings, as is the ultimate failure of the people of Israel under their kings. Reflection is called for at many points. The invitation to think is constantly extended.

FUNDAMENTALISM AND FAITH

Fundamentalism is a complex phenomenon in the history of religious tradition. Fundamentalism often reflects a particular quality of faith: It claims to believe what runs counter to the usual canons of human knowledge. Underpinning this faith and even more central to the fundamentalist drive may be the need for certainty. Certainty about a position is normally a quality of knowledge, not of faith. Scientists, at their best, are often committed to faith rather than knowledge. Evolution and quantum mechanics, for example, place enormous demands on the human capacity for belief. Scientists committed to evolution or to quantum physics know that these are hypotheses that account for much observation or experiential data. Evolutionists and quantum physicists believe that these hypotheses are the best we have at present, so they use them and believe them. They would not claim certainty, only a high degree of probability; at most, certainty would have to be qualified "in the light of our present knowledge."

To all appearances, fundamentalists seem to need certainty. Middle-ground religious faith accepts a degree of doubt. Theist faith cannot escape the whisper, "Perhaps there is no God"; atheist faith cannot escape the whisper, "Perhaps there is a God." Fundamentalist faith—uncomfortable with the uncertainty inherent in belief—seeks to escape this doubt by belief in certainty. (For a full description and discussion of fundamentalism, without entering into the personal needs under-pinning much fundamentalist belief [despite a reference to "the absolute and overweening certainty possessed by fundamentalists," 338], see Barr 1981.)

Faith in God is too important a matter to be shored up by muddled thinking and veiled dishonesty (cf. Job 13:7). This conviction should be the drive that motivates critical study of these books of the Bible.

STRUCTURE OF THIS BOOK

Diamonds need a setting; so do details. The approach to each of the biblical books here will take this into account, with a general overview before the more detailed study involved in reading the sections of the book; toward the end, there will be a review, reading the whole, in which some of the impact of the interpretation may be digested. The sections for detailed discussion will be determined primarily by the sense-units of the text rather than by the division into chapters and verses. That division, done over centuries, largely follows the sense of the text; but, on occasion, it may have been done with a view to other purposes or different interpretations (cf. Tov 1992, 50–53). At the end of each book, a few issues for review are offered as points of departure for reflection on what has been explored in interpreting the book.

AVOWAL

What need do I have for the Bible? Through critical study, I have dis-covered a high level of intelligence at work in the Bible's production; I need that. I have discovered a divine interaction with our world not too different from what I experience today; I need that. I have discovered statements about life and faith and people and God that express what I do believe and want to believe; that too I need. There is much more. Appallingly arrogant as it may sound, I discover in the Bible a God I can live with. I am profoundly uneasy with the God of the fundamen-talists and the fanatics. The God I discover in the Bible I can live with, I can love, I can believe loves me. I need that.

ACKNOWLEDGMENTS

At Westminster John Knox, my thanks to Jon Berquist who had the idea, and Stephanie Egnotovich who deftly brought it to completion.

NOTE

*The asterisk (*) used occasionally with verse numbers in this volume indicates that only the relevant parts of the verse or verses so marked is referred to. In other words, the asterisk (*) is a signal that a part or parts of the text involved is excluded from the reference.

Biblical references are given to the chapter and verse numbering of the Hebrew text and (where different) of the NRSV, thus covering the two sets of numbering in current use. Which set is employed by a given translation will be quickly recognized.

Books and articles will be referred to by author's name and date of publication; full details will be found in the bibliographies at the end of each chapter. Commentaries will be referred to by author's name followed by "comm."; full details are given at the end of the book.

Bibliography of works other than commentaries

Barr, James. 1981. *Fundamentalism*. 2d ed. London: SCM Press.

Campbell, Antony F., and Mark A. O'Brien. 1993. *Sources of the Pentateuch: Texts, Introductions, Annotations*. Minneapolis: Fortress.

Mills, Mary E. 1999. *Historical Israel: Biblical Israel. Studying Joshua to 2 Kings*. London: Cassell.

Nelson, Richard D. 1998. *The Historical Books*. Nashville: Abingdon.

Tov, Emanuel. 1992. *Textual Criticism of the Hebrew Bible*. Minneapolis: Fortress.

1

The Book of Joshua

OVERVIEW

A major task facing the interpreter of Joshua is what to make of the faith claims presented in the book. Is there any way in which they can be acceptable to a modern believer? If the faith claims are unacceptable, is there any value left for us in the book? Did Israel have the right to believe that God disposed of land in its favor that was already occupied by others? If such a claim was acceptable in times past, is it acceptable to us now? Did Israel have the right to believe that God had commanded it to utterly destroy all that breathed (cf. Josh 10:40; also 11:20)? Can we reject such belief and hold to faith without resorting to the facile and naive?

This is not the same thing as asking about the historical worth of the book. Largely under the influence of archaeology, older models—among them, conquest, peaceful infiltration, and peasant revolt—have been abandoned. A traditional archaeologist such as William Dever favors "indigenous origins" and/or "symbiosis" models, which are not compatible with the historical picture in the book of Joshua (cf. Dever 2001, 41, 267). The issue for interpreters of the text is the decisions to be taken about its meaning and the values enshrined in it, rather than the history behind it.

A recent book, *The Bible Unearthed* by Israel Finkelstein, a professional archaeologist, and Neil Asher Silberman, might have provided an up-to-date and balanced report of archaeology's results. To my regret, I find aspects disappointing. I had hoped for more archaeological detail and documentation; instead I found expressions of interpretation and belief (theirs). I think I had a right to expect a more academic and critical approach to the biblical text; instead I found sweeping portrayals that caricatured a past credulity. Perhaps too much should not be asked of a book clearly meant for the popular market. However, the complexity and multiplicity that I find in the biblical text of the Pentateuch and the Deuteronomistic History seems to me most unlikely to have emerged "during the span of two or three generations, about twenty-six hundred years ago" (Finkelstein and Silberman 2001, 1); this complexity and multiplicity fits most uncomfortably with the idea of later fiction. We are looking at a period longer than two or three generations; we have to find better and more sophisticated explanations.

A couple of quotations from Dever, hardly a radical liberal, will help clarify the picture emerging from present archaeological research. As to what must be discarded, he says,

> Today, on the basis of the evidence that Finkelstein and his colleagues have presented . . . , all archaeologists and virtually all biblical scholars have abandoned the older conquest model or even "peaceful infiltration" and peasants' revolt models, for "indigenous origin" and/or "symbiosis" models in attempting to explain the emergence of early Israel in Canaan. (Dever 2001, 41)

As to what is emerging as a new context for historical understanding, he says:

> Extensive surface surveys . . . , together with excavation in depth at a few sites, have revealed that in the heartland of ancient Israel about 300 small agricultural villages were founded *de novo* in the late 13th-12th centuries. . . . These villages are located principally in the central hill country, stretching all the way from the hills of lower Galilee as far south as the northern Negev around Beersheba. None are founded on the ruins of a destroyed Late Bronze Age site. . . . Such a dramatic "population explosion" simply cannot be accounted for by natural increase alone, much less by positing small groups of pastoral nomads settling down. Large numbers of people migrated here from somewhere else, strongly motivated to colonize an underpopulated fringe area of urban Canaan, now in decline at the end of the late Bronze Age. (Dever 2001, 110; for more on these origins, see Finkelstein and Silberman 2001, 101–20)

Not surprisingly, the book of Joshua is one of those books of the Older Testament that gets a particularly bad press. The walls of Jericho come tumbling down at a simple shout, which few find convincing; the local inhabitants are well and truly wiped out, leaving absolutely no survivors, which most find savage, beastly, and inhuman.

The bad reputation is a pity because Joshua offers several fascinating possibilities for theological thought. First, we can see two approaches to the life of faith, which can be summarized as: (a) rely on God for everything; (b) plan everything down to the last detail and, of course, rely on God. The early part of the book of Joshua reflects both approaches. Second, Joshua forces the question, if might is not right, what is? The extermination of the locals—which of course never happened but is all the same reported as commanded and done—makes that question unavoidable. Third, the combination of quite differently styled accounts of the allocation of the land is a good example of biblical composition, with all the issues which that raises.

The book of Joshua opens with the changing of the guard; Moses is dead and Joshua is in charge. His job: to put the people in possession of the land (1:6). There is an insistence on keeping the law of Moses in order to ensure success (1:8). The people are ordered to be ready to cross the Jordan in three days' time. The two and a half east-of-Jordan tribes are reminded of their commitment to the campaign. Their wives and children and flocks live on the other side of the Jordan (1:14). It is not easy to be sure but the impression given by this introductory chapter is that there is no more in view than the "possession" of the land, not looking beyond chapter 12; the land's allocation is mentioned in a phrase (11:23a), and its occupation is not mentioned at all. Later, after chapters recounting allocation to the tribes, Josh 21:43b has Israel take possession of the land and settle in it. Otherwise, oddly enough, Israel's occupation of the land (settling or living in it) is largely passed over in silence. It is scarcely a blatant silence, but it is a silence—and it is surprising.

To move beyond Josh 1 into Josh 2–12 with any security, a form-critical optic needs to be brought into play. Even relatively casual observation reveals a substantially narrative style in Josh 2:1–10:27, whereas in Josh 10:28–12:24 the style is list-like or summarizing rather than narrative. The substantial stylistic difference between 2:1–10:27 and 10:28–12:24 is clear and beyond dispute. The crossing of the Jordan (Josh 3–4) and the capture of Jericho (Josh 6) can be called narrative text, but determining how best to name the type of narrative is not easy. Joshua 5 has three brief narrative episodes that reflect the change from wilderness to settled land—concerning circumcision, Passover, and the commander of the army of the LORD; it is a brave interpreter who would describe them more specifically. The traditions about Ai, Gibeon, and the five-king coalition are standard narrative. On the other hand, Josh 10:28–41 clearly belongs in the list-like category. The account of the northern campaign (Josh 11:1–15), while list-like, is more accurately in a "summarizing" style. This description can be extended to 11:16–23. Joshua 12:1–24 is made up of two lists.

Within 2:1–10:27, spies view the land west of the Jordan (Josh 2), Israel crosses the Jordan (Josh 3–4), three episodes signal the end of the wilderness period (Josh 5), Israel captures Jericho (Josh 6), Israel makes a failed attempt to capture Ai (Josh 7) and a successful one (Josh 8), the people of Gibeon deceive the Israelites into making peace with them (Josh 9), and finally Israel is victorious against a coalition of five kings— the kings of Jerusalem, Hebron, Jarmuth, Lachish, and Eglon (Josh 10:1–27). A conclusion to these traditions can be found in 10:42–43. Anyone familiar with the geography of the area will recognize at once that these traditions cover a remarkably small territory. Jericho, Ai, and Gibeon are all located within a narrow strip of the land later allocated to Benjamin. The sorties are from the Jordan valley and appear to be based on Gilgal, near Jericho (cf. 10:15 or 10:43). The territory involved is far from extensive.

In 10:28–12:24, on the other hand, the territory involved is definitely extensive. List-like material in 10:28–41 covers a sweep of the south— Makkedah, Libnah, Lachish, Gezer, Eglon, Hebron, and Debir. After the battle in the north (Josh 11:1–9), Joshua and Israel are reported to have taken Hazor and the towns of the north. The concluding claims cover a wide extent of territory (cf. Josh 11:16–17) and possession is followed by allocation: "So Joshua took the whole land, according to all that the LORD had spoken to Moses; and Joshua gave it for an inheritance to Israel according to their tribal allotments" (11:23). Finally, two lists are provided of the defeated kings on the east and west of the Jordan—Og and Bashan in the east and a total of thirty-one in the west— indicating Israel's complete possession of the land.

The next major part of the book, Josh 13:1–22:34, is taken up with the issue of allocation of the land in detail. While Josh 11:23 gives this issue just a clause ("Joshua gave it for an inheritance to Israel according to their tribal allotments"), here it gets ten chapters. The blocks are easily identified: Chapter 13 deals mainly with the east-of-Jordan tribes; chapters 14–17 deal mainly with the allocation, at an unspecified location, to Judah (Josh 15) and Joseph (= Ephraim and Manasseh, Josh 16–17); chapters 18–19 deal with the allocation at Shiloh to the other seven tribes; in Josh 20 cities of refuge are established and in chapter 21 provision is made for the Levites. Finally, in Josh 22, the west-of-Jordan tribes (Reuben, Gad, and half of Manasseh) are dismissed and return home.

The book concludes with accounts of speeches by Joshua to two gatherings of all Israel, one at a place that is not named (23:2) and one at Shechem (24:1). The Shechem gathering is concluded with the establishment of a covenant and the dismissal of the people. The last few verses report Joshua's death and burial, the fidelity of Israel under his leadership and that of those who survived him, the burial of Joseph's bones at Shechem, and finally the death and burial of Eleazar son of Aaron.

This overview is summed up in the following outline.

THE POSSESSION AND ALLOCATION OF THE LAND	JOSHUA 1–24
I. Possession of the land	Josh 1–12
A. Introduction	chap. 1
B. Narrative style: the south	2:1–10:27 (42–43)
1. Soldierly focus	chap. 2; 6:1–2; 8; 9:3–27; 10:1–27, 42–43
2. Sacral focus	chaps. 3–4; 6:3–27; chap. 7
3. Neither soldierly nor sacral	chap. 5; 8:30–35; 9:1–2
C. Lists, list-like, and summarizing styles	10:28–12:24
1. List-like: the south	10:28–41
2. Summarizing: the north and the whole of the land	11:1–15, 16–23
3. Lists	12:1–24
II. Allocation of the land	chaps. 13–22
A. Predistribution: east of the Jordan	13:1–33
B. Distribution: west of the Jordan	chaps. 14–19
1. Part one	14–17
2. Part two	18–19
C. Postdistribution	chaps. 20–22
III. Conclusion	chaps. 23–24

God's speech transferring the leadership to Joshua and ordering Joshua to cross the Jordan and take the land is placed at the head of the book. It is important, therefore, to notice what is of substantial importance in the book that is not explicitly mentioned in God's speech. There is no reference to any distribution of the land by lot among the tribes. There is no emphasis on the participation of the east-of-Jordan tribes. There is no mention of the attitude to be taken to the local inhabitants. At this stage, at least, it is inappropriate to draw conclusions from these silences; it would be equally inappropriate not to note them.

MAJOR TEXT SIGNALS

The signals in the text for each section are discussed in their respective sections. At this point, it is important to look closely at the text signals that have a major effect on the book of Joshua as a whole. First, perhaps, the term "text signals" needs explanation. Interpretation should be controlled by the text that is being interpreted; alas, that is not always the case—but it should be. This control is exercised by attention to the presence of certain factors in the text, certain phenomena in the text; here I call them text signals. In close study of a text, such signals may be a change from first to third person or from singular to plural, and so forth. Where, as in the case of the "major text signals," a more extensive stretch of text is under examination, such signals will be features in the text that may be significant for its understanding. The basic understanding should be clear: Text signals are the features observed in a text that ought govern its interpretation.

1. The first major signal may come as a surprise because of its obviousness: The whole move of Israel into the land is placed under the aegis and authority of Moses. Joshua, Moses' assistant, had already been commissioned by Moses to take over command after his death (Deut 31:7–8; cf. 1:38). The figure of Moses is the measure against which Joshua is measured; the authority of Moses is the authority under which Joshua operates. God is reported saying to Joshua: "As I was with Moses, so I will be with you; I will not fail you or forsake you" (1:5; cf. Deut 31:8). Joshua is not the leader of Israel in his own right; he is the leader of Israel in Moses' place. This measure is reflected in 3:7 and 4:14: "The LORD exalted Joshua in the sight of all Israel; and they stood in awe of him, as they had stood in awe of Moses" (4:14). The summary verse toward the end of the first part of the book again returns to the figure of Moses: "So Joshua took the whole land, according to all that the LORD had spoken to Moses" (11:23).

2. A second major signal calls for subtle observation: Moses is hardly prominent in the originating traditions that are central to the book. In the first long narrative section, Josh 2:1–10:27, the exalta-

tion of Joshua to the level of Moses is referred to at 3:7 and 4:14 (where both passages could be editorial), 4:10 has a troublingly super-fluous reference to Moses (the LORD has already commanded Joshua), and 4:12 has an appropriate reference to the orders given by Moses in his lifetime. Four references occur in Josh 8:30–35 (vv. 31, 32, 33, 35), but the passage as a whole is rightly regarded as late. Finally, Josh 9:24 speaks of God's command to Moses in his lifetime. In the originating traditions, Moses is not prominent. Similarly, in the major section concerning the allocation of the land Moses is scarcely mentioned. He is appropriately credited with assigning land east of the Jordan (Josh 13; cf. 18:7), with the promise to Caleb (14:6–15), and with provision for the daughters of Zelophehad (17:4). The cities of refuge go back to Moses (20:2) as does the provision for the Levites (21:2, 8); the dismissal of the east-of-Jordan tribes involves their having fulfilled responsibilities specified by Moses (cf. 22:1–9). The traditions for the allocation of the land to the west-of-Jordan tribes are found in 14:1–19:51; apart from past provisions, Moses' authority is invoked only in the rather uncertain 14:2–5.

This observation suggests a difference between the originating tra-ditions and the later compositional activity responsible for the book regarding the importance of appeal to the authority of Moses.

3. A further signal in this regard relates to the status given Joshua. Early in the book, he is clearly placed on a par with Moses. This is evi-dent in Josh 1:1–6 and is given renewed emphasis in 3:7 and 4:14 (again, with both verses being possible expansions of the tradition). At the end of the traditions of Israel's taking possession of the land, Joshua is the sole leader, achieving all that God had promised Moses (Josh 11:23). In the latter part of the book, Joshua's role is reduced to membership in a committee responsible for the allocation of the land; in 14:1, responsi-bility for the distribution to Judah and Joseph is attributed to Eleazar the priest, Joshua son of Nun, and the heads of the families of the tribes. When the turn of the other seven tribes comes, Joshua is apparently the sole person responsible (cf. 18:1–19:50). However, when the distribu-tion of the land is reported as finished and a particular town has been allocated to Joshua himself (19:49–50), it is duly noted that the same committee—Eleazar, Joshua, and the family heads—was responsible for this distribution by lot at Shiloh (19:51). These differences reflect either a conflict of tradition or the adding of precision. The basic com-mittee is referred to also at 17:4 and 21:1. The tendency to downgrade Joshua's role that is evident in 14:1 and 19:51 is also explicit earlier in the book where a hierarchy or sequence of command is established: "As

the LORD had commanded his servant Moses, so Moses commanded Joshua, and so Joshua did" (11:15).

This suggests a difference regarding the role of Joshua between those responsible in the main for the earlier parts of the book and those responsible for the later parts. In the composition of the early part of the book, it was important to give prominence to Joshua and to see a unity in the leadership of Israel out of Egypt and into the promised land. The text emphasizes a fidelity that is special to the generation that "had known all the work that the LORD did for Israel" (Josh 24:31; cf. Judg 2:7, 10). For these editors, after Moses and Joshua there was no satisfactory succession to the leadership; after them, Israel fell apart, a victim of increasing anarchy. Monarchy might arrest the decline. For those responsible for the latter part of the book, the allocation of the land to the tribes, it is evident that Joshua's role was reduced to membership of the controlling committee—and Eleazar the priest is named first. The reasons for this are not spelled out.

4. The difference has been noted between narrative-style text in Josh 2:1–10:27 and list-like or summarizing text in Josh 10:28–12:24. The text signal is sent by the differing styles of the two sets of text. It is noteworthy that while extermination is present in 2:1–10:27, there is a positive obsession with it in 10:28–41 (cf. also 11:11a, 12, 14b). Our modern revulsion for ethnic cleansing must be handled with care, and we must ensure that ancient texts are assessed by the standards of their time. Nevertheless, these texts fare badly by any standards. The fact that such wholesale extermination did not happen and that Israel knew it did not happen (cf. Josh 23; Judg 2:1–5; 2:20–3:6) does not make the report of it and its attribution to divine command any more palatable.

If the references in Josh 23 to the remaining peoples and the dangers they posed are given weight, it is unlikely that the texts reporting this alleged full-scale extermination of the locals were integral to the book of Joshua at the time Josh 23 was composed.

5. A barely discernible signal in the text is given by a shift of emphasis in the LORD's orders to Joshua at the start of the book. The context shifts from military to moral. Joshua is first ordered to "be strong and courageous; for you shall put this people in possession of the land" (1:6)—clearly a military focus. Next, Joshua is ordered to "be strong and very courageous, being careful to act in accordance with all the law" (1:7)—more evidently a moral focus.

The shift is minor enough and acceptable enough that it could be passed over without further consequences, but for two observations: (1) several stereotyped phrases in verses 7–8 recur in Josh 23; (2) verse

9 provides an envelope structure integrating verses 7–9 into the divine speech. These signals have raised questions. The "book of the law" and the two infinitives associated with observing the law recur in 23:6. Not turning aside from the law, to right or left, is found in the book of Joshua only in 1:7 and 23:6 (cf. Deut 17:11, 20). The whole of Joshua's speech in chapter 23 addresses a radically different situation from that of Josh 1–12; it is possible that the passage in 1:7–9 is to be associated with Josh 23 (originally proposed in Smend 1971).

This observation allows for there to have been a possible revision of the book of Joshua at some stage, which drew attention to the importance of fidelity to God's law and prepared the way for the later attribution of the people's ultimate failure to their loss of faith-identity.

6. Comments on the next major text signal are relatively tentative; they are based on cumulative observations rather than on any single decisive instance. A variety of explanations is possible; it is possibly significant that the text does not invoke any of them. The issue is the place in the text of the traditions of the east-of-Jordan tribes—Reuben, Gad, and the half-tribe of Manasseh. Difficulties begin in the book of Deuteronomy but need not be rehearsed here (cf. Campbell and O'Brien 2000, 46–52). In Josh 1, the difficulty is slight but the observation needs to be made: Joshua's address to the two and a half tribes follows his order to the officers of the people (vv. 10–11); ideally, it should precede this order. If these warriors are regarded as integral to the people (cf. v. 14), then they should be addressed before the order is given to be ready to strike camp and move. The ideal need not be observed; the difficulty is slight.

The difficulty is more acute, however, when the project is viewed as a whole. Wives, little ones, and livestock are to remain east of the Jordan; "all the warriors among you" are to take part in the forthcoming campaign (v. 14). There is no mention of protection for those left behind or of supervision for the flocks and pastures. In Num 32:16–24, the threat from the locals is noted (32:17) and a proposal is made to build sheepfolds and fortified towns; the problem is recognized, even if the solution is inadequately sketched. (Note that Num 32:28 is the only other occurrence in the Hebrew Bible of the committee of Eleazar, Joshua, and the family heads.) The waging of war each summer was common (cf. the traditional view of 2 Sam 11:1). The necessary division of roles between warriors and home guard may be taken for granted, but the text does not exactly invite it. In Josh 1–12, there is nothing to insist on more than a summer's campaign (but cf. Josh 11:18). In the present text, however, the allocation of the land is apparently situated later in

Joshua's life, when Joshua "was old and advanced in years" (13:1; note the identical description in 23:1—despite the NRSV, NJPS, and others, which render "*well* advanced in years"). At the time of the distribution, Caleb claims to be eighty-five (Josh 14:10); Joshua is reported to have died at the age of one hundred and ten (Josh 24:29). Chronological calculations have to be careful of the danger of simply adding up figures from texts; differing traditions may falsify additions. Calculations apart, the distribution of the land is set late in Joshua's life, and the Reubenites, the Gadites, and the half-tribe of Manasseh are not dismissed until after it all (Josh 22:1–9). The idea that they returned home between summers is possible, but it is not invited by the silence of the text. The final episode of the great altar by the Jordan (22:10–34) has a significance that totally escapes us.

It is appropriate that the distribution of the land east of the Jordan (Josh 13) is reported before the distribution in Josh 14–19. It is also appropriate that the dismissal of the east-of-Jordan tribes is reported after all the details of the distribution are complete—although it could be argued that their commitment was to stay only until the land was possessed and rest was achieved (cf. Josh 1:15 and 11:23), not until the land was distributed. However, despite the appropriateness of the placement of these traditions, misgivings about them remain. First, the LORD's speech to Joshua in 13:1–7 ends with an order to proceed to the division of the land among the nine and a half tribes (v. 7). In this it parallels the only other speech of the LORD in the book, at its beginning, where the LORD orders Joshua to cross the Jordan and take possession of the land. Thus, appropriately, God orders the possession and the distribution of the land. Unfortunately, there is no reference to this divine order in Josh 14:1–5. Second, the content of the divine speech in 13:2–6 does not refer to the land to be distributed but lays claim to a considerably broader territory. Third, the east-of-Jordan allocation of land by Moses is reported twice, globally in verses 8–13 and for each tribe in verses 15–31, with a summary in verse 32 and notes on the tribe of Levi in verses 14 and 33, which agree that the tribe did not receive an inheritance and which differ on the reason for this. Misgivings remain.

Finally, in this context, it is appropriate to mention the fragment from Qumran (4QSam^a) associated in the NRSV with 1 Sam 11. It preserves a tradition in which Nahash, king of the Ammonites, oppressed the Gadites and Reubenites, gouging out the right eye of every Israelite east of the Jordan. Only seven thousand escaped to Jabesh-gilead. The place and precise significance of this tradition is disputed, and it is looking less likely to be original here. However, it does record belief in an

Israelite presence east of the Jordan and the threat posed by Nahash and the Ammonites. To complicate matters, however, Nahash is reported to have had loyal relations with David (2 Sam 10:2). Further, the Reubenites, Gadites, and half-tribe of Manasseh remain unmentioned in association with the assault on the Ammonite capital (2 Sam 11–12) or in relation to David and his supporters east of the Jordan (cf. 2 Sam 17:27–29).

The upshot of these observations is to raise questions for reflection concerning the traditions about the east-of-Jordan tribes. Were any of these traditions part of an early core of the book of Joshua? Did any belong integrally with the account of the distribution of the land?

When all these observations about the major text signals are taken into account, they provide something of the horizon within which the book of Joshua needs to be read. In a number of areas, uncertainty exists; certainty does not. Experienced interpreters will be aware of these uncertainties and be wary of coming to any particularly dogmatic conclusions. Wise readers will exercise similar discretion. The invitation to thought is always there.

Reading the Sections

POSSESSION OF THE LAND
JOSHUA 1–12

Introduction
Joshua 1

The introduction to the book of Joshua falls into four parts, each with its own point to make: (1) God's speech ordering the occupation of the land (1:1–6), (2) God's speech ordering obedience to the law (1:7–9), (3) Joshua's speech commanding the officers of the people (1:10–11), and (4) Joshua's speech to the east-of-Jordan tribes with their reply (1:12–18).

Joshua 1:1–6

The first section of God's speech, ordering the occupation of the land, has a concentric pattern. In the center is the description of the territory's extent, which is unbelievably vast (v. 4). On either side is God's assurance of Joshua's success, bolstered by reference to Moses (vv. 3, 5). The speech opens with the command to cross the Jordan into the land that is God's gift; this part of the speech ends with God's encouragement to Joshua and reference to the land as sworn to the ancestors (vv. 2, 6).

The extent of the land is far beyond anything reported in the book itself; it is akin to the opening of Josh 13 describing a situation in which "very much of the land still remains to be possessed" (13:1), with the specifics given in 13:2–6. The echoes of Deut 11:24 are strong. The parameters appear to be the desert in the south and the Lebanon to the north, the Euphrates in the east, and the Mediterranean in the west (cf. Nelson, comm., 33; Soggin, comm., 29–31; also Gen 15:18–21; Deut 1:7; 1 Kgs 4:21, 24 NRSV). The precise rationale for such a traditional ambit claim at this point is not clear; the reality under Joshua falls short of the claim (cf., however, 2 Kgs 14:25).

As noted above, Joshua's association with Moses is marked. What Joshua is to achieve is what has been promised to Moses (v. 3). The support experienced by Moses will be experienced by Joshua (v. 5). There is a juxtaposition of what is to come in the description of God's action as giving the land (v. 2) and the exhortation to Joshua to be strong and courageous (v. 6). The land will be portrayed as God's gift and Joshua will be portrayed fighting for it.

Joshua 1:7–9

The second section of God's speech emphasizes the observance of God's law and the success that will flow from this, an understanding embodied in the story of Achan. The importance given to the book of the law here is not matched by anything in the book of Joshua before 23:6. Constant meditation on the law is not found in Joshua but such meditation has its place in the law of the king (Deut 17:14–20; cf. vv. 18–19). It is highly likely that this material is an expansion of God's speech in order to artic- ulate a particular theological understanding.

Joshua 1:10–11

This third part of the introduction is straightforward. Joshua com- mands the "officers of the people" (cf. Exod 5:10; Deut 20:5, 8, 9) to give the orders to break camp, to be ready to cross the Jordan and enter the land in three days' time. The time factor probably allows a story- teller to correlate this with the following episode's three days of the spies in hiding (Josh 2:16, 22), although this might not suit an actuary.

Joshua 1:12–18

The exchange between Joshua and the Reubenites, Gadites, and the half-tribe of Manasseh brings the introduction to a close. Joshua

emphasizes the instructions given by Moses to these tribes. The allot-
ment of their land is reported in Deut 3:12–17; the charge to assist with
the campaign west of the Jordan is given in Deut 3:18–20. A more
extensive account is given in Num 32:1–42. There is grave doubt
whether this material can be considered to reflect early traditions.

The reply these tribes make to Joshua is at one level simple acquies-
cence (v. 16). Beyond that, they twice invoke Moses as the model for
(1) their obedience to Joshua and (2) God's support of Joshua (v. 17).
Finally, they formally concede to Joshua the power of life and death
over them (v. 18). In his lifetime, although Moses on occasion exercised
such power, nowhere was it ever formally conceded to him. Joshua is
being given high status.

Narrative Style: The South
Joshua 2:1–10:27 (42–43)

As I noted in the overview, to move beyond Josh 1 a form-critical optic
must be used in reading. It is important to recognize that a different
style of text begins with Josh 10:28 and continues until Josh 12:24.
Joshua 2:1–10:27 (42–43) is substantially narrative in style. By contrast,
Joshua 10:28–41 is list-like, Josh 11:1–23 is in a summarizing style, and
Josh 12:1–24 comprises two lists. My decision to treat these two blocks
separately is not a decision about their significance or reliability, but
rather is based simply on the grounds that there is a certain unity evident in the two different focuses of narrative tradition. Given this
unity—Joshua's sorties from Gilgal for one; the sacral nature of the Jordan, Jericho, and Achan traditions for the other—it is helpful to look
at these narrative-style traditions separately from those that are articulated differently.

The activities under Joshua's leadership here reported in narrative
style are conceptualized in two radically different ways. One conceptu-
alization is military, with fighting involved. The other conceptualiza-
tion is sacral, with no fighting involved at all, except for the defeat
caused by Achan. In the military narrative, spies are sent out to reconnoiter the land, Jericho's king and soldiers are mentioned, the battle for
Ai is described in detail, a group from Gibeon is reported deceiving
Joshua into making peace, and finally the fighting with a coalition of
five kings is described. In the sacral portrayal, the Jordan is crossed in
a thoroughly unmilitary fashion (Josh 3–4), Jericho is captured without
a weapon being used for the capture (Josh 6), and Israel's defeat before
Ai is given a single verse (7:5), while the chapter is devoted not to

Israel's strategic or tactical failure in battle but to a people's failure caused by an individual's failure—Achan's breach of sacral law.

Neither portrayal is a complete account. The military focus has no crossing of the Jordan and no capture of Jericho. The sacral focus has no city captured other than Jericho. The suggestion is not that these were complementary accounts of how Israel's occupation of Canaan happened, but rather complementary articulations of how that occupation of Canaan is to be understood. In the former, Israel itself does the fighting; God's role is to help. In the latter, Israel does nothing proportionate to the outcome; God does it all. The separate treatments here allow the different faith understandings to be more fully appreciated. It needs to be stressed that there is not an opposition between the two focuses. In the text constructed around a soldierly focus, the introductory statement is emphatic each time: the LORD has handed over the foe to Joshua and the Israelites (cf. 6:2; 8:1; 10:8). God's help is determinative, but Israel's role is proportionate to the outcome—they fight. In the sacral texts, God's role is determinative and Israel's contribution is totally disproportionate to the outcome—they do not fight.

The nature of the sacral texts for crossing the Jordan and capturing Jericho is also important. It has been suggested that a timely earthquake might have blocked the Jordan's flow and weakened Jericho's walls; interpreters will be aware that the biblical text recounts nothing of the sort. The text is about something else.

Soldierly focus

Joshua 2   Reconnaissance

Joshua sends out two spies from Shittim to reconnoiter the land. The previous attempt at such reconnaissance, under Moses' auspices, had been an unmitigated disaster. That report indicated that the land was exceedingly good but extremely well defended. Israelite morale was abysmal (Num 13:32–14:4); only Joshua and Caleb considered invasion worth a try—and they were nearly stoned for their pains (Num 14:10). This time the results are the exact opposite: The two spies report that morale within the land is abysmal (cf. Josh 2:9–11, 24).

The details are of interest. The two spies go to a brothel in Jericho ("the house of a prostitute"). The action is placed after sunset (cf. vv. 2, 5); nevertheless, the NRSV's "spent the night there" (v. 1) and "before they went to sleep" (v. 8) are both politely misleading. Night would be the best time to be let down through a window and to escape into the hills. The more literal "and lay there" (v. 1) and "before they were laid down" (v. 8) better reflects the flexibility of the Hebrew (JPSV). Whatever of timing and activity, a prostitute's house would be a good place to find reliable information. The house is of sufficient significance—in view of the story's plausibility—that the city ruler can be said to be aware of the comings and goings. (The "king of Jericho" rings a trifle pretentiously in modern ears; the "mayor of Jericho" would presume information on the city's institutions that we do not have.)

"The gate" is mentioned twice (vv. 5, 7). As in most Canaanite cities, the gate was vulnerable to attack. Here it can remind us that we may be familiar with images of the archaeological discovery of the great stone tower of seventh millennium Jericho, thousands of years before Joshua; we know nothing of the city's fortifications in Joshua's time, beyond the location of Rahab's house "on the outer side of the city wall" (v. 15).

Prostitutes do not come very highly accredited in biblical literature. Nevertheless, one ancestress had to play the prostitute in order to be enabled to play her role as ancestress (Tamar); one, with the dubious honor of symbolizing unfaithful Israel, became a prophet's wife (Gomer); Jephthah, the son of a prostitute, was excluded from his family but became "head and commander" in Israel. In this story, Rahab is prophetess and theologian, as well as a driver of good bargains. Her speech opens with a personal confession; she knows that the LORD has given Israel the land, and she knows that fear and dread have possessed its inhabitants (2:9). According to her, the local inhabitants have heard of Israel's deliverance at the Sea of Reeds and of the fate of Sihon and Og. She then drives a bargain for the survival of herself and her family.

The two spies are not reported as reconnoitering the land; they report to Joshua on the confession of faith. We hear of a king in Jericho and a search for the spies. The report the spies can bring to Joshua is exactly what a military commander would want to hear: Enemy morale is nonexistent. The reason is appropriately theological: "Truly the LORD has given all the land into our hands" (2:24).

Joshua 6:1–2   Jericho

Joshua 6:1–2 is straightforward: Jericho and its king have been handed over by the LORD to Joshua and the Israelites. The image of a besieged city is clear (6:1); the bestower of victory is the LORD (6:2).

The reference in verse 2 to "the soldiers" (literally: valiant warriors) is regarded by many as a gloss, since it lacks any connectives (cf. Gray, comm., 76–77; Soggin, comm., 81; Nelson, comm., 86—who notes, however, that it "is present in both OG and MT"). Neither king nor soldiers have any further place in the story. The king alone is mentioned in Josh 8:2 and 10:1, 28, 30; without these later references, we would have no mention of the fate of Jericho's king, unless the ruler is understood to be included in the general statement of 6:21—which would sit uncomfortably with the later references to "Jericho and its king" (8:2; 10:1).

Verse 2 in itself and in its conjunction with 8:2 and 10:1 together point unmistakably to a different story from what follows in Josh 6:3–27. Some form of military campaign is called for. Something of a possible parallel is hinted at in Judg 1:24–25 for the case of Bethel/Luz. If, as I believe, it is correct to differentiate between a military story that we do not have (beyond these two verses) and the sacral story that we do have—although commentators tend not to do so—then a question has to be asked: Why is the reference to Jericho's king (with or without his soldiers) retained at the start of this narrative? It could be omitted without any loss to what follows. The later references could be understood in the light of the fall of Jericho. Once the text explicitly mentions Jericho and singles out "and its king" (with or without his soldiers), questions are inevitably invited by the ruler's absence from the rest of the narrative.

An interpretation that demands serious consideration is that the text invites its readers to hear an echo of a military account in these two verses while encountering a clearly sacral account in what follows. We do not have access to the intentions of compilers, but we might assume that, given the text as it is, its compilers knowingly set side by side a pointer to the soldierly focus and the bulk of the narrative from the sacral focus.

Joshua 8   Ai

With or without any reference to Jericho, Josh 8:1 opens with the LORD's order to Joshua to attack Ai and the assurance that ruler and people, city and land, have been handed over by the LORD (8:1). There is no reference to any prior failure until, in verses 5–6, "as before" occurs twice, clearly referring to the failure narrated in chapter 7. It is possible that the two phrases come from editorial work blending both sacral and military focuses into a single composition. Careful readers will notice that there is no reference in 7:4–5 to the defenders of Ai coming out against the attackers. It must have happened, but it is not made explicit. In chapter 7, strategy was not raised, beyond the spies' assurance that no more than "two or three thousand men" would be needed.

In chapter 8, after the LORD's command, Joshua lays out a careful battle plan: An ambush is to be set in place during the night, and a feint and a feigned flight will draw the defenders away from the city, enabling the force in ambush to move in and take the city. This is the strategy that is executed successfully (vv. 14–24).

However, a repetition in the text may signal the presence of another strategy. Twice it is noted that Joshua did "something" during the night "somewhere" (cf. vv. 9 [spent the night among the people] and 13 [went . . . in the valley]). The most economical interpretation is to recognize two options in the text for setting up the ambush. In verses 3–4, the ambush is established during the night and located not far from the city, without specifics being given. In verses 12–13, it is established during the day and located to the west of the city, specifically between Bethel and Ai. When such options are recognized, a storyteller or reader can be expected to attend to one or the other but not to both. A further option may be expressed by the presence of verses 18 and 26. In verse 7, the ambush force is left to decide the moment of their entry into the fray; in verse 18, the LORD gives Joshua the order to signal this with his sword (or javelin), and in verse 26 the weapon remains in Joshua's outstretched arm until the operation is finished (cf. Moses' hands in the battle with Amalek, Exod 17:8–16). The military strategy can be left to bring about its victory, or the help of God can be made more dramatically evident.

A biblical text may on occasion be dismissed as fearfully difficult (or a fearful mess), or it may be interpreted in ways that go beyond the conventional. It is also possible that a text is meaningless, but this possibility should always be the last resort of an interpreter. Biblical narratives of battle, in my experience, do not set up two ambushes in a story that will only use one, do not discuss the eve of battle as occurring on two separate nights, and do not devote a day to setting up a small ambush (5,000; see 8:12) to be involved in military options only the following day. Without question, the text of Josh 8 is difficult; equally without question, two ambushes are mentioned. In all probability, verses 9b and 13b—which both include a central "Joshua / that night / in" and begin with different verbs ("spent" or "went") and end with different places (the people or the valley)—refer to the same night. Equally, then, the two "early" risings of verse 10 (Joshua) and verse 14 (king and people of Ai) probably refer to the same morning, relating first to the attackers and second to the defenders. If we allow the possibility of this, and if we accept that texts do not always tell stories but on occasion (by including variant versions) enable stories to be told, this text of Josh 8 can be seen to make satisfactory sense. Enabling stories to be told allows the text to include options for the telling, to allude to different ways in which stories have traditionally been told.

We will see examples of this elsewhere in this volume. In this case, one option involves a large ambush set up during the night (vv. 3–4); another option involves a smaller ambush set up early in the day (vv. 12–13). Verse 13b, referring to the same night as verse 9b, signals the duplication of the ambush. The narrative deals with the night ambush on the eve of the battle; naturally, the morning ambush is dealt with after the muster and move of the troops. Verse 13b may be a signal to the storyteller (or the user of the text) of what is happening. We may judge it a most unclear signal, but it is not unprecedented. A similar duplication occurs when 2 Kgs 13:12–13 are virtually repeated in 2 Kgs 14:15–16 so that, among other things, King Joash of Israel dies in 13:13 and visits the ailing prophet Elisha in 13:14. A similar understanding, appealing to a signal that is far from clear, is possible (see Campbell and O'Brien 2000, 433). In the case of Josh 8, without a signal the establishment of two ambushes would be confusing; so perhaps the presence of verse 13b is best read as a signal to the storyteller or the user. Equally in this text, the weapon in Joshua's outstretched hand (v. 18, a signal to attack; v. 26, a symbol enabling victory) may be read as an invitation to invoke divine intervention for those who prefer this to leaving the unfolding of the battle to sheerly strategic considerations.

It may help to follow the narrative from its beginning. It opens with the LORD's exhortation to Joshua, "Do not fear or be dismayed," akin to 10:8, followed by the order to move against Ai. Ai will be treated as Jericho was; only the issue of booty is different. A note of strategy is included in the order: "Set an ambush" (8:2).

The text immediately has Joshua comply with God's order, with a general statement setting things in motion (v. 3a). Thirty thousand are chosen for the ambush, to be put in place during the night, not too far from the town, behind it (as God ordered, v. 2). Joshua then outlines the strategy for the attack. During the night, the ambush is established; Joshua spends the night with the troops, not with the ambush (v. 9). Verses 10–11 report the start of the day's combat. Joshua, the elders, and the army approach Ai and set themselves up (NRSV: "camped") with a valley between themselves and the town. Presumably, therefore, they are on a ridge so that a small ambushing force can be moved off without being seen. Verses 12–13 portray the alternative ambush option (see above): five thousand troops only, moved into position early in the day, to the west of Ai. At this point the NRSV has: "and Joshua spent that night in the valley" (v. 13b). Most Hebrew manuscripts have: "and Joshua went that night in the valley." The Greek does not have the verse at all. Some Hebrew manuscripts have "spent that night"; Noth opts for it, following verse 9 (p. 46). The NRSV is probably right. As noted above, the text may now be meaningless or it may contain a signal taking us back to verse 9, as if to say: remember, storyteller or reader, one ambush or the other. With verse 14, the narrative of the day's combat is resumed, this time from the defenders' point of view.

We need to take a break from the battle for a moment in order to look at two other issues that come to the fore in these texts: military numbers and Septuagint texts.

The numbers in the text vary widely: 36 in 7:5, 30,000 in 8:3, and 5,000 in 8:12. There is broad agreement that the round numbers of ancient Israel's military—hundreds, thousands, etc.—probably represent specific military groups or units, perhaps reflecting recruitment patterns. Ideals for groups and realities for recruitment can be expected to have varied across the history of ancient Israel. Mendenhall, assuming a radical break between the old folk militia and the military organization of David and Solomon, calculated that the figures for Num 1 indicate a range of five to fourteen men per "thousand"—at the time of the book of Numbers (Mendenhall 1958, 63). The picture has to remain uncertain; figures may often be symbolic rather than statistical.

The Septuagint (LXX), speaking broadly, is a translation of Hebrew scriptural texts into Greek, made in the third and second centuries B.C.E., and including books not included in the later canonical Hebrew Bible (= Masoretic Text, MT). It is probably fair to say that the LXX can be most useful in confirming the presence of a word or phrase that it shares with the MT; it is not so useful in determining what the MT might have had when it does not share what is present in the MT. It has become clear in the last few generations that a variety of textual traditions existed in ancient Israel. When the LXX and the MT agree, the LXX may be said to confirm the presence of the text of the MT. When the LXX and the MT disagree, it is often possible that the LXX is following a different text tradition. Careful study of the LXX is a prerequisite for text-critical work. Full analysis of a tradition in the LXX is required before it can be used for text-critical emendation of the MT (J. A. Sanders, in conversation). Major differences between the LXX and the MT in the book of Jeremiah or 1 Sam 16:14–18:16, for example, are well known. Among others, Stanley Walters draws attention to the surprising differences between the telling of the stories of Hannah (MT) and Anna (LXX) in 1 Sam 1 ("Hanna and Anna").

A cursory reading reveals the wide discrepancies between the MT and the LXX in Josh 8 (cf. Nelson, comm., 108–10). The LXX has only the first ambush, makes no mention of either version of Joshua's activities "that night," has Joshua's position east of Ai rather than north, has no daytime ambush, and has Joshua's hand etc. as a signal for the attack but not as a symbol of victory, as well as other differences. While various possibilities can be entertained, it is likely that the LXX here is following its own version of the story, not that of the MT.

Back to the battle. The ruler of Ai and his forces made a sortie from the town to repel the attackers (v. 14), Joshua and the Israelites retreated before them, drawing them away from their base (vv. 15–17), the forces from the ambush moved in and took Ai and then moved out against the defenders who came under attack from front and rear (vv. 18–22). Joshua hanged the ruler, wiped out the population of the town, and burned the town to the ground (vv. 24–29).

The ceremony at Shechem and its consequences are treated separately (see below, pp. 46–47), but the savagery of extermination needs discussion. At Jericho, the attackers wiped out the people and the livestock (cf. 6:21); at Ai, they wiped out the people but not the livestock (8:24–27). Outside the cave at Makkedah, Joshua executed the five kings of the coalition (10:26). This is bad enough. As we will see later, it gets appallingly bloody in 10:28–41 and equivalently but not so emphatically in 11:1–20.

At issue, first, is language and religious belief. The NRSV uses the language of "devoted to destruction," "utterly destroy," and so on. The Hebrew noun is *ḥerem*, often referred to as "the ban," with corresponding verbal forms. The basic meaning of the noun, at its most original, is the qualification of something as forbidden, either because it is particularly holy or particularly unholy. In the Older Testament, the word is usually used in the context of Israel's wars, mainly those in the premonarchic period. In early references, the concept was of enemies (and sometimes plunder) having been exclusively assigned to God— ruling out any boost in captives, livestock, and wealth. Such destruction may have been promised and carried out only in cases where divine help was felt to be especially necessary (cf. Num 21:2–3); to systematize it in association with "holy war," defensive wars, or whatever, is becoming increasingly improbable. In later deuteronomic or deuteronomistic texts, the ban—the destruction of enemies—was invoked in order to protect Israel from syncretism or apostasy. There are some other usages, but these two are the ones that mainly concern us here. (Note: the final chapter of this book may be anticipated to indicate briefly the technically correct use of the terms "deuteronomic" and "deuteronomistic": "deuteronomic" refers to the period, circles, activities, and so forth associated with King Josiah's reform; "deuteronomistic" refers to the circles, texts, activities, and so forth associated with the Deuteronomistic History (found within Deuteronomy through Second Kings [cf. Noth 1991; Campbell and O'Brien 2000]).

Next is the matter of practice in the ancient world. The utter destruction associated with the ban—while it may rightly provoke revulsion—was by no means exclusive to Israel. It is claimed that the kings of Assyria did it "to all lands" (e.g., 2 Kgs 19:11); those ordered to punish Babylon were ordered to do it (Jer 50:26; 51:3); the Ammonites and Moabites did it to the inhabitants of Mount Seir (2 Chr 20:23). The best known example from outside the Bible is in the Mesha Stele from Transjordan, an inscribed black basalt monument a little over a meter high and a little more than half a meter wide, from Moab of the late ninth century B.C.E. The relevant section reads: "I Mesha, son of Chemosh- . . . , king of Moab, . . . went by night and fought against it [Nebo] from the break of dawn until noon, taking it and slaying all, seven thousand men, boys, women, girls and maidservants, for I had devoted them to destruction [*hhrmth*] for (the god) Ashtar-Chemosh" (*ANET*, 320; cf. Gibson 1971, 71–83).

Verdicts on such behaviors, beliefs, or claims can be entrusted to readers. While to some degree motives might allegedly be justifiable, it is of little comfort to the dead that they died for the honor of somebody else's god rather than the greed of a conqueror or to prevent those of little faith from being led astray. It is also of little comfort that the deuteronomic-deuteronomistic idea of exterminating the locals to protect the faith of Israel was apparently wishful thinking; such killings never happened. That they were believed to have been commanded is bad enough. War in the ancient world could be very brutal, but we moderns to our shame have little cause to feel superior to the ancients in this regard. Names such as Coventry or Dresden, Hiroshima or Nagasaki, Rwanda or Bosnia-Herzegovina remind us that in certain aspects warfare has not changed. Where survival is believed to be at stake or issues of family or clan are involved, hostility can be bitter, prolonged, and all too often total. We speak of blood feuds, family feuds, and vendettas; we know of tribal and national conflicts. They are not foreign to biblical belief, whatever the actual biblical practice; they are not foreign to the modern world. They are foreign to basic humaneness (for a comprehensive and pioneering study of the complex issue of war within the Pentateuch, see Lohfink 1994).

Joshua 9:3–27   Gibeon

The story of the Gibeonite decision "to ruse rather than lose" is subtly placed (cf. 10:2). It is the third in a series, after Jericho and Ai. It brings home, as nothing else does, the accuracy of Rahab's statement: "I know that the LORD has given you the land, and that dread of you has fallen on us, and that all the inhabitants of the land melt in fear before you" (Josh 2:9). The LORD gave Jericho, along with its king and soldiers (if the text is right) into Joshua's hand (Josh 6:2). We do not know how, in the military narrative, Jericho was taken; we may assume that a stratagem with Rahab played a role and that the people of Jericho put up a fight (cf. Josh 24:11). If Josh 6:21 reflects tradition, Jericho's people and livestock were destroyed. The king and people of Ai put up a fight, sallying out against their attackers; Ai's people were destroyed, but not its livestock (Josh 8:25–27). In line with Rahab's avowal, the people of Gibeon opted not to fight and were not destroyed. As befits the third city in a series, the surrender of Gibeon is a climax. The next story, the fourth and final one, is not about cities but a coalition. The cause for fear was real because "Gibeon was a large city, like one of the royal cities, and was larger than Ai, and all its men were warriors" (10:2). Climax indeed.

There is a delicious irony in the conjunction of the Ai and Gibeon stories. Ai fell to an Israelite ruse; Israel fell for a Gibeonite ruse.

The Gibeonite ruse was simple enough. They dressed up in worn clothing, made their gear and provisions look the worse for wear, and turned up at Gilgal asking for a treaty. The Israelites are portrayed as skeptical (9:27); it makes for good storytelling. The Gibeonites told a good yarn and the Israelites fell for it. The text suggests Israel yielded to hunger rather than discretion; they tucked into the food "and did not ask direction from the LORD" (9:14).

Three days later, the Israelites discovered the deceit. Too late; the treaty commitment had been made and Gibeonite lives were guaranteed (9:15). So a compromise was reached: Their lives would be spared, but some of them would always be slaves in the service of the LORD, "hewers of wood and drawers of water" for the house of the God of Israel (Josh 9:23; cf. Josh 16:10; 17:13; Judg 1:28, 30, 33, 35).

Clearly this story fascinated or troubled later Israel. Particular attention has been given to the treaty and the compromise following it. Verses 15b and 18–21 reflect this later attention. Variations—the inhabitants of Gibeon (v. 3), the Hivites (v. 7), the four cities (v. 17)—suggest options; traces late in the chapter may reflect the later attention. The details need not detain us.

Joshua 10:1–27, 42–43   Coalition

The sequence of three and then a fourth is proverbial (cf. Amos 1:3, 6, 9, 11, 13; 2:1, 4, 6; Prov 30:15, 18, 21, 29). This soldierly narrative sequence brings us to the fourth story. Fittingly for the final story, it is not about cities but about a coalition of kings. The coalition was assembled by Adoni-zedek of Jerusalem; its other four members came from Hebron, Jarmuth, Lachish, and Eglon. Together the five represented a substantial part of later Judah. Two towns had fallen to the Israelites and this powerful coalition set out to stiffen morale and encourage resistance by attacking Gibeon, the timorous who had made a treaty (cf. 10:4–5). The Gibeonites appealed to Joshua.

If we did not know better, it would seem that this time Joshua was going to be in trouble. One town at a time might be good strategy; a coalition of five kings might be a little too much. The coalition is certainly portrayed as being too much for Gibeon; the Gibeonite appeal to Joshua suggests he has a substantial force at his command. In this case, relative military power is not the focus of the story. God's assurance is given Joshua, as before (10:8; cf. 6:2; 8:1). Joshua's forces make a sudden appearance, after a forced march through the night coming up from Gilgal into the central hilly spine. Victory is not attributed to strategy or tactics; it was the LORD who fought for Israel—"the LORD threw them into a panic before Israel, who inflicted a great slaughter on them" (10:10). The panic was God's doing; the killing and pursuit was Israel's, until the LORD is reported joining in with a hailstorm (big stones from heaven, v. 11a; hailstones, v. 11b). The conjunction of forces is noted: The hailstones killed more than the Israelites did.

A forced march through the night means a daytime battle. Such was the victory that the day needed extending, so Joshua is reputed to have outdone England's King Canute, stopping sun and moon in their tracks "until the nation took vengeance on their enemies" (v. 13).

Tension in the text suggests the possibility of two stories. Verse 15 has Joshua and all Israel return to the camp at Gilgal. According to verse 21, however, after the pursuit "all the people returned safe to Joshua in the camp at Makkedah." A storyteller could easily blend the two operations; the text does not, but leaves open the option of closing at verse 15. The coalition's decision to attack Gibeon points to intimidation of the fearful. Joshua's treatment of the five kings would have had much the same effect, raising the morale of his own commanders and spreading dread and fear throughout the land (just as Rahab had said). The conclusion to this episode is found in verses 42–43. "All these kings" (v. 42) refers to the five (Jerusalem, Hebron, Jarmuth, Lachish, and Eglon) rather than the more general "Kadesh-barnea to Gaza" in the deeper south and "Goshen as far as Gibeon" covering the center and north of Judah (v. 41). Verse 43 concludes the campaign with the return to Gilgal.

With this narrative section at an end, it is appropriate to take stock. The portrayal is clear and surprisingly limited. The Israelites remain based in their camp at Gilgal, in the Jordan valley. The group ("all Israel"?—cf. 8:15, 21, 24; 10:15), led by Joshua and backed by the LORD, is portrayed as the dominant fighting force in the region (i.e., mainly Judah), winning battles, sacking towns, and instilling fear. Nothing has been said, in this narrative, of possession or settled occupation (cf., by way of contrast, Josh 21:43b).

Sacral focus

In turning to the "sacral focus," we are breaking the run of the present text. The reason for this needs to be clear. The texts we have been reading in the "soldierly focus" portray Israel fighting for its land, helped by its God. Each time a battle looms, God is portrayed saying to Joshua: I have handed your enemy over to you (cf. Josh 6:2; 8:1; 10:8). The stories to come in the "sacral focus" offer one view of how this help from God was to be understood. In these texts, the Israelites do not fight; God hands them success—or, in the case of Achan, God hands them failure because of an individual's breach of sacral law. The narrative of the overall campaign needs to be heard: God is on Israel's side. Within it, the stories of the "sacral focus" offer an understanding of how the events of this narrative may be pictured or celebrated.

Joshua 3–4   Jordan crossing

If the account of the crossing of the Jordan is looked at globally, the picture is unproblematic. The priests carrying the ark of the covenant leave the Israelite camp in front of the people. The people keep a respectful distance from the ark, about a thousand yards. As the feet of the priests bearing the ark dip in the edge of the water of the Jordan, the flow of the water stops, piling up at Adam, further up the river. The crossing takes place opposite Jericho. Presumably the people pass on both sides of the ark, maintaining the thousand yard distance, but this is not said. One sanctuary, consisting of twelve stones, is established in the middle of the Jordan, "where the feet of the priests bearing the ark of the covenant had stood" (4:9); another will be established at Gilgal, where they camp that night, consisting of twelve stones taken up from the middle of the Jordan, "from the place where the priests' feet stood" (4:3, cf. v. 22). When the last of the people have crossed, the priests bearing the ark come up out of the middle of the Jordan. As the soles of their feet touch dry ground, the waters of the Jordan return to their place. The people "camped in Gilgal on the east border of Jericho" (4:19).

The text offers us a spectacular liturgy, with the ark of the LORD at its center, borne by Israel's priests, the people respectfully distant, the wonder of the Jordan's stopping and the riverbed dry as the bed of the Reed Sea, with sanctuaries put in place to mark the meaning of the occurrence: The waters of the Jordan were cut off in front of the ark of the covenant of the LORD (4:7); as Israel came out of Egypt, across the dried bed of the Reed Sea, so Israel has entered its promised land, across the dried bed of the Jordan river (4:23). Israel, under the leadership of Joshua and the power and guidance of God, fulfills its destiny.

This is the global picture. A closer look reveals that the text is not a smooth whole cloth, but has numerous lumpy bits, knots, and twists. These rough spots need some attention:

1. 3:1–2   The "three days" of 3:2 is in tension with 3:1, which has Israel overnight at the Jordan before the crossing. The earlier instruction in 2:11 suggests three days before the move from Shittim rather than after it.

2. 3:3–4 + 5   The text falls a little short of the skillful sequencing usually found in Israelite narrative. The officers' instructions (vv. 3–4) are followed by two commands from Joshua, one to the people (v. 5) and one to the priests (v. 6). Since Joshua's command to the people refers to the eve of departure, it would more normally precede the instructions from the officers; Joshua's command to the priests would then give the signal for the move to begin. The ideal sequence would be Joshua to the people: "sanctify yourselves" for tomorrow the move will happen (v. 5); then the officers to the people: move when the ark moves and follow it at a respectful distance (vv. 3–4); finally, Joshua to the priests: "take up the ark . . . and pass on in front of the people" (v. 6). Narrative need not be perfectly sequenced, but this sequence is clumsy, and clumsiness is often editorial activity drawing attention to itself.

3. 3:9–10   The call to hear "the words of the LORD your God" (v. 9) is not followed by a divine speech or anything that might be described as "the words of the LORD your God." Instead, verse 10 concerns the driving out of local peoples and verses 11–13 concern the ark of the covenant and the waters of the Jordan.

4. 3:11, 13   These two verses alone use a very rare title for God—
"the Lord of all the earth"—which occurs elsewhere only four times
(Mic 4:13; Zech 4:14; 6:5; and Ps 97:5). Its use as part of the title of the
ark is found only here. The verses are addressed by Joshua to the
Israelites and can be understood as a repetition and appropriate expansion of God's words to Joshua (cf. v. 8). Verse 12 remains problematic.

5. 3:12   The command to select twelve men, one from each tribe,
is strangely isolated. Usually some purpose is indicated; here there is
none. No attempt is made to associate the action with or incorporate it
into what follows. Of course, if two sanctuaries are involved, it may be
appropriate to have two sets of bearers.

6. 4:2   The verse is an almost identical duplication of 3:12. Again,
two sanctuaries may require two sets of bearers.

7. 4:4–7   This catechesis, associated with the mid-river sanctuary,
concerns the stopping of the Jordan's flow for the crossing of the ark.
It is not to be confused with the later catechesis reflecting on God's dry-
ing up of the waters of the Jordan for Israel as God had dried up the
Reed Sea for Israel to cross (4:21–24).

8. 4:9   This verse, referring to the mid-river sanctuary, is oddly
out of place following the comment in 4:8 about the stones being laid
down where Israel camped (i.e., Gilgal). For both sanctuaries to be
accommodated, careful logistical planning would be necessary.
Instructions are given in 4:3 and 4:8 to the bearers of the stones for
the Gilgal sanctuary; in between, instructions are given to bearers for
the mid-river sanctuary (4:4–5). Verse 9 establishes the mid-river
sanctuary.

9. 4:10–11   Correlation of these verses with 4:1 requires something
of the following sequence: the crossing by the people (*haggôy*) is completed (v. 1); the stones for the two sanctuaries are removed or established (vv. 2–9); the people (*hā'ām*) cross in haste (v. 10b); finally, the ark
and its priests cross (v. 11). It is possible, but the duplication of *haggôy*
and *hā'ām* is troublesome.

Whatever the sequence, a crossing "in haste" is completely at odds
with the tenor of the surrounding stately ceremony in which a respectful distance is kept from the ark and the Jordan's flow is stopped from
Adam, well to the north. A hurried crossing is more in keeping with
verses 12–13, associated with a battle that is not to be reported.

10. 4:12–13   As noted, the place of the east-of-Jordan tribes in these
texts is uncertain. These tribes cross over "before the Israelites," without reference to the ark. In verse 13, the 40,000 cross over "before the
LORD," also without reference to the ark. They are described as armed

for battle, but no battle eventuates. Their place in the sequence and their role in the story are difficult to understand.

11. 4:15–17 Joshua commands the priests to come up out of the Jordan and, when they have done so, the Jordan's flow resumes. There is tension with the report of the priests' crossing in 4:11.

12. We may also note that the exaltation of Joshua is promised by God in 3:7–8 and accomplished in 4:14. It is far from clear that this "exaltation" is integral to the intervening text.

Regarding these compositional issues, Richard Nelson has observed: "The logical digression and persistent reiterations in chapters 3 and 4 are undoubtedly the result of a complicated history of composition and redaction, but no hypothesis to unravel the history of their formation has met with general acceptance. . . . Any generally acceptable comprehensive solution to this compositional tangle is probably unattainable" (Nelson, comm., 55–56). To open up an avenue to the possibly "unattainable," it may be necessary to abandon a search for the origins of the material (via composition and redaction) and turn rather to the literary genre and the function of the text in chapters 3–4.

When we have looked at these signals in the text, we need to pause and remind ourselves of what in an ancient world was not as we would automatically expect it to have been. We, in today's media-saturated world, take it for granted that texts are written to be read by people. In the ancient world that was not the case. In ancient Israel, for example, sophisticated texts such as these may have been read to people; stories may have been told from the texts; the texts may have been used by specialists—but they were not written to be read by ordinary people. The issue is not so much one of literacy, but more significantly of distribution. Without printing, texts could be copied but could not be distributed widely and were therefore restricted to an elite (for more, see Niditch 1996). "Elite" in this context has to refer simply to a few rather than a chosen few or a powerful few. In medieval times, texts were available to monks in choir, but not to people in the body of the church. Texts might be available to a teacher in a community, but not to the people in the street. Texts were, instead, mediated to a wider public, and we need to allow for the role of the mediators. Typical mediators would have been storytellers, thinkers, and other users—such as presiders at festivals, organizers of liturgies, advocates for reform, and so on. We need to examine texts for what they offer us rather than for what we expect to find in them. With this in mind, we can turn back to the text (for a visually helpful layout, cf. Campbell and O'Brien 2000, 112–17).

The storyteller or presider over an ancient festival or communal gathering, as also today's reader, would have had little difficulty being aware of the story line of the Jordan crossing. The distractions are not hard to identify and ignore. The ark left the camp, followed by the people at a respectful distance; the Jordan's flow stopped at the arrival of the ark, which stood in the middle of the Jordan while the entire people crossed over; the ark then came up out of the Jordan, the memorial stones were attended to, and the entire group moved on to camp for the night at Gilgal, on the east border of Jericho.

The chapters may well derive from the historicizing (i.e., transforming into historical narrative) of an organizer's guide to the liturgies associated with the Jordan crossing. The organizer of a liturgy would have been well aware of the story and appreciative of notes that indicated the points he would be wise to attend to. A ceremony of sanctification on the eve of the celebration is a possibility (3:5). It would be important to have a leader figure who controls the movements and the pauses (3:6, 7–8). With an uninitiated group, it would help to give a preview of events (3:9, 11, 13); the group to carry the stones can be selected ahead of time, especially if there was the long journey back from the river's edge to Gilgal (3:12). If the midriver memorial is to be celebrated in some way (aided by a low water level perhaps), it needs to be attended to at the appropriate time (4:4–7, 9). The leader, Joshua, would signal the completion of the ceremony and the return to the Gilgal sanctuary (4:14–15).

The thinker and theologian can ponder the two catecheses: the role of the ark (4:7) and the parallel between the departure from Egypt and the entry into Canaan (4:22–24). Or they may ponder the majestic solemnity of the crossing with priests and ark contrasted with the mention of the people crossing in haste, accompanied by armed troops (4:10b, 12–13). Does Israel receive its land as gift from God, or must Israel fight for it with God's help? Maybe thinkers or theologians simply reflected on the preservation of the *multiple* traditions that made up Israel's sacred memories of its past.

Joshua 6:3–27   Capture of Jericho

In the story of the capture of Jericho, there is little doubt that Israel receives the town as a gift from God. Jericho's king and his soldiers (if the text is right) are mentioned (v. 2), but they have no place in the story—similar in this regard to the armed troops at the crossing. It is a sacral text in which the action is God's.

Two contrasting patterns of behavior are evident in the Jericho text. In one, the warriors circle the town once a day for six days and seven times on the seventh, in silence, enjoined by Joshua: "You shall not shout or let your voice be heard, nor shall you utter a word" (6:10). At the right moment, a shout is to bring the walls down. In the other, there are seven priests with seven trumpets, with a military escort and the trumpets being blown continually (cf. 6:8–9, 13). At the right moment, a shout is to bring the walls down. We might imagine the first as a silent, suspenseful story, told by Alfred Hitchcock, culminating in the mighty shout of these wild nomads and the collapse of a fortified city's walls. We might imagine the second as an opulent and color-filled spectacle, orchestrated by Cecil B. de Mille, with priests and trumpets and a mighty shout bringing down a fortified city's walls. We might even imagine both blended into one, with the bulk of the people being silent and only the honor guard of troops and priests around the ark sounding their trumpets, until the final mighty shout is given.

While this combined option is possible, the text does not give it to us. Two signals are reported for the shout (Joshua's command, v. 16, and a trumpet blast, cf. vv. 5, 20); two shouts are reported (v. 20: NRSV, "shouted," "raised a great shout"). Just to confuse matters a little more, four commands are located between Joshua's order, "Shout! For the LORD has given you the city" (v. 16) and the people's shout in reply, "So the people shouted" (v. 20; for a visually helpful layout, see Campbell and O'Brien 2000, 119–23).

None of this matters much when we realize that the story, however it is told or reenacted, is summed up in Joshua's words: "For the LORD has given you the city" (v. 19). If there is to be reenactment, at least two versions are preserved for the purpose. There is no more to be said; this version is sacral.

Rahab and her family are taken care of. Perhaps this is a reminder of a more military conquest story, like the king and soldiers; perhaps not. The issue of devoted things (v. 24) is a good preparation for the sacral story to come.

Joshua 7   Achan fiasco

Chapter 7 is not a story of battle. Verse 1 is a summary in anticipation of the story's core; it tells us that Israel broke faith over the devoted things, identifies Achan and his action, and speaks of God's anger. The "devoted things" are mentioned twice in verse 1 and do not recur in the text until verses 11–12. Achan is fully identified in verse 1, but in the body of the text, he is not identified until verse 18, after preparation in verse 14 and painstaking procedures in verses 16–17. God's anger is mentioned in verse 1 and not again until verse 26.

The body of the text begins with Joshua sending men from Jericho to Ai. There is no assurance of success from God, as there is in other cases (cf. Josh 6:2 [Jericho]; 8:1 [Ai]; 10:8 [the coalition]). There is no battle whatsoever, just ignominious flight—they "went up . . . and they fled before the men of Ai" (7:4). This flight is all the more surprising when we look at what precedes and follows it. In the preceding verse, the spies insist that "not all the people" should bother being in the assault party. The text has them say it twice: "The whole people" should not go up. A small attack group is enough; the inhabitants of Ai "are so few." What follows is probably worse. There are some thirty-six casualties on Israel's side and "the hearts of the people melted and turned to water" (7:5). The language of hearts melting is used only twice elsewhere in Joshua—for the local inhabitants, afraid of Israel (2:11), and for all the local kings, afraid of Israel (5:1). At this point in the story, Israel has been reduced to the condition of its enemies.

Joshua and the elders mourn until evening (for the only time in the book of Joshua). God is portrayed as rather surprised (vv. 10–11). Surely it is obvious: Israel has sinned; things devoted to destruction have been stolen. It is no wonder that Israel cannot stand before its enemies. "I will be with you no more, unless you destroy the devoted things from among you" (7:12).

The point is painfully clear. Victory is God's gift; when the law is broken, the gift will not be given. Joshua receives his orders for how matters are to be set right (7:13–15). The next day, the orders are carried out: Achan is identified and stoned to death. This is indeed a sacral story. For one individual's sin, "the Israelites are unable to stand before their enemies" (7:12). Victory is not gained by Israel, with God's help; victory is given by God, with Israel's observance.

Neither soldierly nor sacral

Chapter 5 marks the change of epochs. A generation ago, Israel had come out of Egypt and a new epoch had begun—the desert time. Now Israel has entered Canaan and again a new epoch has begun—life in the land. Identity and commitment need to be reaffirmed with circumcision. The new land provides food; the manna has stopped. The new land is holy ground; Joshua stands in Moses' place.

Joshua 5:1 The new epoch

The portrayal of the Jordan crossing parallels aspects of the crossing of the Reed Sea at the Exodus. These two crossings are depicted as defining moments in the early history of Israel. Joshua 3–4 presents the moment as Israel celebrated it. Joshua 5:1 presents it as Israel's foes across the Jordan saw it: "Their hearts melted, and there was no longer any spirit in them"—just as Rahab had said. While the precise geographical designations may be vague, the intention is clear. The kings west of the Jordan and east of the Mediterranean cover the whole land that Israel is now entering. Further specification is unnecessary; when the text says the whole, it has said it all.

Joshua 5:2–9   Circumcision

In these verses too, the intent is clear; there is some haggling over the specifics. The generation entering this new land must undergo the rite of circumcision. The need for it causes the haggling. At the beginning (v. 2), the Hebrew is unambiguous; the Israelites are to be circumcised "a second time"—two words, both the verb and the number, are involved. At the end (v. 9), "they were uncircumcised, because they had not been circumcised on the way." The LXX may have found the second circumcision a bit mind-boggling; in verse 2, it reinterprets the verb and omits "a second time." The introduction of the idea that an entire generation died in the desert made a more palatable understanding possible.

Like all good symbolism, this has to be open to multiple interpretation. The crossing of the Jordan is not the mere crossing of a river. It is Israel's move into the totality of a new existence. Circumcision that became a central symbol of Israel's existence had somehow to be brought to the fore for this entry into new existence. It symbolized the newness; the old is transformed, not abandoned. Identity and commitment are reaffirmed.

Joshua 5:10–12   Passover/Manna

No times are given for the crossing of the Jordan. According to 5:10, while camped at Gilgal, Pesach (= Passover, with no linguistic association with crossing) was celebrated on the fourteenth day of the month (cf. Exod 12). Specialists will note that the association with unleavened bread (*maṣṣâ*) is taken for granted. That is probably incidental to the mention of Pesach and the manna here. Pesach (Passover) is first and foremost the celebration of Israel's departure from Egypt; the manna is symbolic of Israel's sojourn in the wilderness. Both express God's care for the people, bringing them out of Egypt and feeding them in the desert. Pesach is given special mention because the coming out of Egypt has been balanced here by the coming into the land. It marks a new beginning (cf. Exod 12:2). The manna is mentioned because its ceasing signals the end of an epoch. The time of the wilderness wandering is past; the time of Israel's life in the land has begun.

Joshua 5:13–15   Commander

These are a fascinating three verses. The imposing figure of the "commander of the army of the LORD" has never been heard of before and will never be heard of again in the Hebrew Scriptures. He appears before Joshua with drawn sword in his hand. He has only one command to give: "Remove the sandals from your feet, for the place where you stand is holy" (v. 15). That is all. No promise of help in the task ahead, no challenging command, no real answer to the (literal) question, "Are you for us or for our adversaries?"

"I have now come" (5:14). Why? The import of the appearance is greater than any promise or challenge. Joshua is placed on an equal footing with Moses; Joshua's role in leading the people into the land is put on the same footing as Moses' role in leading the people out of Egypt. The command to both men is identical: "Remove the sandals from your feet" (Exod 3:5 and Josh 5:15). It occurs nowhere else in the Hebrew Scriptures. The formulation of the reason is almost identical, again restricted to these two occasions—you stand on holy ground. As Moses led Israel once, so will Joshua lead them now. The new land is holy ground.

Joshua 8:30–35 + 9:1–2   Shechem

A painstaking study of Josh 8:30–35 has concluded that this passage is late and post-deuteronomistic (L'Hour 1962). Nelson notes that the passage is "known to occur in three different locations" (Nelson, comm., 116). The LXX places it after Josh 9:1–2; a Hebrew text from Qumran, 4QJosh[a] places it just before Josh 5:2—that is, "closely after the Jordan crossing and immediately before the circumcision" (Nelson, comm., 117). Our concern is not so much with issues involving date or origin as with meaning. Once the meaning is scrutinized, the various locations fall into place.

According to verses 30–35, Joshua built an altar on Mount Ebal (which is in the vicinity of Shechem, itself unmentioned in the text), made offerings to the LORD, and wrote the law on the stones before all Israel—just as Moses had commanded (cf. Deut 11:29–30; 27:2–13). For those who set great store by the observance of the law—and we have seen the emphasis in Josh 1:7–9 and in the Achan story—this account of the exact observance of Moses' command and of Israel's scrupulous attention to "all that is written in the book of the law" (vv.

31, 34) would have been a guarantee of Israel's total success. No wonder then that when the local rulers heard, they united in a major coalition against Joshua (Josh 9:1–2). The coalition was organized, according to the text, because of something that the kings heard. In Josh 10:1 a coalition is organized when Adoni-zedek of Jerusalem heard what had happened to Jericho, and Ai, and Gibeon. Joshua 9:1 simply has "heard" (the NRSV's "heard of this" correctly reflects the vagueness of the reference). For the purposes of the text, it suits perfectly that the kings beyond the Jordan had heard of the ceremony on Mount Ebal and—wisely but vainly—mustered all their forces "to fight Joshua and Israel" (9:2).

The tradition reflected in the LXX may be understood slightly differently. There the ceremony at Mount Ebal follows the mustering of the coalition. Against overwhelming forces, the guarantee of God's help and Israel's success would have been urgent. The location of the passage as close as possible after the crossing of the Jordan (cf. 4QJosh^a) may reflect a strict interpretation of Deut 27:2 (so Nelson, comm., 117); also, the sooner Israel has the down payment on God's benevolence, the better. Faced with such urgency, the impracticalities associated with the location of Ebal and Gerizim are unimportant. (For the difficulties of the passage, see particularly Nelson, comm., 115–20.)

List-Like and Summarizing Styles
Joshua 10:28–12:24

List-like: the south

Joshua 10:28–41   Southern conquests

These fourteen verses are unique in the Bible. Before deciding on a stance toward them, we need to look at their distinctive qualities. In these verses, six towns—Makkedah, Libnah, Lachish, Eglon, Hebron, Debir—are destroyed, their rulers and populations exterminated, and the ruler and his people from a seventh town are wiped out (Gezer, v. 33). Within these verses, there is no reference to leaving or returning to camp, no reference to strategy, no speeches of the LORD giving assurance. However, the LORD's help is reported, in the third person, for Libnah and Lachish (vv. 30, 32). There is a limited overlap with the towns of the five-king coalition—Jerusalem, Hebron, Jarmuth, Lachish, Eglon; three are common to both lists, two are exclusive to the earlier list (10:3), and three are exclusive to the later list (10:28–41).

The first list, of course, describes the defeat of a coalition, begun in the neighborhood of Gibeon; the second list describes towns captured, with the destruction of rulers and populations. The name linking the two is the town of Makkedah; however, three of the kings killed in the second list had already been put to death in the earlier action against the coalition (10:26).

The material is described as "list-like." It is not the same as the two lists in chapter 12, both beginning "these are the kings" (12:1, 7). On the other hand, the fourteen verses are devoid of any of the characteristics of narrative or story: no trace of plot, no circumstantial details, no discussion of strategy, and so on. The central feature appears to be that Joshua and all Israel destroyed every person and "left no one remaining" (vv. 28, 30, 33, 37, 39, 40). Verse 40 extends the claim from six towns to "the hill country and the Negeb and lowland and the slopes." Assessment of the location of the six towns reveals just how far this claim goes beyond the details described. Lachish, Libnah, and Eglon are clustered together in the southern lowlands (or Shephelah). Makkedah's location is unknown; it is usually located in the Lachish region (cf. Josh 15:41; Aharoni 1967, 195 n. 59), putting it a long way from Gibeon. The other two towns to make up the six are Hebron in the mountains of Judah and Debir a little further south. A small cluster hardly represents "the lowlands," any more than the towns of Jericho, Ai, and Gibeon represent the central highlands of Ephraim or two towns represent the hill country of Judah. The claim is symbolic; the towns named relate to the claim as do parts to a whole.

The language of destruction is extremely dense. This is not surprising for fourteen verses that report the destruction of six towns and the death of the ruler and people of a seventh. Nevertheless, it is worth noting. "Took" occurs five times (not for Libnah); "the edge of the sword" occurs six times; "utterly destroyed" occurs six times (not for Libnah); "every person" occurs six times; the combination "utterly destroyed . . . every person" occurs five times (not for Libnah); that there were no survivors ("no one remaining") is specified six times—for Makkedah, Libnah, King Horam of Gezer, Hebron, and Debir (not for Lachish and Eglon)—and with "utterly destroyed" in the final summary in verse 40.

This language of destruction is not easily situated within the language of Israel. The specification of "no survivors" occurs a dozen times in the Hebrew Scriptures—for Sihon and Og in Deut 2:34 and 3:3 (cf. also Num 21:21–35); for the warriors at Ai (Josh 8:22) and the victory in the north (Josh 11:8); and for the house of Ahab in Jehu's revolt (2 Kgs 10:11). The combination "utterly destroyed . . . every person" occurs only in these fourteen verses (cf. Josh 11:11). The concept of God's "removing" the local peoples (cf. Deut 7:1, 22) does not occur in Joshua—the only things "removed" are Joshua's sandals (Josh 5:15). Utter destruction is the fate of these peoples (Deut 7:2), but beyond this the key concerns of Deut 7:1–6 are not repeated in Josh 10:28–41. Deuteronomy manifests a strong concern for the inner purity of Israel; the evil is to be purged from Israel's midst (cf. Deut 13:5 [NRSV, 13:6]; 17:7, 12; 19:19; 21:21; 22:21, 22, 24; 24:7). None of this language is found in Joshua.

The outcome of these considerations is that Josh 10:28–41 is an independent fragment of tradition. As an independent fragment, it has been skillfully inserted into the account of Joshua's campaign against the southern coalition (10:7–27, 42–43), with its execution of the kings in the cave at Makkedah and its more restrained conclusion and report of the return to camp at Gilgal. Reaching this conclusion is not to make a claim about the authenticity or authority of the tradition. That task is left to the reader.

Summarizing: the north and the whole of the land

Joshua 11:1–15   Hazor and northern conquests

With Joshua 11:1–15, we turn to the north of the country. Hazor, "the head of all those kingdoms" (11:10), is to the north of the Sea of Galilee. The description we are using for these texts of chapter 11 is "summarizing." They are not technically lists, like the two in chapter 12. They are not as patterned and repetitive (list-like) as Josh 10:28–41. On the other hand, there is no narrative being told; we are given the bare bones of people and places. The battle is given four verses (11:6–9); the enemy coalition, five verses (11:1–5); the generalized fate of the northern towns, six verses (11:10–15). By comparison with the extensive texts earlier in the book of Joshua (2:1–10:27), these are summaries at best.

The coalition is portrayed as representing a wide extent of territory in the north. At the head is Jabin of Hazor (cf. Judg 4–5); the identifications of Madon and Shimron are both uncertain, but both are northern (cf. Aharoni 1967, 106, 206); Achshaph is in the plain of Acco, the "northernmost coastal plain," just north of the Carmel range (cf. Aharoni 1967, 21, 206). Overall, the lands range from the Sea of Galilee to Mount Hermon in Lebanon. The gathering point of the coalition,

Merom, is situated in Upper Galilee, a little to the north of Hazor (cf. Aharoni 1967, 206).

The verses related to the battle are remarkably structured. At the center is verse 7: Joshua and his troops fell upon the enemy "suddenly," a surprise attack. Before this, a speech from the LORD gives assurance and a strategic instruction: Hamstring the horses. After it, the LORD is reported handing over the enemy to Israel's pursuit (v. 8), and Joshua follows the strategic instruction, hamstringing the horses and burning the chariots (v. 9). The verb "to give" (NRSV here, "to hand over") is, of course, common in the book of Joshua. However, its use for enemies is not common; it occurs for Jericho (6:2), Ai (8:1, also vv. 7, 18), and the southern coalition (10:8, also v. 19) and for Libnah and Lachish (10:30, 32). Otherwise, after 11:6 and 8, we do not come across it again in this context of enemies until Josh 24:8 and 11. God's assurance is only given three times in the book: Josh 8:1 (Ai), 10:8 (the southern coalition), and here in 11:6. Tactics are involved—hamstring the horses—but they are not tactics to win the battle; instead, they serve to disarm the enemy after the defeat (v. 9). What the LORD promises in verse 6 ("I will hand over all of them, slain, to Israel") is done in verse 8 ("and the LORD handed them over to Israel"). The victory is the LORD's.

The aftermath of the battle is succinctly reported (vv. 10–15). Hazor is burned, the other towns depopulated, and valuables and livestock plundered. It is in these verses that the language of 10:28–41 recurs. Joshua "took" (root: *l-k-d*) Hazor and all the towns; the utter destruction of every person is reported for Hazor and all the towns. The destruction of "all that breathed" is reported twice, for Hazor (v. 11) and for all the peoples (v. 14); otherwise it only occurs in Joshua at 10:40 (cf. Deut 20:16). The phrase, the "edge of the sword," which occurs once each for Jericho (6:21) and Ai (8:24), occurs six times in 10:28–41 and three times here (11:11, 12, 14). Conclusion: the same spirit that breathed in 10:28–41 is recognizable here.

The final verse puts an unusual emphasis on the chain of command; it is more emphatic than 11:23. As YHWH commanded Moses, so Moses commanded Joshua, and so Joshua did (v. 15). Literally (in both Hebrew and NRSV), Moses has the last word. The source for such a concern is obscure.

Joshua 11:16–23 The whole of the land

These verses, perhaps with the exception of verses 21–22, provide a conclusion to the account of Israel's entry into possession of the land.

What is most remarkable is the absence of any dependence on the texts
that precede, with the sole exception of the reference to the
Gibeonites. The land described hardly corresponds with any details
from the preceding chapters. There are some links to the generalizing
of 10:40–41, but hardly a close correspondence. The death of the kings
is reported, but not of their peoples; nothing is said of booty. A long
war is specified (v. 18), rather to the contrary of what has preceded.
The theology of YHWH hardening the hearts of Israel's enemies is not
expressed anywhere in the book of Joshua. It belongs rather with the
plague accounts of Exodus (cf. Exod 4:21; 7:13, 22; 8:19; 9:12, 35;
10:20, 27; 11:10; 14:4, 8, 17).

Apart from the two verses here, the Anakim are mentioned only in
Josh 14:12, 15 and twice directly in Deuteronomy (1:28; 9:2; three
other references are comparative).

The final verse of the chapter, 11:23, clearly reflects the earlier
generalizing presentation of YHWH's commission to Joshua in 1:1–6.
Although it may not reflect accurately the detail of the sources compiled within the early part of the book of Joshua, it reflects accurately
enough the overall accomplishment of the promise with which the
book began. The concluding clause cannot be overlooked. It reads literally: "And the land was undisturbed, without war" (was quiet from
war: *wĕhā'āreṣ šāqĕṭâ mimmilḥāmâ*). This is not to be confused with
the deuteronomistic concern for rest, expressed through the root
n-w-ḥ and the noun *mĕnûḥâ*. The "undisturbed" clause here occurs
again in Josh 14:15 and then in the Deliverance Collection in Judges
at Judg 3:11, 30; 5:31; and 8:28. The deuteronomistic ("rest") clause
is used in Deut 3:20; 12:9–10; 25:19; Josh 1:13, 15; 21:44; 22:4; 23:1;
Judg 2:23; 3:1; 2 Sam 7:1, 11; 1 Kgs 5:4; 8:56. The two different
expressions describe the same state of peace and can refer to much the
same periods of time, but they reflect different patterns of language
and almost certainly derive from different circles. Here the conclusion that "the land was undisturbed, without war" links these traditions to a stage of the Deliverance Collection (in Judges) that is
pre-deuteronomistic. It may be noteworthy that here (Josh 11:23) a
claim is made without any time limit being set on it. The same statement is repeated four times in the Deliverance Collection, always
associated with a forty-year time limit. Does such a limit imply
remembrance of and insight into human frailty? Nothing of the kind
is noted for Joshua's generation.

The texts about north and south hardly add up to an occupation of
the "whole land" and yet that is what Joshua is reported to have taken

(11:23). The tenor of generalizing passages has been in this direction. In such a case, it may be important not to confuse science with symbol. When a description of the parts does not add up to the whole, the issue is often not error or deception but an appeal to symbol. The detail of the parts selected can cast light on the way the whole was reached. The parts may not equate to the whole, but they may facilitate the understanding of the whole. The parts highlighted may symbolize something of the whole. In this regard, the last word may be given to Soggin: "The redactor did not want to give us so much an account of historical facts, as to bear witness to the mighty acts of Yahweh in history" (Soggin, comm., 144).

When all this has been said, it should be noted that our task here has been an interpretation of the text of the book of Joshua. This is not a history of Israel's occupation of its land. That would be a different task, drawing on a far wider range of sources.

Lists

Joshua 12:1–6 and 7–24   Defeated kings

Joshua 12 gives us two lists of the kings defeated by Israel, those east of the Jordan and those west of it. Both begin with the formulaic "these are the kings of the land" (*'ēlleh malkê hā'āreṣ*). Despite its six-verse length, the first list has only two names—Sihon and Og—while the second list has some thirty (MT: thirty-one). The first list notes allocation by Moses (v. 6); the second list notes allocation by Joshua for the land west of the Jordan (v. 7). The extent of the territory is noted for both sides of the Jordan. On the east, the descriptors tally with those of Deuteronomy; on the west, 12:7 repeats the information of 11:17 (Mount Halak occurs in these two verses only) and 12:8 draws much of its information from 10:40.

The introductions need not have the same origins as the lists, naturally. The second list is clearly independent of the traditions in the book of Joshua. It may have the value of an independent source, or it may not. We frankly do not know. For Noth, it is deuteronomistic (Noth, comm., 71–72), but, beyond Sihon and Og, interest in the Canaanite kings is not characteristically deuteronomistic. Nelson remarks that "because it is not merely a rehash of the book's narratives, it clearly reflects to some degree a genuine source with a previous history of its own," but he comments that its literary history "remains clouded . . . remains an enigma" (Nelson, comm., 162). We actually know nothing of its historical worth.

ALLOCATION OF THE LAND
JOSHUA 13–22

The conclusion of the book of Joshua, above all the "assembly at Shechem" (chap. 24), has attracted plenty of attention. Before chapter 24, the distribution of the land and associated traditions may be of considerable interest to specialists, but they do not arouse the interest of most readers. The structural blocks make us aware of what is going on, but we will not linger on them. There are two major blocks of tradition for the west-of-Jordan distribution of land: chapters 14–17 (Judah and Ephraim/Manasseh) and chapters 18–19 (the other seven tribes). An introduction and the situation east-of-Jordan come before these two, and after them some further traditions are added.

It is not unlikely that Josh 21:43–45 formed the conclusion of the basic Josianic deuteronomistic book of Joshua, following on 12:24, and presumably followed by Josh 24:29–31. A pre-deuteronomistic collection of traditions appears to have existed, now within chapters 2–12, which the Deuteronomists incorporated into a larger work, giving particular emphasis to the role of Joshua in carrying on what had been begun under Moses. Subsequently, more traditions were added to this nucleus. I discuss further details in the final chapter.

Predistribution: East of the Jordan
Joshua 13:1–33

Joshua 13:1–7   Introduction

This little introduction is troublesome in three respects. First, it begins with a reference to Joshua's age—"Now Joshua was old and advanced in years" (13:1)—that is identical with Josh 23:1b (*wiyhôšuʿa zāqēn bāʿ bayyāmîm*). This leaves a lengthy period between the occupation of the land (Josh 1–12) and its distribution to the tribes. It also renders absurd the claimed participation of "all the warriors" of the east-of-Jordan tribes, leaving their wives, their little ones, and their livestock undefended across the Jordan (cf. Josh 1:14). Second, the promise of further occupation in the future (Josh 23:4–5) is even more explicit in 13:1b ("very much of the land still remains to be possessed"). This is in troubling contrast with the confident claim in 11:23 that "Joshua took the whole land." Third, the territory described extends roughly from the border with Egypt to the north of Lebanon. This does not correspond at all with the land to be divided in verse 7. Thus, the introduction brings together rather unharmoniously the chronological concern (late in Joshua's life), the territorial concern (much to be possessed), and the issue of distribution of the land (cf. Soggin, comm., 151–53).

Joshua 13:8–14, 15–31   East-of-Jordan tribes: globally and separately

The allocation of land to the two-and-a-half tribes east of the Jordan is reported in two stages. First, verses 8–13 give a global description of the land allocated to the Reubenites, the Gadites, and the half-tribe of Manasseh—all the territories of Sihon and Og. It is noted that Geshur and Maacath were not driven out (v. 13) and that no inheritance was given by Moses to the tribe of Levi (v. 14—because "the offerings of fire" were their inheritance).

Second, verses 15–31 give a separate, and not entirely troublefree, description of the territory for each group—Reubenites (vv. 15–23), Gadites (vv. 24–28), and the half-tribe of Manasseh (vv. 28–31).

Joshua 13:31–32   Conclusion

Verses 31–32 provide a conclusion. This allocation was done by Moses (v. 32). An inheritance for the tribe of Levi was not part of this Mosaic allocation; "the LORD the God of Israel" was their inheritance (v. 33). The absence of an inheritance for the tribe of Levi is the same as in verse 14; the reason given is different.

Joshua 13 gives the impression of an assemblage of traditions rather than a piece composed for the purpose of accounting for the east-of-Jordan situation (cf. Soggin, comm., 151–59). Whether this enhances or detracts from the traditional value of these texts remains uncertain.

Distribution: West of the Jordan
Joshua 14:1–19:51

Joshua 14–17   Judah and Joseph (= Ephraim and Manasseh)

In this first block of tradition concerning the distribution of the inheritances west of the Jordan, the task is attributed to a small group: the priest Eleazar, Joshua son of Nun, and the heads of the families of the tribes of the Israelites (14:1). The distribution was to be by lot. There is no reference to Shiloh in association with this first distribution. Shiloh is first mentioned in the introductory material to the distribution by Joshua to the seven tribes (Josh 18:1, 8, 9, 10) and then in 19:51, in association with the same small group (the priest Eleazar, Joshua son of Nun, and the heads of the families). Coming after the completion of

the distribution by Joshua and the allocation by the Israelites of Timnath-
serah to Joshua (19:49–50), the origin of 19:51 has to be suspect (cf.
Gray: "the secondary, redactional character of the Shiloh tradition is
clearly indicated by the fact that . . ." (Gray, comm., 159–60).

The report of the distribution by lot to Judah and Joseph (Ephraim
and Manasseh) is not begun until chapter 15. Chapter 14 begins with a
rather unsatisfactory introduction which reports the Mosaic allocation
of land to the east-of-Jordan tribes and the situation of the Levites.
This information will be repeated again at 18:7. A tradition is then
reported that Joshua, at Gilgal, gave Hebron to Caleb (14:6–15; cf.
Campbell and O'Brien 2000, 136, 144–45). After that, the distribution
gets under way, and land (15:1–12) and towns (15:21–62) are listed for
Judah separately, and territory with towns for Ephraim (16:5–9) and for
Manasseh (17:7–11). A variety of assorted traditions are interspersed
among these.

Joshua 18–19   Seven tribes

In this second block of tradition concerning distribution of the inheritances west of the Jordan, the task is attributed to Joshua (18:10).
The casting of lots is preceded by a note that the whole congregation
of Israel assembled at Shiloh and set up the tent of meeting there
(18:1). Joshua sent out a survey party, three men from each of the
seven tribes as yet without inheritances, to divide into seven parts the
land between Joseph in the north and Judah in the south (18:2–9).
Once again it is noted that the Levites are to have no portion; this
time a third reason is given: "The priesthood of the LORD is their
heritage" (18:7a).

The seven tribes are Benjamin (territory before towns, 18:11–28; cf.
Nelson, 212), Simeon (within Judah, 19:1–9), Zebulun (19:10–16),
Issachar (19:17–23), Asher (19:24–31), Naphtali (19:32–39), and Dan
(19:40–48).

The overall assessment of the texts on the allocation of the land
(chaps. 13–19) is controverted and can be debated in great detail. Nelson's comment is fair: "This geographic information rests on source
material, some of which originally had an administrative purpose. . . .
On the other hand, much of this material seems to have been concocted
by scribal erudition on the basis of traditions and source lists of uncertain origin" (Nelson, comm., 8). There are great differences in the
potential age and authenticity of various traditions, to say nothing of
the way that they have been adjusted to suit the present composition
(cf. Campbell and O'Brien 2000, 141–43). To conclude, with Nelson:

"The ideological map given in Joshua is certainly more realistic than that of Ezekiel, but the literary and theological purposes are similar" (Nelson, comm., 12).

Postdistribution
Joshua 20–22

Joshua 20   Cities of refuge

Without permanent structures for law enforcement, punitive action was the responsibility of the next-of-kin (*gō'ēl*). Manslaughter (unplanned homicide) was distinguished in law from premeditated murder (e.g., Exod 21:12–14). To allow time for this legal distinction to be investigated, cities of refuge were established where a killer could shelter temporarily from the next-of-kin (cf. Deut 19:1–13; Num 35:9–12, 16–28).

In Josh 20, the law is formulated (vv. 3–6) and the six cities designated for this purpose (vv. 7–9).

Joshua 21:1–42   Levites

When we turn to the establishment of the cities for the Levites, it is comforting to be aware of what John McKenzie notes: "The OT data concerning Levi are not consistent and present a number of problems which scholars have not yet solved. . . . The preexilic history of the Levites includes a complex historical process which thus far has defied analysis" (McKenzie 1965, 504–5). Confirming this, we may note various dates suggested for the levitical cities by scholars: David's time, Albright; Solomon's, Mazar; Josiah's, Alt; at least preexilic, de Vaux, Haran (from Rehm 1992, 304). (For further details and the likelihood that this list is "a creation from the post-exilic period," see Spencer, 1992. See also Nelson on Josh 21: "Presented in the format of a town list, this has the earmarks of a scholarly imitation rather than an actual archival source" [Nelson, comm., 237].)

The Levites were mentioned previously in Joshua as receiving no inheritance (see Josh 13:14, 33; 14:3, 4; 18:7). Their allocation consisted of towns and pasture lands within the inheritances of other tribes. The list has its complexity, however, and the summary in verses 41–42 is a systematized simplification.

Joshua 21:43–45   Conclusion

Verses 43–45 are a summary of the whole book of Joshua: The land has been given by God as promised to the ancestors, possessed by the Israelites, and settled by them (v. 41; cf. 1:6). God has given rest to

Israel from all its enemies, none of whom had withstood its attacks (v. 42; cf. 1:5a and 23:9b). All God's good promises to Israel have come to pass (v. 43; cf. 23:14–15).

Noth remarks that this passage (in fact 21:43–22:6) is "so close to Dtr. in style that one could attribute it to Dtr. himself," except that 11:23ab anticipates it and it anticipates 23:9b and 14b (Noth 1991, 67). In the present circumstances, we can concede these verses to the Deuteronomists and see them, as noted earlier, following on 12:24. With the insertion of the allocation texts, 21:41–43 (with its reference to possession and settlement) forms a suitable conclusion at this point.

Joshua 22   Dismissal of east-of-Jordan tribes

With possession, allocation, and settlement accounted for, it is appropriate for the east-of-Jordan tribes to be dismissed and return to their lands. As is the case for so much of this material, considerable uncertainty about chapter 22 remains unresolved. It is likely that the episode of the "altar of great size" was already formulated in verses 9–34, almost certainly in priestly circles, before being incorporated here. Verses 1–6 and 7–8 form the bridging link. While there are strong signals of deuteronomistic language in verses 1–6, a number come from late in the deuteronomistic movement. Overall, despite uncertainty, it is likely that those interested in verses 9–34 incorporated the episode here, shaping their introduction around issues of late deuteronomistic concern and language, blending it in skillfully with 21:43–45 (cf. Campbell and O'Brien 2000, 156–57).

Nelson brings out the potential meaning of an otherwise difficult text: "The intention of this story is to promote an awareness of and commitment to national unity in the face of opposing attitudes and circumstances. . . . In whatever period this story originated, it must have persuaded generations of readers [author: hearers/users] to hold fast to national unity in spite of geographic separation and the dangers of diverse viewpoints. The unity of Yahweh's people is founded not on geographic proximity, but on shared faith and fidelity in worship" (Nelson, comm., 249–50).

The gist of the story is not difficult to tell, and its refractoriness is not difficult to see. The east-of-Jordan tribes on their way home build an altar of great size near the Jordan. The west-of-Jordan tribes are alarmed, gather for war at Shiloh, and send a deputation to negotiate. The meeting is "in the land of Gilead" (22:13). The delegation speaks of the land east-of-Jordan as unclean and of the altar-building as treachery (ma'al) and rebellion (root: m-r-d) against the LORD. The builders reply that the altar is not for rebellion or sacrifice but is evidence for future generations of their belonging to YHWH, God of Israel (22:26–30). The response satisfies the delegation, and the project of war is abandoned. The problems lie in the text's silence about where Joshua was when he dismissed the east-of-Jordan tribes (Shiloh? Timnath-serah?) and its obscurity about where the altar was built; in the idea of an altar "not for burnt offering, nor for sacrifice" (v. 26); about the period when building an altar might be thought of as "treachery" and "rebellion against the LORD" (v. 16); in the idea that the land allocated by Moses might be described as "unclean"; and about any setting known to us that might make suitable sense for such a story, whatever the age of its tradition or the time of its present formulation (late).

Conclusion
Joshua 23–24

One of the mysteries of biblical studies is where the unity of Israel came from. Biblical tradition made a sterling effort to derive it from Abraham and Sarah, Isaac and Rebekah, and Jacob, Leah, and Rachel. Generations of scholars have smiled wistfully and sadly shaken their heads. It is a commonplace of modern biblical scholarship that all of Israel did not participate in the exodus. The evidence for this is not so much from the exodus texts themselves but from the texts and traditions concerning the settlement of Israel in the land of Canaan. Simply put, not all the Israelites entered the land with Joshua; some of them were already there. The origins of Israel and the times of their entry into Canaan are regarded as considerably diverse.

The question remains: Where did the unity of Israel come from? For a long time, Josh 24 answered that question: The unity of Israel came from an assembly under Joshua at Shechem. Such a unity-forging assembly was a suitable conclusion to the life of Joshua, who had led a significant group of the people into Canaan. When it became clear that Josh 24 could not reflect the closing activity of Joshua's life, attention shifted to Josh 23 as the final speech closing off his career, but that too has been shown to be unacceptable. So we are left with the freedom to read both chapters for what they have to say in relation to the book they conclude, without worrying unduly about hypotheses of history.

Joshua 23   Speech of Joshua

With Josh 23, the book of Joshua undergoes a sudden shift of major significance. It is not just that Joshua is old; that was noted back in 13:1.

Even extensive territorial claims had been flagged back at 13:2–6. In Josh 23, however, not only is the task incomplete but the risk of failure is introduced for the first time: "Know assuredly that the LORD your God will not continue to drive out these nations before you" (v. 13); "you shall perish quickly from the good land" (v. 16).

In 21:45, the word was that "not one of all the good promises that the LORD had made to the house of Israel had failed; all came to pass." Now, suddenly, the past is not completed and the future is uncertain. A caution had been sounded in chapter 1: "Do not turn from the law to right or left, so that you may be successful" (1:7), but now the caution has changed to downright threat: "so the LORD will bring upon you all the bad things, until he has destroyed you from this good land that the LORD your God has given you" (23:15). The book has moved from the ideal world where obedience might be envisaged to the real world where transgression was to be feared.

Noth was the scholar who, against past practice (including his own), dropped Josh 24 from the Deuteronomistic History. His long-held view was that it showed no knowledge of the version of the conquest given earlier in Joshua, and so he concluded that "this passage was apparently unknown to Dtr." (Noth 1991, 23 n. 1). That allows Noth to have his Deuteronomist finish off the whole occupation story with Joshua's long speech in chapter 23, "looking back to the great events now at an end," going on "to warn the people against the gods and cults of the land," and culminating in "a threat of retribution" (Noth 1991, 66). He might have been warned by the parallel he drew with Deut 4:25–28, widely regarded as part of a later expansion of Deuteronomy.

Instead, it was Rudolf Smend (1971) who studied Josh 1:7–9; 13:1bß–6; 23; and Judg 1:1–2:9; 2:17, 20–21, 23, and concluded that all these passages, including Josh 23, belonged to a second and later level of the Deuteronomistic History. His initial study was followed up, on Samuel and Kings, by two of his students, Walter Dietrich and Timo Veijola (see chap. 5 in this volume). For all three, the Deuteronomistic History and its later revisions belonged in the time of exile. A different view was first advocated by Frank Cross, arguing for a Josianic Deuteronomistic History and a later exilic revision. His exilic revision included Deut 4:27–31 and Josh 23:11–13, 15–16 (Cross 1973, 287). For a full-scale study advocating a Josianic Deuteronomistic History with two focuses in an exilic revision see Campbell and O'Brien (2000). Further discussion is in chapter 5.

The upshot for Josh 23 is clear. The shift in the tenor of the book is marked and may reflect a looking back to the past and forward to the future or a difference in authorship. Close observation of the language, thought, and context suggests a difference in authorship. The shift in tenor is unaffected. The theology, however, must be read carefully. Israel's disobedience does not mean that God's commitment to Israel ceases. Disobedience means that Israel may not be successful (cf. 1:7). Disobedience will bring God's anger (23:16); Israel, however, remains God's people.

Joshua 24:1–28   Assembly at Shechem

In chapter 23, Joshua summoned all Israel, but the text does not say where they were summoned to and does not have them dismissed. Joshua 24 tells us both. They are summoned to Shechem (24:1) and, after the assembly, they are sent away to their inheritances (24:28).

In his address to this assembly, Joshua traces the story of the people, from their ancestors to the present (vv. 2–13). Then Joshua exhorts the people to serve YHWH, offers them a choice, and, when they choose to serve YHWH, Joshua argues that they are unable to (vv. 14–21). The people insist, their commitment is solemnized, a covenant made and written on stone, and the people dismissed.

There are problems. The tracing of Israel's story—a short historical credo—is a literary achievement that comes late in Israel's literature. As Noth commented, the account of the conquest does not tally with the traditions of the book of Joshua (cf. vv. 11–12). "The gods that your ancestors served beyond the River" sounds remarkably odd for a people whose ancestors had left Mesopotamia centuries before. The offer of a choice between YHWH and the gods of Mesopotamia or the gods of Canaan (v. 15) sounds most odd after the strictures of Josh 23.

The demand for a choice, not between life and death but between gods, hardly makes Josh 24 suitable as a report of the final assembly of Joshua's generation. Could the demand for a choice reflect the rallying of elements to the unity of Israel in premonarchical times? While this is possible, the references to the gods beyond the River mean that the substance of the present text has to be much later than premonarchical. Several options offer more immediate association with these gods beyond the River. Lothar Perlitt (1969, 273–79) suggests three options with deuteronomistic associations, where the threat from Assyria demands reaffirmation of commitment to YHWH: (1) the Assyrian takeover of northern Israel (cf. 2 Kgs 17); (2) the Assyrian threat to Judah (cf. under Ahaz, 2 Kgs 16:7–18; under Manasseh, 2 Kgs 21:1–16);

(3) the weakening of Assyria and reform of Josiah (2 Kgs 21:1–6, 12). Dennis McCarthy, arguing against any deuteronomistic association, suggests the earlier and enduring threat of Aramean power from east of the Euphrates after the collapse of the Davidic empire, akin to Elijah's challenge to Baalism on Mount Carmel (McCarthy 1978, 283). A likely option is the situation of the deracinated peoples from beyond the River, transplanted by the Assyrians into northern Israel, who needed to come to terms with YHWH (cf. 2 Kgs 17:24–41; for discussion of this problematic and difficult passage, see Campbell and O'Brien 2000, 443–46).

Joshua 24:29–33   Concluding traditions

The book concludes with the death and burial of Joshua, along with the evaluation that "Israel served the LORD all the days of Joshua, and all the days of the elders who outlived Joshua and had known all the work that the LORD did for Israel" (24:31). A comment of this kind already has in sight a new generation that did not know the works of the LORD (cf. Judg 2:10). Traditions are added concerning the burial at Shechem of Joseph's bones and the burial of Eleazar at Gibeah.

For Noth, "we must assume that this information was taken over by a secondary hand from Judg. 2 into Josh. 24:29–31 when the book of Joshua was made into an independent literary unit" (Noth 1991, 22 n. 3). Campbell and O'Brien adduce reasons for attributing Josh 24:29–31 to their Josianic Deuteronomist (2000, 163).

It is important to note here that the LXX has an extensive addition after Josh 24:31:

> In that day, the Israelites took the ark of God and carried it around among them; and Phinehas exercised the priest's role in place of his father Eleazar until he died and was buried in his own Gibeah. The Israelites departed each to their own place and to their own town. And the Israelites worshiped Astarte, and the Ashtaroth, and the gods of the nations round about them. And the Lord delivered them into the hands of Eglon, King of Moab, and he ruled over them eighteen years.

Auld comments: "If we reverse the argument and consider this to be an uncorrected fragment of an earlier version of the text, then it also preserves precious evidence of how the longer text was expanded from it" (Auld 1998, 125). Such decisions can be left to specialists, but if the LXX reflects an older fragment, its presence gives added weight to what will be seen in the next chapter: the move from experience to reflection and further development.

READING THE WHOLE

In many ways, the book of Joshua can be seen, for Israel, as a pool of light, with a bit of smudge in the middle and an ominous shadow at the end. God's clear program was established at the start and implemented throughout the book. The unity of the people was underscored by the participation of the east-of-Jordan people in the action of taking possession of the territory across the Jordan. Something of the permanence and divine ordinance for all this is symbolized in the allocation by lot of the land to the various tribes. An understanding is clear throughout the book: God's help gave Israel its land. The correlative of that is occasionally explicit: Without commitment to God's law, God's help cannot be counted on. By and large, however, Joshua has led an Israel without blemish to the successful conclusion of God's design: "All came to pass" (21:45).

The smudge in the middle is where terse texts take over from extensive narrative and the extermination of peoples is presented as God's will. Historically, we know it did not happen (so did they). Theologically, it may seem a most appalling support for those of little faith; what constitutes possible occasions for the loss of unity in faith must be eliminated rather than overcome. Symbolically, it may point to fanaticism rather than faith. It bulks large enough to be a cause of scandal for many, but it is also a small enough part of the program to be easily overlooked.

The shadow cast at the end of the book is worrying, because of our awareness that it is a very long shadow indeed. There are unquestionably further pools of light, but the shadows will gather until the future is dark. The demand of the aging Joshua, "Hold fast to the LORD your God" (23:8), is a demand that in his last assembly of the people Joshua will claim they cannot meet (24:19). We might hope that this "you cannot" was merely a rhetorical flourish given Joshua. Unfortunately, the texts and the generations to come will prove it right.

Viewed as the reflection of the development in Israel's thinking, the book of Joshua offers traditions of how the Israelites came into their land: God gave it to them. It is not certain, but not unlikely, that these traditions, both warlike and sacral, were brought together in some sort of composition before the creation of a Josianic Deuteronomistic History (i.e., much of Josh 2–10). This Deuteronomistic History, with its sweeping range from Moses to Josiah, brought together the Mosaic leadership for Israel coming out of Egypt and the leadership of Joshua for Israel coming into Canaan. "As I was with Moses, so I will be with you" (1:5). For Israel, this is the image of a perfect world; "Joshua took the whole land" (11:23) and "not one of all the good promises that the LORD had made to the house of Israel had failed" (21:45). The suggestion that Josiah is reflected in the portrayal of Joshua is attractive (see Nelson 1981), but too many of the texts involved are either post-Josianic or of uncertain origin for the case to be satisfactory. At best, it reflects an editing of a base text that is left to be explained. Further developments are added after the Josianic Deuteronomistic History. Joshua 1:7–9 and Josh 23 bring the cold light of realism into the warm glow of success. Allocation of land is the consequence of its occupation; distribution by lot at the Shiloh sanctuary is a further symbol of the whole program's being of God. Texts of extermination may be indicative of the desperation that is spurred by fear for survival. There is more, but this will do.

For many serious readers today, Josh 1–12 is a puzzling text, to put it politely. Archaeological evidence makes it clear that what is portrayed in Josh 1–12 is not how Israel emerged in Canaan. Critical reading of the biblical text reveals Josh 1–12 as a highly inadequate portrayal of taking "the whole land" (Josh 11:23). In the not-too-distant past, believers viewed the chapters as a reliable portrayal; in the far distant past, the same could have been true. ("Could have been" is possible; it is not necessary.) We may assume that the bulk of Josh 1–12 had been put together by the time of the Deuteronomistic History. The faith articulated in the "sacral" texts is clear enough; the experience undergirding the "soldierly" texts is elusive; where the fanaticism of the ethnic cleansing came from we are not sure. Above all, the need met by this composition evades us. It is not simply a matter of preserving traditions. More than preservation has happened. If traditions have been drawn on, some have also been fragmented in order to be blended into a sequential text of considerable complexity. What needs are met by this image of Israel? What function is served by this picture of conquest? What gap is bridged? Why have these chapters more troubling unevenness than comparable biblical compositions? Hypotheses are possible; certainty is not.

Such a book has interesting consequences for Israel's time and ours. In Israel's time, the weaving of a narrative or telling of a story, where more than one view is offered, allowed for focus on one view or on an alternative or on the fact that several views existed. In our time, a plurality of views in the text requires us to accept the existence of a plurality of views in ancient Israel, and where they differ we may not be able to avoid exploring our evaluation of them. These different views are often not compartmentalized into separate chapters but blended together. The book of Joshua amalgamates these differing traditions; it does not adjudicate between them. Traditions are juxtaposed, not evaluated. To the best of our knowledge today, that is part of the nature of biblical text.

REVIEW ISSUES

1. What different viewpoints are offered within the book of Joshua?
2. What is the value of the book of Joshua to a historian or to a theologian?
3. In medieval Islam, the view was held that a ruler had the right to rule until a stronger dispossessed him and ruled in his place; Machiavelli and Mao would not have disagreed. Has world opinion changed? Has there been a profound deepening of the human spirit, or has there been a sad shift from "what we want, we get" to "what we've got, we keep"?

Bibliography of works other than commentaries

Aharoni, Yohanan. 1967. *The Land of the Bible: A Historical Geography*. London: Burns & Oates.

Auld, A. Graeme. 1998. *Joshua Retold: Synoptic Perspectives*. OTS. Edinburgh: T. & T. Clark.

Campbell, Antony F., and Mark A. O'Brien. 2000. *Unfolding the Deuteronomistic History: Origins, Upgrades, Present Text*. Minneapolis: Fortress.

Cross, Frank Moore. 1973. "The Themes of the Book of Kings and the Structure of the Deuteronomistic History." Pages 274–89 in F. M. Cross, *Canaanite Myth and Hebrew Epic: Essays in the History of the Religion of Israel*. Cambridge, Mass.: Harvard Univ. Press.

Dever, William G. 2001. *What Did the Biblical Writers Know and When Did They Know It? What Archaeology Can Tell Us about the Reality of Ancient Israel*. Grand Rapids: Eerdmans.

Finkelstein, Israel, and Neil Asher Silberman. 2001. *The Bible Unearthed: Archaeology's New Vision of Ancient Israel and the Origin of Sacred Texts*. New York: Simon & Schuster.

Gibson, John C. L. 1971 *Hebrew and Moabite Inscriptions*. Vol. 1 of *Textbook of Syrian Semitic Inscriptions*. Oxford: Clarendon.

L'Hour, Jean. 1962. "L'Alliance de Sichem." *RB* 69:5–36; 161–84; 350–568.

Lohfink, Norbert. 1994. "The Strata of the Pentateuch and the Question of War." Pages 173–226 in *Theology of the Pentateuch: Themes of the Priestly Narrative and Deuteronomy*. Translated by Linda M. Maloney. Edinburgh: T. & T. Clark.

McCarthy, Dennis J. 1978. *Treaty and Covenant: A Study in Form in the Ancient Oriental Documents and in the Old Testament*. AnBib 21A. New ed. completely rewritten. Rome: Biblical Institute.

McKenzie, John L. 1965. *Dictionary of the Bible*. New York: Macmillan.

Mendenhall, George E. 1958. "The Census Lists of Numbers 1 and 26." *JBL* 77:52–66.

Nelson, Richard D. 1981. "Josiah in the Book of Joshua." *JBL* 100:531–40.

Niditch, Susan. 1996. *Oral World and Written Word: Ancient Israelite Literature*. Library of Ancient Israel. Louisville, Ky.: Westminster John Knox.

Noth, Martin. 1991. *The Deuteronomistic History*. JSOTSup 15. 2d ed. Sheffield: JSOT Press. German original, 1943.

Perlitt, Lothar. 1969. *Bundestheologie im Alten Testament*. WMANT 36. Neukirchen-Vluyn: Neukirchener Verlag.

Rehm, Merlin D. 1992. "Levites and Priests." *ABD* 4:297–310.

Smend, Rudolf. 1971. "Das Gesetz und die Völker: Ein Beitrag zur deuteronomistischen Redaktionsgeschichte." Pages 494–509 in *Probleme biblischer Theologie: Gerhard von Rad zum 70. Geburtstag*. Edited by H. W. Wolff. Munich: Kaiser.

Spencer, John R. 1992. "Levitical Cities." *ABD* 4:310–11.

Walters, Stanley D. 1988. "Hanna and Anna: The Greek and Hebrew Texts of 1 Samuel 1." *JBL* 107:385–412.

2

The Book of Judges

OVERVIEW

The book of Judges opens with traditions of Israel's occupation of Canaan that are surprisingly different from those just concluded in the book of Joshua. Perhaps not so surprisingly, they are both preceded and followed by a note of Joshua's death. Following these traditions, several fragments offer explanations for the presence of those locals left in Israel's midst (cf. Judg 2:1–3:6).

Judges 2:11–19*, in the middle of these fragments, serves as an overview of a carefully organized series of stories in 3:12–8:35. The stories are of the deliverance of Israel in campaigns led by hero figures— Ehud, the trio of Deborah, Barak, and Jael, and finally Gideon. The careful organization is found in framing activity that expresses a theological understanding of what can be learned from these stories of deliverance. It has been traditional to read the stories as ideals of divine

---

*The asterisk (*) used occasionally with verse numbers in this volume indicates that only the relevant parts of the verse or verses so marked is referred to. In other words, the asterisk (*) is a signal that a part or parts of the text involved is excluded from the reference.

Biblical references are given to the chapter and verse numbering of the Hebrew text and (where different) of the NRSV, thus covering the two sets of numbering in current use. Which set is employed by a given translation will be quickly recognized.

Books and articles will be referred to by author's name and date of publication; full details will be found in the bibliographies at the end of each chapter. Commentaries will be referred to by author's name followed by "comm."; full details are given at the end of the book.

grace and guidance; for example, von Rad (with a quotation from Martin Buber): "The real point at issue is Israel's proper ordering under God's rule, and it is understandable that the Book of Judges has been designated as the 'Plato's *Republic*' [Buber] of the Bible" (von Rad 1962, 1:332). It is more realistic, however, to read the collection as a witness to the failure of leadership after Joshua.

Israel is portrayed as remaining on the "straight and narrow" during the generation of the deliverer. Following the deliverer's death, however, Israel is portrayed doing evil and being punished for it by God, enduring foreign domination for substantial periods of time. The deliverers then are raised up by God or are commissioned by God to liberate the people, but the deliverance is portrayed as liberation from a punishment that God has visited on the people. With regrettable regularity, Israel reverts to evil, is punished by God, and then is liberated from the punishing oppressor. The institutional leadership is lacking that could have given Israel some stability in fidelity. The echo of the comment after Joshua's death is clear: The people of Joshua's generation worshiped the LORD; after all, they had seen "all the great work that the LORD had done for Israel" (Judg 2:7; cf. Josh 24:31). But Joshua's generation was followed by another that "did not know the LORD or the work that he had done for Israel" (Judg 2:10). The series of deliverance stories points out that this happened again and again. The experience of God did not seem to survive the generation gap. Left to themselves, the Israelites did what humans usually do: They messed up. And after the death of each deliverer, they were left to themselves.

Gideon, the last of these deliverer figures, ends up strangely. He is portrayed as declining dynastic rule (root: *m-š-l*) over Israel on the grounds that it is not himself or his son or grandson but the LORD who will rule over Israel (Judg 8:22–23). Immediately following this noble act, however, he is shown leading Israel into apostasy, making an ephod out of seventeen hundred shekels of gold and more: "All Israel prostituted themselves to it . . . and it became a snare to Gideon and to his family" (8:27). Surpassing strange! There is ambivalence in the story that follows. Abimelech, Gideon's son by a "concubine" (secondary wife: *pîlagšô*, 8:31), makes the citizens of Shechem an offer that they cannot refuse, they consent to back him, he eliminates the competition by murdering his seventy brothers, and he becomes king (*melek*, 9:6) at Shechem. The ambivalence lies in the fact that verses 22 and 55 reflect a claim to kingship over Israel. The story is restricted to rivalry for rule over Shechem (cf. 9:2), but with a couple of references to Israel (9:22,

55). Abimelech's murderous attempt at rule, whether in Shechem alone or in Israel, is a dismal failure.

The next block in the book is associated with Israel's renewed apostasy (10:6) and God's punishment of surrendering them "into the hand of the Philistines and into the hand of the Ammonites" (9:7). The figure of Jephthah is centered on the Ammonite oppression; Samson is associated with the Philistine oppression. Before each, there is a fragment of tradition about so-called minor judges: Tola and Jair in 10:1–5 and Jephthah, Ibzan, Elon, and Abdon in 11:7–15, about whom we know nothing—neither who they were nor what they did. There is just enough detail in the traditions to arouse curiosity and leave it unsatisfied. Before the introduction of Jephthah, there is a theological reflection on Israel in 10:6–16, similar to the overview in 2:11–19.

There is a marked difference between the two, however. The passage starts with a repeat of a familiar theme—"The Israelites again did what was evil in the sight of the LORD"—specifically involving apostasy (10:6). It goes on to have God act dismissively: "Go and cry to the gods whom you have chosen; let them deliver you in the time of your distress" (10:14) and ends on an ambivalent note. The traditional translation reads that God could "no longer bear to see Israel suffer" (10:16). The Hebrew is susceptible to another and radically different rendering: "God could no longer bear the burden of Israel." The first translation signals the continuation of what has been; the second need not mean divine abandonment but may signal a radical change of situation. As in many of the best ambivalences, there is truth in both. Life will go on and God will be part of the deliverance of Israel from the Ammonites. God will begin the deliverance of Israel from the Philistines, but there will be radical change before it is achieved.

Something else too is discordant here. God was part of Jephthah's victory and Israel's deliverance—"The LORD gave them into his hand" (11:32; cf. 11:29, 30–31, 36; 12:3)—yet Jephthah's commission was not from God but from the elders of Gilead (11:9–11). Samson, in contrast, has a truly remarkable birth story (Judg 13), in which he is said to be one "who shall begin to deliver Israel from the hand of the Philistines" (13:5). He may have begun the task; he certainly did not complete it. As von Rad comments: "The oddest figure amongst the judges is Samson: the reader will indeed find it absolutely impossible to understand him as judge over Israel" (von Rad 1962, 1:333). It is King David who delivers Israel from the Philistines, completing the task that Samson only began. Echoes of the traditions of Israel's origins haunt the figures of Jephthah and Samson. Jephthah is driven off by his brothers much as Abraham was ordered by Sarah to drive off Hagar and Ishmael (cf. Judg 11:2 and Gen 21:10; the NRSV's "drive off" reflects the same verb in both [root: *g-r-š*]; its "inherit" translates two different verbs [roots: *yrš* and *nḥl*]; similar situation, slightly different language). Samson, of course, was born to a mother who was "barren, having borne no children" (Judg 13:2). The birth-to-be is announced by the angel of the LORD (cf. 13:21–23). The echoes of Sarah in the past are clear. Birth to a barren mother has meaning for Israel. It will be evident in the destiny of Samuel, the prophet to anoint David king.

With the stories of Samson, the language of the judge ceases. Judges 13:1 echoes the refrain of the earlier stories. Judges 15:20 and 16:31b have Samson judge Israel for twenty years; those twenty years can hardly be said to be worth much, and with them the judge language stops. Another refrain takes its place and forms an envelope around the remaining chapters of the book: "In those days there was no king in Israel; all the people did what was right in their own eyes" (Judg 17:6; 21:25; cf. also the short form, Judg 18:1 and 19:1). The traditions preserved in these chapters are rightly called "texts of terror" (Trible 1984); they are appalling. Leadership and deliverance are absent; the strong oppress the weak. For example: "The Danites, having taken what Micah had made, and the priest who belonged to him, came to Laish, to a people quiet and unsuspecting, put them to the sword, and burned down the city. There was no deliverer (*wĕ'ên maṣṣîl*)" (18:27–28). The traditions that follow are worse; wrongs are righted by even more terrible wrongs. This is surely a generation that did not know YHWH.

If the book of Judges is to be characterized under a single term, it is "the book of dysfunction." The conquest was a failure—at least as far as emphasis on occupation of "the whole land" goes. The pattern of deliverer-judges was a failure—at least as far as assuring a fidelity in Israel akin to that of Joshua's generation. The minor judges and Abimelech, Jephthah, and Samson were no better. The book ends in abysmal anarchy. Overall, it portrays a picture of intensifying dysfunction. The final refrain is unavoidable: "There was no king in Israel." The period portrayed in the book of Judges is a horrible hinge between the Israel of Moses and Joshua and the Israel of prophets and kings. If the Deuteronomistic History is understood as exilic and hostile to Israel's monarchy, the book of Judges fits uncomfortably within it. If the basic Deuteronomistic History is understood as Josianic and favorable to Israel's monarchy, the book of Judges witnesses powerfully to the need for that monarchy. For an application of recent literary theory to the interpretation of Judges as a book, "an integrated work . . . a complex work, that was reshaped in various stages and sub-stages, and had a long, complicated editorial history," see Amit 1999, 358. For a variety of approaches, see Yee 1995.

This overview can be summed up in the following outline. Details emerge in the discussion below; for example, "force and failure" may be applied to both Jephthah and Samson, but the meaning for each is quite different.

ISRAEL IN THE BOOK OF JUDGES	JUDGES 1–21
I. Occupation of the land: a different picture	Judg 1:1–2:5
II. Transition of generations	2:6–10
III. Life in the land: new generations and degeneration	2:11–21:25
A. God's action	2:11–16:31
1. Repeated regularly	2:11–9:57
a. Overview and reflections	2:11–3:6
b. Organized traditions of deliverance	3:7–8:35
c. Abimelech: force and failure	9:1–57
2. Repeated sporadically	10:1–16:31
a. Introduction and reflection	10:1–16
b. Jephthah and minor judges	10:17–12:15
c. Samson: force and failure	13:1–16:31
B. God's absence	chaps. 17–21
1. From south to north: might is right	17–18
2. From Dan to Beer-sheba: threefold outrage	19–21
a. Rape and murder	19
b. Civil war and extermination	20
c. Murder and rape	21

MAJOR TEXT SIGNALS

1. The first major signal in the book of Judges is the references to the death of Joshua. The book opens with one: "After the death of Joshua . . . " (Judg 1:1). This is hardly surprising, as Joshua's death was reported at the end of the previous book (Josh 24:29), but it is reported again at Judg 2:8. That is surprising, and its implications demand thought.

The two statements of Joshua's death bracket off Judg 1:1–2:5. There is a sense in which these traditions are set outside the flow of time. They belong as part of the narrative text, even though they are not part of the narrative sequence.

The introductory phrase, "after the death of Joshua," situates what follows as occurring after the events of Joshua's life. The two references to "the territory allotted" (*gôrāl*) confirm this view (v. 3), but the term does not occur again. Other aspects of 1:1–2:5 suggest a different picture. The reference in Judges to Joshua's dismissing the people and to Joshua's death and burial (Judg 2:6–9) has to be seen as odd coming after 1:1. It is important in terms of the transition to new generations. To stop with this observation, however, would be to neglect a further signal.

2. The second signal is sent by 2:7 and 2:10. Judges 2:7 speaks of the fidelity of Joshua's generation and offers a reason for it: They had "seen all the great work that the LORD had done for Israel" (cf. Josh 24:31). Judges 2:10 refers to the emergence of a new generation, of whom it is said only that they "did not know the LORD or the work that he had done for Israel." The implications of this change of generations is yet to be unfolded; the signals, however, are there.

3. A third signal relates primarily to the material between 2:11 and 8:35. There is a very strong patterning of elements within these texts, which reveals multiple stages of reflection. In the past, the historical-critical approach to biblical texts has identified such stages of reflection with stages of authorship. This may well be correct, but for us the issue needs to be researched rather than assumed. The patterning revolves around five elements:

a. Israel's activity	doing evil in the eyes of YHWH
b. God's activity	punishment, handing over to an oppressor
c. Israel's activity	a cry to God
d. God's activity	deliverance, subduing the oppressor
e. Outcome	tranquillity for a generation

The stages of reflection are visible in the language used for these elements, the presence or absence of these elements, and the presence of other elements. All this will need to be looked at closely when we attend to the texts; the signals are there and cannot be ignored. (For an overview of these elements, see the table "Patterns and Judges" in Campbell and O'Brien 2000, 477.)

One other signal has to be flagged in this regard, for it is easily overlooked: There is a vast diversity among the traditions incorporated within the framing; yet for all the differences, there is remarkable uniformity in the pattern that makes up the framing.

4. A further signal, relating above all to Judg 10:1–16:31, can be formulated as the absence of the pattern but the presence of some of the elements. None of the elements are present in Judg 9:1–57, and it is difficult to situate. The language of judging is present in a number of cases: Judg 10:2, 3; 11:27; 12:7, 8, 9, 11, 13, 14; 15:20; and 16:31. The language of Israel's doing evil recurs in 10:6 and 13:1. The language of punishment is found at 10:7. Israel's cry to God is found in 10:10 (cf. 10:14). The language of deliverance is found at 10:1, 11, 12, 13, 14, 15; also 11:26; and 13:5. The specific language of the subduing of the oppressor occurs at 11:33 (cf. 12:3).

Two things are notable in this inventory. First is the absence of any reference to tranquillity. Second is the clustering of elements in 10:6–16, although even there the patterning of 2:11–8:35 is absent. When this cluster is set aside, along with the language of judging which involves a variety of functions, the key occurrences are only 10:1; 11:33; 13:1; and 13:5. The whiff of presence is overwhelmed by the odor of absence.

5. The final chapters of the book of Judges send a fifth signal. The earlier patterning and its elements are totally absent. A different pattern has taken their place, the pattern of the refrain. The refrain—"In those days there was no king in Israel; all the people did what was right in their own eyes"—occurs at Judg 17:6 and 21:25; its first half occurs at Judg 18:1 and 19:1. The signal points to something common to all five chapters. It may do more.

Reading the Sections

OCCUPATION OF THE LAND:
A DIFFERENT PICTURE
JUDGES 1:1–2:5

This block of text has three parts: traditions of assault (1:1–26), an extensive tradition of default (1:27–36), and a somewhat dissociated explanation (2:1–5). As noted earlier, the parts are held together by the envelope formed by statements of Joshua's death before and after.

The traditions of the first part (1:1–26) can be characterized as "traditions of assault," for the idea of "going up against" is dominant (cf. 1:1, 2, 3, 4, 15, 22; also LXX of 1:11). First of all, Judah goes up against the Canaanites, defeats them at Bezek, captures Jerusalem, and then goes down against the Canaanites in the hill country, the Negeb, and the lowland, with particular mention of Hebron and Debir. Further traditions associated with Judah have the Kenites settle in the Negeb with the Amalekites (v. 16). Judah and Simeon sack Zephath/Hormah (v. 17), and Judah takes Gaza, Ashkelon, and Ekron, with their surrounding territory (v. 18). A note follows that anticipates the second part, to wit, that Judah took the hill country but could not drive out the chariot-owning inhabitants of the plain (v. 19). Hebron is mentioned again (v. 20) and the statement made that the Benjaminites did not drive out the Jebusites who lived in Jerusalem (v. 21). The tradition that concludes this first part notes that the house of Joseph went up against Bethel and sketches the strategy of its capture (vv. 22–26).

In whatever way they are understood, the issues raised by these Judahite traditions need to be noted. First, the inquiry put to the LORD by the Israelites asks literally: Who shall go up for us against the Canaanites in the beginning? This does not sit comfortably with Joshua's activity either in Josh 1–12 or 13–23. Verse 3, with its references to the territory allotted to Judah and then to Simeon, implies an understanding in which the "allotted" territory had to be conquered; despite Josh 11:18, this can hardly be said to be the understanding of the book of Joshua. Judah is said to have defeated the Canaanites at Bezek (Judg 1:4). Bezek is identified with Khirbet Ibziq in the northeastern part of Mount Ephraim (Aharoni 1967, 197); this is not the picture presented in the book of Joshua. The status of Jerusalem is uncertain; it is captured and burned by the people of Judah (Judg 1:8), but the Benjaminites did not drive out the Jebusites there (Judg 1:21; cf. Josh 15:63, where this is said of the people of Judah, and Josh 18:28, where Jerusalem is listed in the inheritance of Benjamin). The view that Judah destroyed Jerusalem, that the Jebusites later occupied it and held it against the Benjaminites till David's time (e.g., Aharoni 1967, 197) does not resolve the totality of these difficulties. The report that Judah took Gaza, Ashkelon, and Ekron (Judg 1:18) is unlikely to be accurate, both because (1) these are three of the five Philistine towns (but cf. 1 Sam 7:14) and (2) Gaza and Ashkelon are on the coastal plain, while Ekron is a little farther east, in the Shephelah (cf. v. 19). The LXX has a negative in verse 18 and a change of verb—did not inherit/take possession—which is, perhaps, harmonizing, but is more realistic (see Aharoni 1967, 198).

These traditions can be looked at in two ways. On the one hand, as fragmentary memories of a distant past, they should not be seen as incompatible with the more systematized presentation in the book of Joshua; much can be brought into harmony. Alternatively, they are seen as fragmentary memories of a different picture of Israel's occupation of its land. All things considered, the latter is more likely.

The second part of the block (1:27–36) is a list-like summary of the activities of seven of the tribes: Manasseh, Ephraim, Zebulun, Asher, Naphtali, and the house of Joseph—after reference to the displacement of Dan. Often referred to as the "negative conquest" because of the emphasis on towns whose inhabitants were not driven out, the tradition in fact implies a situation of settlement in specific areas for various tribes of Israel. If Reuben, Gad, and the half-tribe of Manasseh are located east of the Jordan, and Judah, Simeon, and Benjamin are reckoned as dealt with in the first part of the block, this leaves only Issachar (in the valley of Esdraelon) unaccounted for from the Joshua traditions (cf. Josh 19:17–23).

At least three factors justify characterizing Judg 2:1–5 as a "dissociated" explanation of the incomplete nature of Israel's occupation in the preceding chapter: (1) There is no reference to those addressed by the angel of the LORD after going up from Gilgal; (2) there is no reference in the preceding chapter to any covenants made by Israel with the inhabitants of the land; and (3) the statement, "I will not drive them out before you," places this within Joshua's generation, elsewhere affirmed to have faithfully worshiped the Lord (cf. Josh 11:15; 21:45; 24:31; Judg 2:7). It looks as though an independent, and relatively late, tradition has been pressed into service to account for the incomplete aspect of Israel's occupation of the land.

Uncertainty over the whole is unavoidable, given the conflict of fragmentary traditions. Some of the conflict can be reconciled; some remains. The fragmentary state of the evidence prohibits certainty. Two levels of evaluation need to be differentiated. One relates to historical recovery of the past; the other relates to the expression of meaning in the present.

As to recovery of the past, at one end some opt for obscure but evident historical value in these traditions while, at the other, some opt for the evident absence of historical value. In between, many struggle with conflicting factors: "another picture of the occupation . . . and but partially completed" (Bright 1960, 117–18); "the editor's reconciliation of faith and fact" (Gray, comm., 212); "unlike anything else in the book[;] . . . certainly not a unified literary composition, but . . . built up of preformed narrative units together with archival details and notices of various sorts" (Boling, comm., 63). Boling attributes Judg 1:1–36 with chapters 19–21, as a framing preview and postview, to a sixth-century deuteronomistic editor (Boling, comm., 30). While all things are possible, unfortunately there is no trace of characteristic deuteronomistic language or thought as evidence to substantiate this assertion; it is too schematic to be even probable.

The emphasis on Judah for the south, although starting at Bezek, and the emphasis on the incompleteness for so much of the north, although present to a lesser degree in Joshua, taken together suggest a core of alternative traditions—in all their complexity. (The Joshua passages are: for east of the Jordan, Josh 13:13; for Judah and Jerusalem, 15:63; for Ephraim and Gezer, 16:10; for Manasseh and Beth-shean, Ibleam, Dor, En-dor, Taanach, and Megiddo, 17:11–13.)

As to the expression of meaning in Judg 1:1–2:5, given the tenor of what is to follow, the tone is set by 2:1–5, giving infidelity as the cause that accounts for incompleteness. The presence of these traditions sandwiched between reports of Joshua's death, whatever the factors of textual growth, cast the block in an uncanny light; it has a ghostly air of insubstantial unreality. In evaluating its contribution, apart from the case of 2 Kgs 13–14 (cf. Campbell and O'Brien 2000, 170), two other areas need consideration. In the book of Numbers, Israel arrives at the plains of Moab before chapter 25; chapters 26–36 reflect traditions that were to be located in the Mosaic period but before the book of Deuteronomy. In the books of Samuel, a collection in 2 Sam 21–24 contains traditions of David's military organization that are otherwise unknown to us in the extensive traditions about David as military leader.

Here, in the book of Judges, the theme of failure resulting from infidelity is introduced from the outset. Given Judg 2:17, this infidelity is insinuated even into Joshua's generation. In the rest of the book to come, it will permeate the whole story of Israel. Conflict remains; infidelity and the worship of the LORD go hand in hand.

TRANSITION OF GENERATIONS
JUDGES 2:6–10

The on-again off-again oddity of the reporting of Joshua's death is significant for what it envelops; however, it does not affect these five verses. Judges 2:10 would be enough on its own, but it is helped by Judg 2:7 (cf. Josh 24:31). Without Judg 2:7, we would still have known that Joshua's was a near-perfect generation. Achan's is the only sin in the book. Some writers include the dealings with Rahab and Gibeon in the category of Israel's sin, but this is wrongheaded. The deal with Rahab was a smart move on Israel's part; the deal with Gibeon was a smart move on Gibeon's part. Neither is named sin. What Achan did is named a sin (Josh 7:20) and attributed to Israel (Josh 7:11). Sin is not mentioned elsewhere in the book. So Joshua's was a near-perfect generation.

But there is a new generation. That is obvious; that had to happen. This new generation "did not know the LORD or the work that he had done for Israel" (Judg 2:10). This is not so obvious, not so inevitable. It is a theological observation from which no conclusion is yet drawn; the conclusion lies in the experience ahead.

Judges 2:10 (or indeed 2:6–10) is not merely a transition from Judg 1:1–2:5. It is a transition from the whole generation of Joshua, including those who outlived him. It is a transition from the Israel of Moses and Joshua to the generations afterward. It is the transition from "them" to "us," from the past to the present. It is a transition that is constant and real.

LIFE IN THE LAND:
NEW GENERATIONS AND DEGENERATION
JUDGES 2:11–21:25

God's action
Judges 2:11–16:31

Repeated regularly

Judg 2:11–9:57   The whole

Before we plunge into the component parts of this text, it is helpful to stand back and survey the whole. It is one of the more thoroughly patterned pieces of biblical text and it is also one of the more difficult (the elements of the pattern are listed earlier, under "Major Text Signals"). The intensity of the patterning is hardly surprising; at issue is the life of a human community before God. The difficulties are surprising, but they are there. It will make reference and discussion easier if we put names on the four major blocks of text (in relation to the patterning): (1) the *overview* (Judg 2:11–19*, with the asterisk to remind us that vv. 12–13 are variations of v. 11, and that v. 17 expresses a radically different view of human life); (2) *Othniel* (Judg 3:7–11, made up of the framing elements and no core story); (3) the *collection* (Judg 3:12–8:35, with framing elements around three passages: the story of Ehud, the story with Deborah, Barak, and Jael, and the traditions about Gideon); and (4) the *aftermath* (to be found within Judg 9:1–16:31). These names have been chosen to be as neutrally descriptive as possible.

I explore the significance and difficulties of these chapters under three areas of difference: theology, terminology, and what, for lack of a better term, can be called sequence.

THEOLOGY

Nature of the evil	apostasy—occurs in overview and Othniel only (also 10:6)
God's anger	expressed—occurs in overview and Othniel only (also 10:7)
Israel's repentance	never expressed (but see 10:16)
Israel's cry to God	always expressed—except for the overview

TERMINOLOGY: THE RESCUERS ARE NAMED AS—

Judges	in overview only
Deliverer who judges	in Othniel only
Deliverers	in collection only (expressly there, only Ehud)

SEQUENCE OF THE PASSAGES

Israel did evil	in overview, Othniel, and Gideon (6:1)
Israel continued to do evil	in Ehud (3:12) and Deborah/ Barak/Jael (4:1)

The most fully articulated position is expressed in the initial overview (2:11–19*).

These three sets of differences raise two questions. The first is how the present text of 2:11–16:31 is to be read or used. Initially, information is encoded in the text; subsequently, it is not present; it is either presumed or left latent. The first option ("presumed") allows for a synchronic reading, reading what has become in its form as the final and fully developed text. What is expressed initially (in the overview) is taken for granted in what follows and is not repeated there. The second option ("left latent") allows for a diachronic reading, reading what is becoming in its development toward final text. What is expressed initially (in the overview) has been derived from what follows, but is left latent there.

The second question is whether these differences signal no more than stages of reflection or whether instead they signal stages of authorship. A "stages of reflection" view assumes a single author, whose final reflections have been expressed at the beginning (in the overview). A "stages of authorship" view assumes several authors, each responsible for one of the parts of the text.

We are not obliged to choose between these two. Here as elsewhere, we can read the present text as it is (synchronic), while remaining aware of the potential process of its development (diachronic). In such a case, the final author (responsible for 2:11–19*, the most fully articulated position) makes the entire text their own.

Technically, the patterning of the "collection" ends with 8:28: "So the land had rest forty years in the days of Gideon." However, fragments from the framing elements occur within 9:1–16:31, and I use the term "aftermath" for this material. The "judging" element is frequent; other elements are more sporadic. Examples in this "aftermath" are:

JUDGING		OTHER	
10:2	Tola "judged Israel"	10:1	Tola "rose to deliver"
10:3	Jair "judged Israel"	10:6	Israel continued to do evil (apostasy)
12:7	Jephthah "judged Israel"	10:7	God's anger kindled and Israel punished
12:8	Ibzan "judged Israel"	10:8	Oppression for eighteen years
12:11	Elon "judged Israel"	10:10	Israel "cried to the LORD" (confession of apostasy)
12:13	Abdon "judged Israel"	10:11–15	Issues of apostasy and deliverance
15:20	Samson "judged Israel"	10:16	Israel's repentance (of apostasy)
16:31	Samson "judged Israel"	11:33	Jephthah: "Ammonites were subdued"
		13:1	Israel continued to do evil
		13:5	Samson: "begin to deliver"

With these observations available to us, it is time to look more closely at the component parts of the text.

Judges 2:11–3:6 Overview and reflections

Given the observations above (with substantial indebtedness to Richter 1964 and 1966, balanced with Bal 1988b), it is possible to look more closely at an aspect of 2:11–19* that has not so far received enough attention. As an overview of the text to come, it goes beyond it and quite radically transforms it. The overview portrays, first, a period of repeated activity that is regularly met by failure (2:15), and, second, when the LORD raised up a judge, they were delivered from their enemies "all the days of the judge," such deliverance leaving open the possibility of repeated activity that is regularly met by success (2:18). What is clear in verse 15 is echoed, though less evidently, in verse 18. This portrayal reflects an understanding radically different from that of the collection (3:12–8:35), where a situation of sustained passivity (oppression) is punctured by a single activity of deliverance after which the land is tranquil for a generation.

Without doubt, the overview surveys a situation of patterned activity: "Whenever they marched out, the hand of the LORD was against them" (2:15). "Whenever" (*běkol 'ǎšer*) points to the multiplicity of experience; the elements of the pattern have been noted earlier. The overview takes up the elements of the pattern to come, describing what was seen as Israel's repeated behavior: Israel did evil (v. 11), God gave them over to plunderers (v. 14), God delivered them (v. 16), there was deliverance for the generation of the judge (v. 18), after the death of the judge, they would relapse (v. 19). However, the overview envisages a more active and repetitive situation than the oppression and single campaigns of deliverance tell in the collection.

Viewed in the light of this difference, it is important to note that the overview opens by emphatically asserting that the evil the Israelites did in the eyes of the LORD was apostasy—to worship the Baals, abandon YHWH the God of their ancestors, and follow other gods (vv. 11–13). Few of us today are hassled by the idea of apostasy; fewer still have any inkling of what the experience involves. We may have been trained to identify the Baals with power, prestige, and wealth, or whatever illusion energizes life. That is fine, but to have any feeling for this apostasy, we have to experience the seductive power of what it is that could entice Israel—and can entice us—away from real life. In an agricultural society, grounded in the remorseless cycle of sowing and reaping, the attraction of Baal, the dying and rising god, can be the all-powerful attraction of survival. Survival is an irresistible need, irresistibly attractive. The survival of the human spirit always involves some form of faith, going beyond the merely material. The human spirit is not fulfilled simply by what we can touch. Augustine was right to say, "You have made us for yourself, O God, and our hearts can find no rest until they rest in you." The struggle for faith is the struggle to identify that "you" for our hearts to rest in. That was Israel's struggle. Nothing petty—just the utter essence of human living.

Jeremiah put it well for Israel:

> Be appalled, O heavens, at this,
>   be shocked, be utterly desolate, says the LORD,
> for my people have committed two evils:
>   they have forsaken me,
> the fountain of living water
>   and dug out cisterns for themselves,
> cracked cisterns
>   that can hold no water.
>
>   (Jer 2:12–13)

For Jeremiah—and for Israel—YHWH, their God, is a fountain or source of living water. Any gardener, anyone who knows a desert—and Israel lived close to the desert—knows the impact of water as a source of life. Water is the difference between the barren and the green. Come upon an oasis in the desert and the impact is felt. Broken cisterns that can hold no water—these are the forces that seduce us with the illusion of life, but it is a lifeless illusion. For those of YHWH-faith, Baalism was such an illusion. Israel's struggle with it was a struggle with life and death, the struggle for living water, the seduction of tangible cisterns—that are cracked.

What is surprising in this repeated pattern is that only two texts name Israel's evil as apostasy (the overview and Othniel, as noted earlier). In the three cases of Ehud, Deborah, and Gideon, it is merely said that Israel "did what was evil in the sight of the LORD." According to 2:11–13, this "evil" was to be understood as apostasy. The fact that this is passed over in silence in the three story passages raises the question whether the "evil" in these three cases (3:12; 4:1; 6:1) was or is to be understood as apostasy. Various forms of injustice might well attract punishment.

It is equally surprising that only two texts within this pattern—again, the overview and Othniel—speak of God's anger being kindled (here, v. 14). The phrase occurs four times in Deuteronomy, invariably in the context of apostasy (Deut 6:15; 7:4; 11:17; 29:27). It is likely that the occurrences here are associated with the charge of apostasy. (Other occurrences associating God's anger with Israel's apostasy are Num 25:3 [Baal Peor]; Josh 23:16; Judg 10:7; Ps 106:40; 2 Chr 25:15; note also 2 Kgs 13:3–5.) The relationship to what follows has to remain uncertain. Whether a different understanding is expressed, a corrective is made, or what was already latent is made explicit remains uncertain.

Users of the text can hardly escape the understanding expressed in the envelope of 2:11 and 3:7 at the beginning and later in 10:6–7; whether they accept this understanding for the three stories remains an open option.

The confession of sin and the expression of repentance in putting away the foreign gods is expressed later (e.g., confession of sin: Judg 10:10, 15; 1 Sam 7:6; 12:10; 1 Kgs 8:47; putting away of foreign gods: Judg 10:16; 1 Sam 7:3). Neither is expressed within the patterned narrative (2:11–8:35). Throughout the patterned narrative, a cry to God precedes the deliverance (3:9, 15; 4:3; 6:6). Here in the overview, it is not expressed. It is perhaps latent at the end of 2:18, but the stereotyped phrase of the other passages is absent from the overview. A reason for this silence is not easily available.

Also peculiar to the overview is the description of the rescuers as "judges" raised up by God to deliver Israel from their oppression (2:16). It is thought that the use of the term "judges" here allows for an association of these deliverer-figures with the so-called minor judges, where judging and deliverance are associated with both Tola and Jephthah (cf. Noth 1991, 69–72). It is important to notice the balance in God's activity. God's deliverance of Israel *from* oppression is in each case preceded by God's deliverance of Israel *to* oppression as punishment for the evil done.

It is also worth noting that the designation of the oppressors as "plunderers" (2:14, 16) occurs nowhere else in the book of Judges. The term is rare enough (eleven occurrences in the Older Testament) that nothing points to its potential origin (cf., e.g., 1 Sam 14:48; 23:1; 2 Kgs 17:20).

A final difference between this overview and the following patterned narrative is tranquillity versus deliverance. In the narrative, the statement that the land had quiet for forty years is repeated four times (3:11, 30 [80 years, assumed to account for Shamgar as well]; 5:31; 8:28). In the overview, in contrast, it is said that the Israelites were delivered "from the hand of their enemies all the days of the judge" (2:18). To be delivered from the power of enemies can imply wars fought and victories won, rather than the presence of tranquillity. The difference of expression is unexplained.

Within the overview, a different stage of reflection clamors to be heard. Verse 17 expresses a nuance in relation to verses 18–19. In verses 18–19, there is a generation gap; one generation is faithful and the next is not. Verse 17 says that it is not so easy, that infidelity is present within every generation. Even in the generation of the judge, "They lusted after other gods" (2:17). This is no minor gloss, irritatingly inserted by some later misguided soul. It presents a major theological alternative in its claim that the idea of a transition—from a faithful generation that knew the LORD to an unfaithful generation that did not—is an illusion. According to the theological understanding of verse 17, there is no such transition in real life; both fidelity and infidelity are present in the hearts of each generation. The judges were not merely deliverers, working political wonders with the aid of God. The judges were also leader figures, to be heard or listened to, whose values could be absorbed or rejected. In hard times, the deliverer's values will be absorbed; in gentler times, the same leader's values will be ignored. Verse 17 denies the portrayal of verses 18–19; the text invites us to our own reflecting. Is conversion of the essence (vv. 18–19), or are we as we are (v. 17)—and God is committed to us?

Other stages of reflection are attached to the idea of God's anger. Theologians latched on to God's anger and had God say, "I will not drive them [the local inhabitants] out before you" (Judg 2:3; cf. 2:20–21). Reflection ponders this. Judges 2:3 says, "Their gods shall be a snare to you"—without spelling out specifics. One stage of reflection spells out the presence of the locals as God's testing Israel, "whether or not they would take care to walk in the way of the LORD" (2:22; cf. 3:4)—exposure to the seduction of the illusory. A different stage of reflection puts the presence of the locals in more positive light for Israel (not so positive for the locals): They were left to test Israel in war, "that successive generations of Israelites might know war, to teach those who had no experience of it before" (3:1–2). These reflections are intertwined in the text in ways that need not be detailed here (cf. Campbell and O'Brien 2000, 175–76).

Judges 3:7–8:35   *Organized traditions of deliverance*

Within these organized traditions of apostasy and deliverance, more happens than the telling of the framed stories of three campaigns; three groups of tradition are rehearsed and three more stages of reflection are revealed. The telling of the stories is one stage of reflection. That events happen is experience; that their stories are told is a further stage, deeming the events worth consideration and reflection. The framing of the stories is a further stage; it distills a single pattern of existence from the diverse experiences of the stories. The initial example of Othniel (Judg 3:7–11) is a compilation of the framing elements, with no core story. It too, however, mirrors another stage of reflection, and its changes of language mirror subtle changes of thought.

Because the Othniel episode has no story as its core, the question has to be asked why it should exist. It agrees with the overview in understanding Israel's evil as apostasy at which God's anger is kindled and in God's "raising up" the deliverer. It agrees with the collection in describing the rescuer figure as a deliverer (3:9). It is also said of the deliverer that "he judged Israel" (3:10). There are links to Gideon and Jephthah: "The spirit of the LORD came upon him" (3:10), as it did for Gideon (6:34) and Jephthah (11:29). His hand "prevailed" over Cushan-rishathaim (3:10) as "the hand of Midian prevailed over Israel" (6:2). In its terminology, above all "judge" and "deliverer," the Othniel episode stands midway between the overview and the collection. It could be said to have a bridging function.

The link to Jephthah, although tenuous, leaves open the possibility that the Othniel passage was formulated as some sort of preface, bringing the collection into association with the Jephthah story. It begins with the direct introduction that "the Israelites did what was evil"; the verbal "again" (= verb + infinitive; tag: the "continuation formula") is not employed. The passage now serves as a bridge between the overview and the collection, and it is likely that it was formulated for this purpose. The concern to see the "deliverers" as "judges" is attributed to the Deuteronomist, in the composition of the Deuteronomistic History. As a bridge, whether originally part of the composition or inserted subsequently, the Othniel passage could be from the Deuteronomist or could be later. For Noth, his Deuteronomist was responsible for the overview, Othniel, and the framing of the collection—"a series of stories . . . probably collected together before Dtr." (Noth 1991, 69). Noth passed over the differences discussed here. Richter, who brings these differences to the fore, saw the Othniel episode (emended) as pre-deuteronomistic (Richter 1964, 114–15, cf. 24–25; also pre-deuteronomistic, Campbell and O'Brien 2000, 176). Given its bridging function, a post-deuteronomistic formulation has to be a possibility.

Beyond the elements of the framing, there may be interest in the names. Othniel, son of Kenaz, is mentioned earlier as capturing Kiriath-sepher and so winning Achsah for his wife (Josh 15:17; Judg 1:13). Cushan is mentioned as "the tents of Cushan," in parallel with Midian (Hab 3:7), evidently a place name. Rishathaim does not occur outside Judg 3:8, 10; it may be a piece of creative fantasy. Boling suggests something like "Cushan Double-Wickedness" (Boling, comm., 80) and Gray, noting that "the passage has all the appearance of artificiality," has "Cushan of the Double Iniquity" (Gray, comm., 213). Noth simply labels it "an unsolved mystery" (Noth 1991, 73).

When we move off the Othniel bridge, we move into new territory, where the making of theology has been the primary focus in the making of text. We watch Israel treading its winepress and squeezing the juices of theology out of the grapes of experience. The grapes of experience are held in the stories of three campaigns: against Moab, Canaan, and Midian. The deliverer heroes are Ehud, in a single story; Deborah and Barak with Jael, in a story with a double focus; and Gideon, in a collection of traditions. The theology is expressed in the interpretative framing placed around these three campaigns. The same three theological elements precede the story of each campaign. First, the people of Israel did what was evil in the sight of the LORD. Second, the LORD punished them with foreign oppression. Third, they cried out to the LORD. The response to this cry is basically contained in the stories of the three campaigns of deliverance. At the end of each, two further elements are added: The oppressor was subdued, and the land was undisturbed (NRSV: "had rest") for forty years.

Three things seem to be central here: first, the claim that oppression was God's punishment for Israel's evil; second, that deliverance was God's gift in response to Israel's need; third, the land's tranquillity lasted the deliverer's lifetime. Some today will wish to disagree with all three. The interpreter recognizes their place in the text and weighs up the relationship between the theology and the experiences in which it originated. The presence of the overview and Othniel is a reminder that the same experience can generate theology which is conceptualized and expressed in different ways.

In these three cases, the evil is not specified. From what has preceded, we may presume that it is apostasy, or we may ignore the earlier claim. There is plenty of evil available beyond apostasy. The Ehud framing says it twice in the opening verse (3:12): once as the bald statement that Israel continued to do evil (note the continuation formula), and a second time as the explicit reason for the LORD's "strengthening" of King Eglon of Moab against Israel. This repetition does not recur later; perhaps it is presumed. The oppression is noted as lasting eighteen years. It is then said that "when the Israelites cried out to the LORD, the LORD raised up for them a deliverer, Ehud son of Gera" (3:15). The idea (and the language) of the LORD "raising up" a deliverer is shared with the overview and Othniel (2:16, 18; 3:9); it does not occur after this. Interestingly, it is part of the framing of the story. In this initial part of the frame, Ehud is named as the deliverer. In the story itself, the phrase "by him" (v. 15) refers back to this name. A frame is not imposed on the hard-and-fast form of the stories; the framing becomes part of the narrative.

Ehud is a Benjaminite and left-handed. He heads the party bringing
Israel's tribute to King Eglon and seizes the chance to assassinate
Eglon, escape, and raise a revolt against the demoralized Moabites.
The story is totally secular. The play on words in his "message from
God" (*děbar 'ělōhîm*, which can be a "thing from God") does not alter
the story's secularity. This may account in Ehud's case for the framing's
statement that the LORD raised up for them a deliverer; Deborah is
already prophetess and judge and Gideon is associated with an elaborate commissioning tradition. One way or the other, the act of deliverance is claimed for God. The interpreter must ask whether this faith
claim is imposed on the experience or whether it is derived from the
experience and, if so, how.

Two realities are latent beneath the surface of this text. First, Ehud's
action in assassinating Eglon was high risk; it was very dangerous. Second, it is remarkable that a single individual and a single killing could
trigger a revolt to reverse eighteen years of oppression. As to the risk,
swords were worn on the thigh; that was standard (cf. Exod 32:27; Ps
45:3; Song 3:8). A short sword, on the right thigh, under the man's
clothes, would if discovered have meant instant death. Eglon's body-
guards were slack (cf. David's comment to Abner, 1 Sam 26:15–16).
The story does not tell us why Ehud left and came back (loss of nerve,
inauspicious circumstances, better chance for privacy?). As to the
revolt, we are simply told that Ehud rallied the hill-country folk,
blocked the Jordan fords, and broke the Moabite yoke. In all of this, the
narrator saw the hand of God; we are not told why.

The potential is there for great storytelling: Ehud's preparations for
the assassination (far from uncommon; cf. Joab of Abner [2 Sam 3:27],
Absalom of Amnon [2 Sam 13:28–29], Joab of Amasa [2 Sam 20:10—
another left-handed blow]); Eglon's obesity; the royal court and the
presentation of tribute; Ehud's return and Eglon's mistake in ordering
everybody out (cf. Amnon, 2 Sam 13:9); the moment of the killing;
Israelite enjoyment of the embarrassed discussions among the dead
Eglon's courtiers outside the locked doors. Nothing is known of
Seirah.

About Shamgar too, nothing is known (despite Judg 5:6). It is a widespread assumption that the eighty years noted in 3:30 includes a forty-
year span in association with Shamgar (cf. Noth 1991, 38 n. 2). We may
note Gray's comments: The verse "has every appearance of a tradition
introduced by the Deuteronomic historian into the narratives of the
judges to make a round twelve judges. . . . It may further be noted that
Shamgar is not actually called a judge, and the words 'and he too deliv-

ered Israel' certainly suggest that the passage is secondary" (Gray, comm., 215–16).

Once again, in the framing elements the continuation formula is used to say that "the Israelites again did what was evil in the sight of the LORD"; again, the evil is unspecified. The punishment is noted as "the LORD sold them into the hand of King Jabin of Canaan," whose army commander is Sisera. Note that Jabin was featured as king of Hazor in Josh 11:1 (cf. Judg 4:17) and reputedly was struck down in Josh 11:10; we have to accept discordance between traditions. The verb of "selling" is used four times in Judges with Israel as the object sold (overview [2:14], Othniel [3:8], here, and in the aftermath [10:7]); it is also used for Sisera's fate at Jael's hands (4:9). Israel's cry for help is noted in 4:3, along with Sisera's nine hundred chariots and the twenty years of oppression.

The story proper begins with Deborah's role description; she is a prophetess who was judging Israel (4:4). The judging activity is described as taking place under a palm tree between Ramah and Bethel (4:5); we assume it involved the settling of disputes. None of this really prepares us for what follows. She summons Barak ben Abinoam (unmentioned beyond 4:6, 12; 5:1) and communicates God's command: Barak is to take troops to Mount Tabor; God will bring Sisera to battle at the Wadi Kishon (4:6–7). Most surprisingly in biblical text, Barak manifests independence of God and dependence on Deborah: Despite God's command, he will not go without her. Her reply is almost equally surprising: She will go with him, but the road he travels will not lead to his glory, for the LORD will sell Sisera into a woman's hand (4:9). At this point, the entire plot of the story has been laid out; all that is left is the unfolding of its accomplishment. Beyond verse 4, no mention has been made or will be made of judging or deliverance. Yet at the end, Jabin will be subdued (4:23) and the land will be undisturbed for forty years (5:31).

Barak shows up as instructed, with troops from Naphtali and Kedesh, and Deborah is with him; Sisera hears of it and takes his chariots to Wadi Kishon. Deborah sends Barak into battle with the assurance of the LORD's victory; the LORD provides the victory and Sisera heads off on foot (4:14–16).

The episode with Jael is succinctly but brilliantly told. Jael goes out to meet the fugitive Sisera and brings him to her tent; she beds him down and gives him milk. He asks her to stand guard. Instead, she drives a tent peg through his head "and he died" (4:21). Barak arrives in time to be shown the corpse. The scene is more evocatively rehearsed in the poem (5:24–27). The death scene is superbly sung:

> Between her feet
>   he sank, he fell, he lay;
> between her feet he sank, he fell;
>   where he sank, there he fell—dead.
>   (5:27, au. trans.)

Barak deserves credit; at Deborah's word from the LORD, he left the high ground to engage Sisera and his chariots on the plain. The LORD deserves credit; as promised, he panicked the enemy with a flooded wadi (combining 4:15 and 5:20–21) and provided victory. Jael deserves credit; the risk she took was extremely dangerous. Had anxious sweat made either tent peg or mallet slip in her hand, or had anything wakened Sisera as she prepared to strike, he would surely have killed her mercilessly, strangled her probably with one hand. Like Ehud, she risked her life.

The song tells the story of both Deborah with Barak and Jael, with the details and images expected of poetry. Its intricacies lead to remarkable divergences in interpretation, rather too complex to concern us here. At least three new elements are introduced: the situation around the time of Deborah, with the puzzling reference to the choice of new gods (v. 8); the issue of tribal absence and presence in relation to the campaign; and the fearfully ironic reflections of Sisera's mother, waiting for the arrival of her assassinated son.

The divergences between prose and poem are also worth nothing. In the prose story, no mention occurs of issues of tribal participation in the campaign. In the poem, there is no particularly explicit mention of any twenty-year oppression of Israel. Traditions differ and remind us just how dependent we are on the fragments of memory and interest.

For the theologian, there is plenty of interest in the story of this campaign. God's command is not reported as given to anybody. It is reported as given by Deborah to Barak, whose obedience to it is surprisingly conditional. There is no reference to any intended deliverance of Israel from oppressive Canaan. The victory at the Wadi Kishon is clearly attributed to God. The killing of Sisera by Jael is as devoid of any reference to God as was Ehud's killing of Eglon.

The framing is slightly out of alignment. Verse 23 has King Jabin of Canaan "subdued . . . before the Israelites" exactly as might be expected (cf. 3:30 and 8:28). But then the realistic note of an extended struggle is sounded: "The hand of the Israelites bore harder and harder on King Jabin of Canaan" (v. 24). What avenues are opened here we do not know; they are avenues that do not normally appear on our maps of deliverance here. The statement that the land was undisturbed for forty years follows the poem (5:31b).

Finally we come to the traditions of Gideon (6:1–8:35). The passages have grown steadily: less than a chapter for Ehud; two chapters for Deborah, Barak, and Jael; now three chapters for Gideon. First there is the statement that "the Israelites did what was evil in the sight of the LORD" (6:1). There is no continuation formula, no "again" in the NRSV. As we will see, the treatment of God's deliverance of Israel is more explicit in the Gideon traditions than in the preceding two, yet they both open with the continuation formula (3:12; 4:1) and the Gideon passage does not. The beginning cannot be located in the overview (2:11); its "whenever" (v. 15) contains the again and again within it—it is an overview of the collection (chaps. 3–9). A beginning with Othniel is unlikely, but not wholly impossible. The attempt to account for the exceptional aspects of the Gideon tradition by giving it an originating role in the collection becomes mired in the hypotheses involved. The text must be read as it is, with due awareness of the oddities. No suggestion of apostasy is made in 6:1; perhaps just as well, given Gideon's ephod at the end of it all (cf. 8:24–27).

The report of oppression follows immediately: "The LORD gave them into the hand of Midian seven years." Israel's cry (v. 6; the Hebrew does not have "for help," cf. 3:9, 15; 6:7; 10:10) is preceded by a vivid description of the oppression (vv. 2–5).

It will help to have a brief summary of the episodes that follow. A prophetic message explains the oppression (6:7–10). Gideon is called to "deliver Israel from the hand of Midian" (6:11–24). Gideon pulls down his father's altar for Baal and replaces it with an altar to the LORD (6:25–32), a tradition introducing the name Jerubbaal. Further traditions prepare for the deliverance of Israel (6:33–40) and report the downsizing of Gideon's force (7:1–8). There are preparations for the attack (7:9–14), the report of the attack itself (7:15–23), and the call to Ephraim for help with the mopping up (7:24–25). A quarrel with the Ephraimites is avoided (8:1–3), and the pursuit of Zebah and Zalmunna involves quarrels with Succoth and Penuel before both Midianite kings are reported killed (8:4–21). Gideon refuses the kingship (8:22–23) and then makes an ephod that leads the Israelites to prostitute themselves and that is a snare (*môkēš*) to Gideon and his house (8:24–27). The last two elements of the framing pattern are reported (8:28), and a cluster of disparate traditions concludes the passage (8:29–35).

Attending to all these lies well outside the scope of this book. Among others, there are traditions associated with two names, Gideon and

Jerubbaal—the latter particularly linked to altars at Ophrah—and issues of participation in the campaign flare again, as they did earlier.

Where the deliverance traditions are concerned, two aspects are worth emphasizing. First, Gideon's commissioning is explicitly related to Israel's oppression at the hand of Midian. "Go in this might of yours and deliver Israel from the hand of Midian; I hereby commission you" (6:14). No answer is given here to Gideon's question, "Why then has all this happened to us?" (6:13); perhaps that is the role of 6:7–10. The "spirit of the LORD" comes upon him (6:34, as on Othniel, Jephthah, and Samson). Second, Gideon's attack that achieves Israel's deliverance is an extremely risky night assault, in the days before handheld radios and modern communications. A theological reason is given for downsizing the military force, namely, the fear that Israel might take the credit away from God (7:2). There is a military reason as well. The successful prosecution of a night attack, using trumpets, shouts, and flares to spread panic, demands a small group of near nerveless troops. Three companies of a hundred each (7:16) make for plausible storytelling; much more would have turned a specialized commando attack into a probable debacle. Theology and military strategy in this case are complementary.

The episode of the altar of Baal, belonging to Gideon's father at Ophrah, is a reminder of the actuality of apostasy in the Israel of the time. The overview and Othniel were not importing a foreign concern. Equally, the issue of tribal dissension over participation in the campaign echoes that theme in the Song of Deborah (Judg 5). The theme of deliverance from Midianite oppression is explicit in the call of Gideon (6:11–24). The part played by God in the lead-up to the deliverance is extensively developed (6:36–40; 7:2–8, 9–14). The killing of the two captains, Oreb and Zeeb, and the two kings, Zebah and Zalmunna, gives a sharp edge to the subduing of Midian (8:28).

A link to the Abimelech story could have played its part in the present placing of the Gideon texts. As noted above, the absence of any continuation formula and the extensive traditions that appropriately form part of the Gideon passage raise the issue whether the collection might have begun with Gideon and been extrapolated to the campaigns of Ehud and of Deborah, Barak, and Jael. However, the history of the Abimelech story itself is uncertain enough. Overall, the uncertainties associated with these texts are too many and the hypothetical aspect of any reconstruction is too great to do more than observe the signals in the text and ponder.

A theological reflection is in place. The stories in the collection speak of oppression and deliverance from it. They do not trace its origin to God or its cause to Israel's evil. This is done in the framing elements and taken further in the overview and the Othniel passage. If the collection and its framing are seen as pre-deuteronomistic, the question remains as to the origin of the theology, but the emphasis on apostasy can perhaps be attributed to deuteronomistic concerns. The forty years' tranquillity after the deliverance belongs with the framing elements; it is not integral to the stories. It may result from reflections, in the first place, on faith's rootedness in experience and, second, on the transfer of experience between generations.

Judges 9:1–57 Abimelech: force and failure

The story of Abimelech is a thoroughly nasty one; it starts badly and does not get any better. Abimelech is portrayed as a thug who seizes power in Shechem with an act of ruthless fratricidal slaughter. It is not unlike the gory start to Jehu's regime, where two kings died, a queen, some forty relatives, and seventy sons of Ahab in Samaria (2 Kgs 9–10). The ending for Abimelech and the people of Shechem is none too happy; God repaid Abimelech's crime, and the wickedness of the people of Shechem fell back on their heads (Judg 9:56–57).

If all this sounds a little grim and impiously cynical, it is worth recognizing the context of the book of Judges and of Abimelech in particular. For a Josianic Deuteronomistic History, the book of Judges served very well to highlight the need for appropriate kingship. A self-appointed king was worse than none. The prophetic movement chose to endorse Jehu with an account of anointing (2 Kgs 9:1–10); previously, a prophet had anointed Saul and then David. An appropriate candidate for kingship needed prophetic anointing; Saul and David had it. An appropriate candidate for kingship needed to be obedient to the word of God; Saul was not but Josiah was (cf. 2 Kgs 23:1–3). How David kept his crown under these conditions ranks as a mystery. After the failure of the hopes of the Josianic Deuteronomistic History, emphasis was given to the shadow side of kingship (cf. 1 Sam 7–8); Abimelech's "reign" served the purpose well. Emphasis too was given to the people's role and their failure in fidelity; the Deliverance Collection served this purpose well. As a counter to despair, we may bear in mind Churchill's description of a certain political order as the least undesirable of the available options. What in ancient Israel was "the least undesirable" is not easily discerned. The book of Judges is a book of dysfunction, covering a period portrayed as the nadir of Israel's political fortunes.

The origins of the Abimelech story and the time of its incorporation into the present text escape us. It clearly belongs in the Jerubbaal strand of tradition (outside Judg 9; cf. Judg 6:32; 7:1; 8:29–30, 35; and 1 Sam 12:11). It is untouched by the framing elements; there is no evidence of deuteronomistic editing. An association with the Gideon story is obvious, but the link could be made at any time. Abimelech and Jephthah have a couple of points in common. First, both have diminished status as sons of their fathers and were looked down on by their brothers. Abimelech was the son of a "concubine" (*pîlegeš*, Judg 8:31; his brother's view: 9:18), and Jephthah the son of a prostitute (*'iššâ zônâ*, 11:1; his brothers' view: 11:2). Second, both came to power through strictly secular power-brokering deals (9:2–3; 11:5–10). But while Abimelech did nothing for Israel, Jephthah won victory for Israel and was Israel's judge (12:7).

Abimelech's status is imprecise. He is said to have been made "king" at Shechem (9:6); Jotham speaks of "king" (9:8 etc., 16) and specifically of Abimelech as king over the citizens of Shechem (9:18). (The NRSV's "lords of Shechem" is unfortunate. According to Boling, the *ba'alê šĕkem* are the "city fathers" or "prominent citizens" [comm., 170]. In English usage, "lords" does not normally have this connotation; "citizens" is more satisfactory and less idiosyncratic.) However, in 9:22 it is said that "Abimelech ruled (*wayyāśar*) over Israel three years"; in 9:55, when the men of Israel (*'îš yiśrā'ēl*) "saw that Abimelech was dead, they all went home." Somehow in the text, there is a will to relate Abimelech's kingship to Israel (despite Boling, comm., 175). But two verses do not a national king make—and all Beth-millo (v. 6) does not help.

This is all the more puzzling when we take into account the extremely limited scope of the chapter on Abimelech. After he is made king at/of Shechem and after Jotham's antimonarchical tirade, the text has God send an evil spirit between Abimelech and the citizens of Shechem (9:23). The rest of the narrative is about the petty intrigues of a local power struggle associated with Shechem. It would be a brave interpreter, but unwise, who might seek to identify Shechem with Israel, significant as Shechem must surely have been. We are left puzzled.

"Force and failure" are right for Abimelech. His kingship, however extensive or limited it might have been, appears to have been achieved by force or the fear of force. Whatever he did with it, which does not appear to have been much, can be rightly described as failure.

Repeated sporadically

Judges 10:1–16   Introduction and reflection

There are six so-called minor judges here (Judg 10:1–5; 12:7–15). The details preserved about them are bizarre and fascinating; despite a variety of learned suggestions, the truth is that we know nothing about them or their office. They are reported to have judged Israel (the length of time is always given and does not seem schematic: twenty-three years, twenty-two years, six years, seven years, ten years, eight years); their death and place of burial is recorded in each case. The bizarre details: Jair had thirty sons who rode on thirty donkeys (10:4); Abdon had forty sons and thirty grandsons who rode on seventy donkeys (12:14); Ibzan had thirty sons and thirty daughters and gave his daughters in marriage outside the clan while bringing in brides from outside for his sons (12:9). All six of them are reported to have "judged Israel." Of two only is it also said that they "rose," echoing the overview and Othniel (Tola and Jair, in Hebrew; the NRSV has "came" for Jair's "rose"). For these two, with two verbs, the name (Tola, Jair) comes after the "rose" verb and before the "judged" verb; for the other four, the name comes after the "judged" verb. For Tola only there is a reference to his "delivering" Israel (10:1); apart from Jephthah, Jair is the only one from east of the Jordan, perhaps offering a link to the Jephthah traditions to come.

These observations suggest that for all their similarity, the traditions have been formulated in two distinct groups. The first of these groups functions as an introduction; the second follows on the Jephthah narrative, perhaps as a conclusion to the section.

Tola and Jair may serve to smooth the way to what follows, which is a midway pause in the text for reflection, akin to a second overview. The opening verses, 10:6–9, are fairly standard: With the continuation formula, the text has Israel again doing what was evil, characterized as apostasy, positively (the gods worshiped) and negatively (the LORD not worshiped). The LORD's anger is said to have been kindled, and Israel is delivered to oppression at the hands of Philistines and Ammonites. The Ammonite oppression is noted as lasting eighteen years and causing Israel great distress (10:8–9); we may assume that the Philistine oppression relates to 13:1.

What happens in 10:10–16 is totally unexpected. First, Israel's cry is given words and they are words of confession: "We have sinned . . . abandoned our God . . . worshiped the Baals" (10:10). Such a confession has not been made before. Second, God gives up on Israel, "I will deliver you no more" (10:13) and pushes them off on to the gods they have been worshiping (10:14). Third, Israel's confession is repeated and borne out by reform, previously unmentioned (10:15–16a). Finally, God's reaction is expressed in a two-edged phrase: *wattiqṣar napšô ba'ămal yiśrā'ēl* (10:16b). The traditional rendering is valid and acceptable: "And he could no longer bear to see Israel suffer"—literally, his being was shortened *at* the burden of Israel. However, the more usual connotation of such a phrase is impatience rather than sympathy, and the burden can be God's or Israel's. So an alternative rendering is equally valid and possible: "And he could no longer bear the burden of Israel"; literally, his being was shortened *by* the burden of Israel (cf. Exod 6:9; Num 21:4; Judg 16:16; Mic 2:7; Zech 11:8; Job 21:4; Prov 14:29). The context should decide the issue, but it too is ambiguous. Jephthah is victorious over the Ammonites, "the LORD gave them into his hand" (11:32), but it is not quite the deliverance of before. Jephthah's leadership is the outcome of a deal done with the elders of Gilead (11:4–11), and, at the end, there is no forty-year period of tranquillity. Uncertainty remains. The future may hold reconciliation or divorce. In fact, in terms of context, the future holds kingship established by God's prophet, Samuel—not a relationship that is terminated, but one that undergoes radical reconstruction.

Judges 10:17–12:15   Jephthah and minor judges

The response to the Ammonites pictured in the biblical text is not found in earlier episodes. The Jephthah narrative is set east of the Jordan (emphasized by the incursions alleged in Judg 10:9a), ending in serious dissension with Ephraim; this alone sets it apart. There is trouble with the Ammonites (10:17; 11:4); this "trouble" is not necessarily in tension with an eighteen-year oppression, but it is not brought into harmony with it. The issue of leadership is raised and no reference is made to God (10:18); it becomes a matter of hiring a mercenary (cf. 11:8–10).

Jephthah's story begins with the ostracism from his brothers and his heading up a guerrilla band (11:1–3), a bad omen: His followers are described in similar terms to Abimelech's hired thugs (cf. 9:4). The local elders strike a deal with him to head a campaign against the Ammonites; the deal is sealed "before the LORD at Mizpah," in Gilead, of course (11:11).

The negotiations (vv. 12–28) form a block of their own and are controverted. For Boling, they reflect "a high historicity" (comm., 205); for

Gray, "it is very doubtful" if historicity is to be accorded to "more than the bare fact of Jephthah's negotiation with the Ammonite king" (comm., 334). For Noth, this is a separate section and was "probably interpolated after Dtr.'s day" (Noth 1991, 76 n. 2). He dates the passage to the time when Ammon was the name for the province bordering Judah on the east and "including the region between the Arnon, the Jabbok and the Jordan" (ibid.; i.e., the time of Nehemiah). The passage rehearses biblical history to argue for Israel's right to "all the territory of the Amorites from the Arnon to the Jabbok and from the wilderness to the Jordan" (11:22). Without a final response from the Ammonite king, the narrative is unaffected. Jephthah's might is strengthened with right.

Jephthah's victory is entwined with the story of his vow. The spirit of the LORD comes on him in verse 29; in verses 30–31 he vows a sacrifice should he return victorious. Totally apart from the object of his vow, the procedure is dubious. Empowered by the spirit of the LORD, he is assured of victory; any vow is superfluous. When battle was joined, "the LORD gave them into his hand" (v. 32), and he inflicted a massive defeat on the Ammonites (for Aroer, note Josh 13:25).

Then comes the puzzling story of Jephthah's vow. His daughter insists on its fulfillment: "Do to me according to what has gone out of your mouth" (11:36). Nothing is said about negotiating a substitution. Regulations such as Lev 27:1–8 may very probably be from a late period; they witness to a difficulty that may be timeless. For Jephthah's daughter, the text does not even raise the issue.

Finally, the episode with the Ephraimites brings out the dissension and divisiveness that has dogged these texts since the Song of Deborah (Judg 5). The reality of the rivalry between west and east of the Jordan is unknown. It is expressed as the west's failure to help when asked (12:2–3), but the text has no such request. There is an irony in the language of deliverance and deliverer, given the past, but we are not in a position to pin it down. The language of crossing over (root: '-b-r) is also troubling; there are rivers to be crossed in the east (e.g., the Jabbok), but more seems to be at stake than that.

Most troubling of all, the Jephthah episode ends with a reference that aligns him with the "minor judges" of Israel—and nothing more. There is no reference to the land having been undisturbed for forty years. Instead, there is strife with Ephraim. We cannot put precise numbers on biblical figures, but forty-two thousand dead is a significant figure (12:6); it is around a thirty percent increase on Gideon's thirty-two thousand warriors who were "too many" (7:2). Jephthah defeated the Ammonites, but deliverance seems to have escaped Israel.

The judges who are listed after him—Ibzan, Elon, and Abdon—may complete some archival memory. They contribute nothing, either positive or negative, to our knowledge of the story of Israel.

Judges 13:1–16:31   Samson: force and failure

Samson is a troubled figure. We have already seen von Rad's opinion. For Gray, we have to deal with "the local, sporadic and often trivial nature of Samson's exploits . . . so often motivated by his personal whims and impulses"; his verdict on Samson: "a reckless and irresponsible practical joker" (comm., 236). In many ways, the Samson traditions are a microcosm of ancient Israel's. The start is great; the follow-up is a failure. Samson's birth narrative begins well, but the high point of the rest of his story is that, avenging the loss of his eyes (16:28), in his death he killed "more than those he had killed during his life" (16:30). For Israel, its start under Moses and Joshua was impeccable; the follow-up has so far been an unfaithful failure, with worse to come.

Instead of Israel enjoying forty undisturbed years under Jephthah, the text wheels out forty years of punishment from the LORD, at the hand of the Philistines. Judges 13:1 returns to the continuation formula: "The Israelites again did what was evil in the sight of the LORD." God's response will reach a long way into the biblical text: "The LORD gave them into the hand of the Philistines forty years." The final report of the Philistines being "subdued" occurs in 2 Sam 8:1, following their defeats by David in 2 Sam 5. A divine intervention lasting for Samuel's lifetime is reported in 1 Sam 7:13. Israel's cry to God, long silent, is referred to when Saul's imminent arrival is reported to Samuel and deliverance is spoken of again: "He shall save ($h\hat{o}\check{s}\hat{\imath}\,'a$) my people from the hand of the Philistines" (1 Sam 9:16; cf. 1 Sam 7:8). Saul, of course, fails and David takes up the task. Samson has no lasting contribution to offer (despite Judg 13:5).

This is all the more surprising when we look at Samson's birth narrative, apart from one ominous note: "It is he who shall begin to deliver Israel from the hand of the Philistines" (13:5). That is, the boy to be born will only begin what we know will be a long process. The angel of the LORD appears to both woman and man; she who is barren will bear a son. She is to be careful of food and drink; he will be a Nazirite. All this was announced and it happened: "The woman bore a son, and named him Samson. The boy grew, and the LORD blessed him" (13:24). But not much came of the beginning.

Three major stories make up the Samson cycle; all three involve women. In the first and third (Judg 14; 16), Samson makes a right fool of himself. Something of the attraction of the Samson legends is visible in the contrast between the subservience of the men of Judah and the defiance of Samson (15:11). In chapter 14, he kills thirty Philistines; in chapter 15, he kills a thousand or so; in chapter 16, he kills some three thousand. He is described by Philistines as "the ravager of our country, who has killed many of us" (16:24). Small wonder he went into tradition as a hero. But the picture painted of him is scarcely heroic. In chapter 14, he is portrayed losing big because he blabs his secret to his wife; in chapter 15, he has lost his wife; in chapter 16, he is smart three times when he lies but besottedly stupid on the fourth when he tells the truth of his secret to Delilah, whom he knows has informed his enemies the three previous times. His plea before he dies is savage and selfish, devoid of any concern for Israel or God: "so that with this one act of revenge I may pay back the Philistines for my two eyes" (16:28). What a far cry this is from David's prebattle speech to the Philistine (1 Sam 17:45–47). Of his reputed twenty years' judging Israel (15:20; 16:31) we are told nothing at all. Physical force is central to the cycle; failure as deliverer is evident.

God's Absence
Judges 17–21

It is not possible in the space here to do justice to the traditions of these five chapters. Nowhere in the Bible has a sustained narrative depicted life in ancient Israel as so filled with infidelity and brutality. The refrain that recurs in the chapters sets the tone for the whole block: "In those days there was no king in Israel" (17:6; 18:1; 19:1; 21:25). Unrestrained, humanity comes off a lot uglier than sin.

The geographical focus for these traditions is uncomfortably extensive. The first, Judg 17–18, starts in the center, the hill country of Ephraim, and then touches Zorah and Eshtaol in the south and Laish/Dan in the north. The second, Judg 19–21, moves from Ephraim to Bethlehem to Gibeah, then involves all Israel from Dan to Beersheba, and culminates in a concern again involving all Israel—concern that a tribe should not be blotted out from Israel.

Judges 17–18   From south to north: might is right

The first story has two parts: (1) how the sort of man who would steal from his mother created his own certainty and prosperity and (2)

how he lost both and a "quiet and unsuspecting people" had their
lives stolen—they were put to the sword and their city burned
(18:27).

The man is Micah, from the hill country of Ephraim, and the first
part of the story ends with his comment ironic enough in itself: "Now
I know that the LORD will prosper me, because the Levite has become
my priest" (17:13). The irony here is that God is not bought and sold,
above all not with an idol of once-stolen silver. While this irony may
be latent in the narrative, it is not brought explicitly to the fore.

The story is that eleven hundred pieces of silver have been stolen
from Micah's mother and she has uttered a curse in his presence. He
confesses he stole the silver. Three times it is mentioned: "I took it"
(v. 2); he returned it (v. 3); she took it to the silversmith (v. 4). A cast-
metal idol is made from the stolen silver that once was cursed. The idol
is set up in Micah's shrine (literally, "house of God") and one of his sons
installed as its priest. No judgment is passed, just the comment that "in
those days there was no king in Israel; all the people did what was right
in their own eyes" (17:6). Looking for a job, a young Levite from Bethlehem in Judah happens by. Micah hires him for ten pieces of silver a
year, a set of clothes, and his keep (17:10). Micah assures himself of his
security and prosperity: "Now I know that the LORD will prosper me,
because the Levite has become my priest" (17:13).

The second part of the story starts with a double hint of insecurity:
"In those days" there was no king in Israel; "in those days" the tribe of
Dan was looking for territory (18:1). Society was ungoverned and
unstable. Five Danites, commissioned to look for land, stop by Micah's
house and have the Levite consult God for them. He tells them, "Go
in peace"; the LORD is favorable toward them (18:6). Neither idol nor
priest were at the service of justice.

The five promptly find a land inhabited by "quiet and trusting" folk,
without allies or connections. Six hundred armed Danites move north
to take the land, and on the way they acquire both Micah's priest and
his idol. His remonstrances are met with a threat to his life, and Micah
realized that they were too strong for him (18:26); might was right.
Might was right at the next stop too. With the god Micah had made
and his priest too, the Danites came to quiet and trusting Laish, killed
the people, burned the town, and took over the territory.

The last two verses (vv. 30–31) are uncertain, and are likely compiled
from various traditions. The overall impact is of insecurity and anarchy, with the weak oppressed by the strong.

Judges 19–21   From Dan to Beer-sheba: murder, extermination,
               and rape

The three chapters that end Judges are among the strangest and most
unpleasant—in fact, the most abominable—in all of biblical literature.
The evident compilation of traditions almost doubles the impact. A
woman is raped and murdered and her body dismembered. A tribe in
Israel is all but exterminated. Mass murder and mass rape are practiced
to observe an oath and preserve a tribe. "In those days there was no king
in Israel; all the people did what was right in their own eyes."

Comments such as Boling's—extolling, in the context of the last
episodes, "the shrewd thinking of the elders and the administrative
grace of Yahweh" (comm., 277; cf. 278–79, 294)—are, in my judgment,
inaccurate, unacceptable, and typical of what rightly gives religion a
bad name.

The very oddness of these chapters demands an attention that they
have seldom received. Rather than a purportedly historical report,
they may well constitute a cautionary tale: the horrors of life without
kings. A modern genre might be the sci-fi horror story that is known
to be totally unreal but still sends shivers down the spine. Hot in pursuit of historical tidbits and lost in awe of an appalling God, we may
miss what was obvious to those who originated these tales—they may
be just as meaningful and no more real than the story of Bluebeard.
Such an understanding may shed light on the plurality of traditions in
the composition of these stories of horror. It has also been argued that
some of these stories can be seen to engage the masked but massive
forces of social conflict, surging around such central issues as marriage
bonding that is "patrilocal" or "virilocal" (i.e., living with her father or
her husband; cf. Bal 1988a). If so, the horrors of the masks may mirror the horrors submerged in the society—in Bal's words, "the repre-
sentation of the unrepresentable" (Bal 1988a, 191). After it all, Bal
remarks, "I conclude with the suggestion that the political violence of
wars and conquests is secondary in relation to the institutional violence of the social order" (Bal 1988a, 231). Cautionary tales? Historical residues? One thing only is certain: Judges is increasingly an
enigma. The blatant unreality of the narrative has to be accounted for
in any understanding.

(In the twentieth century, the frightening reality of the human
potential for inhumanity has been scientifically documented in experiments necessarily involving *unreality*—for example, the *simulated* learning under torture at Yale University [Stanley Milgram in 1963; cf.

Schwartz 1987, 112–21] or the *simulated* prison situation at Stanford
University [Philip Zimbardo in 1971].)

We can find a couple of pointers to the unreality of the story in its
echoes from the beginnings of Israel's story and the beginnings of
Israel's monarchy. There is no avoiding the resonances of the story of
the angels who visited Lot and were demanded for intercourse by the
men of the city (Gen 19). The alternative in both cases is spending the
night in the square (Gen 19:2b; Judg 19:20b). The demand for intercourse is the same (Gen 19:5b; Judg 19:22b). The same offer is made
in both cases: two women (Gen 19:8; Judg 19:24). The outcome is ominous: Sodom and Gomorrah are destroyed; the fate of a tribe in Israel
may be symbolic of more. There is also no avoiding the resonance of
the story of Saul's summoning of Israel to the rescue of Jabesh-gilead
(1 Sam 11). It may be no accident that one option toward the end of
these stories is the slaughter of the inhabitants of Jabesh-gilead (Judg
21:8–12). The dismembering of the woman's body, whether symbolic
or literal, is ugly beyond revulsion. The image is horrible enough without invoking the verb but, outside sacrificial contexts, the verb here (to
cut in pieces; root: *n-t-ḥ*; Judg 19:29; 20:6) is only found at 1 Sam 11:7.

The echo of other traditions rather than a dependence on alleged
events for the shaping of these traditions confirms the perception that
their significance lies in the realm of symbol rather than history. In this
case, the full impact of the symbolic still remains for us in shadow. The
evocation of past horror, punished by destruction, is evident; the evocation of rescue through the monarchy is possible. There may be much
more.

The clinching pointer, however, to the unreality of the story lies in
what follows: the gathering of all Israel, from Dan to Beer-sheba
including Transjordan (Gilead), in one body before the LORD at Mizpah. It is unheard of in biblical narrative that a single solitary individual, such as this Levite from the backwoods of Ephraim (19:1, *gār*
běyarkětê har 'epraîm), in an unsupported situation, should bring about
an assembly of all Israel—from north to south and both west and east
of the Jordan. In 1 Samuel, Saul's summons is to war, not to an assembly, and the response is less immodestly specific: "The dread of the
LORD fell upon the people, and they came out as one" (1 Sam 11:7),
with a headcount for Israel and Judah. In Judg 19:29–20:1, the territory
is the same ("all the territory of Israel"), but the universality of the
response is far more specific (Dan to Beer-sheba, including Gilead),
and the "as one" is applied to the congregation [NRSV: "in one body"].
In his immediate context, the spirit of God has come upon Saul in

power (11:6) and "the dread of the LORD" has fallen on the people (11:7). In the broader context of the narrative, Saul has been anointed by the prophet Samuel (9:1–10:16). The summons sent out by Saul points up the unreality of the action associated with the Levite.

Any such assembly in premonarchic Israel is unheard of. Of course, there are assemblies of the elders and assemblies of all Israel in the texts, whether symbolic or real, but this one has a specificity (Dan, Beer-sheba, and Gilead) that takes it out of the realm of the real. Modern biblical scholarship does not know of any circumstance where this might be predicated of premonarchic Israel. The concept of an amphictyony (an association around a common shrine), cautiously advanced by Noth (1960, 85–97, 104–5; note: "one must be careful how one uses this material" [90–91]) was enthusiastically seized on by the next generation of scholarship (e.g., for Judges: Gray, comm., passim; Boling, comm., 19–23 and passim). It has, however, been treated as much more uncertain in succeeding generations as it has come under closer scrutiny (e.g., de Vaux 1961, 7, 93; Gottwald 1979, 345–57, 376–86; Gottwald 1985, 280–84; Mayes 1992)—and any detailed certainty still remains out of reach. Some early sense of belonging that can be appealed to is unquestionably present in the traditions of Deborah and Barak, Gideon, Jephthah, and Saul; much more than that is hypothetical reconstruction, all too often unjustified. The actions of this particular assembly do not in any way enhance a claim to reality. It is too bad to be true.

In chapters 17–18, humanity unrestrained comes off a lot uglier than sin. In chapters 19–21, Israel unrestrained risks self-mutilation and self-destruction. Justice is needed to protect the weak from the strong; wisdom is needed to give prudent governance. Kings become attractive.

Is there a historical core in these traditions (see, e.g., Mayes 1974, 79–83)? We must ask two questions: First, do we, the interpreters, need such a historical core? For Bluebeard, there may be one, but we hardly need it. Second, does the text and its associations demand such a historical core? It is a composite text, composed from a variety of traditions. Does this necessitate a historical core? Any answer will be complex, but "unlikely" is the more likely.

Judges 19   Rape and murder

According to the narrative of chapter 19, the house in Gibeah where a Levite, on his way home, is spending the night is surrounded by locals demanding sex with the visitor. The Levite shoves out his concubine to them. Raped and abused all night, she collapses at the door of the house as dawn is breaking. The incident has been brutal; the narrative is no less brutal now. The Levite opens the door to leave and complete his journey and there is his concubine (secondary wife), collapsed on the threshold. The LXX adds that she was dead; the Hebrew is silent (see Trible 1984, 79–82). He puts her on his donkey, takes her home, cuts up her body, and sends the twelve pieces throughout all the territory of Israel, evoking horror.

Judges 20   Civil war and extermination

The response of all Israel is portrayed here as an immediate assembly at Mizpah: "All the Israelites came out, from Dan to Beer-sheba, including the land of Gilead" (20:1). It is an extraordinary assembly, with the "chiefs of all the people" (cf. 1 Sam 14:38) presenting themselves in an "assembly of the people of God" (without parallel), along with four hundred thousand armed infantry (20:2). The regimented process for provisioning the troops (v. 10) is unparalleled in ancient Israel.

This unheard-of assembly proceeds along lines also unheard of in any account of Israelite law. The Levite is asked how the crime occurred. The victim is described as "murdered" (*hannirṣāḥâ*); presumably the crime is viewed more widely, but it has not been reported as such since its narration in the text (19:25–28). The Levite tells his story and asks for counsel. Immediately, the people "as one" pass sentence on Gibeah "for all the disgrace that they have done in Israel" (20:8–10).

Two issues are important here. First, the Levite has either lied or inculpated himself. He testifies, "They intended to kill me" (v. 5). This has not been reported previously, and either he is lying or he refers to the demand for sex with him. If the latter, he is in part responsibile for the woman's murder, if in shoving his concubine out to the mob he had good reason to believe it could lead to her death. Second, no questions are asked and no corroboration sought. In the present formulation of the law, two or three witnesses are required in capital cases (Deut 17:6; for any crime, cf. Deut 19:15); here, a city and then a tribe will be eliminated on the unsupported word of a single Levite. If this were not meant as a pitiful caricature, such a procedure would be abhorrent.

Sentence has been passed against the city (v. 9). Now the demand is made for the perpetrators of the crime to be handed over to be put to death and to "purge the evil from Israel" (v. 13; the phrase with the noun [*rāʿâ*] is only here; with the adjective [and article] [*hārāʿ*] it is found exclusively in Deuteronomy, nine times). This may suggest a more lawful version; it does not set right the wrongful legal procedure.

What follows when the Benjaminites refuse to hand over the accused is a display of misplaced divine cruelty unheard of in the annals of ancient Israel. According to the text, the odds are stacked against Benjamin, about fifteen to one. With God's encouragement, three times the Israelite force attacks Benjamin; twice they are thoroughly defeated with substantial losses (vv. 21, 25). The third time, the Israelites use an ambush strategy (cf. Josh 8) and practically wipe out the Benjaminite force. Verses 36b–44 give a different and more detailed account of the battle, in particular in relation to strategy. The outcome: six hundred warriors flee to the wilderness; Benjamin, towns and all, is wiped out.

Judges 21   Murder and rape

The near extermination of Benjamin—without wives, it will soon be total—is bad enough. What follows is worse. The text reports a hitherto unreported oath sworn at Mizpah that no Israelite would give his daughter in marriage to Benjamin (21:1). To observe this oath and still keep the tribe alive, the Israelites are portrayed resorting to unbelievable casuistry. In the first version (vv. 5–14), they appeal to another solemn oath—hitherto unreported—passing sentence of death on whoever did not come to the Mizpah assembly. This allows for the slaughter of the inhabitants of Jabesh-gilead, with four hundred unmarried women kept alive to save the future of Benjamin.

In the second version, equally appalling (vv. 15–23, combined with the preceding by a negative in the Hebrew at the end of v. 14; cf. the LXX), the Israelites "compassionately" encourage the Benjaminites to abduct the wives they need during a festival at Shiloh.

The conclusion in verse 24 is about as banal as "and they lived happily ever after" at the end of some folktales. Maybe that is how it should be. The refrain returns to close it all off: "In those days there was no king in Israel; all the people did what was right in their own eyes" (21:25).

READING THE WHOLE

Read as a total text, the book of Judges paints an increasingly miserable picture of a dysfunctional Israel, portrayed as a very creaky hinge between the heroic past of Moses and Joshua and the possible future under prophets and kings. Mieke Bal is right to open her wide-ranging studies in Judges with the sentence: "The Book of Judges is about death" (Bal 1988a, 1).

The reflections on the occupation of Canaan are less sanguine than those in the book of Joshua. The chapters focused around the deliverer-judges reveal, in fact, the portrayal of an unstable Israel, unable to achieve the unfaltering adherence to their faith and their God that might allow life to flourish. They are seduced by the attractiveness of other gods. Foreign oppression is used by God to punish them; God's deliverance is from the oppression that has been God's punishment. Tranquillity is sporadic, interrupted by bursts of oppression. Divisive forces are visible in the background of the narratives.

Abimelech's regime is the reverse of tranquillity or stability. Jephthah achieves a victory in the east, but division with the west comes to the fore. Samson is born in the brightness of hope and dies in the darkness of the blind. He leaves Israel no better off. The final chapters mirror the wretchedness of the Israelites left to themselves. They bully others; they destroy themselves. Poor things, they have no king.

REVIEW ISSUES

1. Where do we find the biblical text preserving remarkably different traditions?

2. What is the evidence suggesting that ancient Israel worked out some theology by the organization of experience?

3. What strengths are portrayed for this period of the Judges and what weaknesses?

Bibliography of works other than commentaries

Aharoni, Yohanan. 1967. *The Land of the Bible: A Historical Geography*. London: Burns & Oates.

Amit, Yairah. 1999. *The Book of Judges: The Art of Editing*. BibInt Series 38. Leiden: E. J. Brill.

Bal, Mieke. 1988a. *Death and Dissymmetry: The Politics of Coherence in the Book of Judges*. Chicago: University of Chicago Press.

———. 1988b. *Murder and Difference: Gender, Genre, and Scholarship on Sisera's Death*. Bloomington. Ind.: Indiana University Press.

Bright, John. 1960. *A History of Israel*. London: SCM Press.

Campbell, Antony F., and Mark A. O'Brien. 2000. *Unfolding the Deuteronomistic History: Origins, Upgrades, Present Text*. Minneapolis: Fortress.

Gottwald, Norman K. 1979. *The Tribes of Yahweh: A Sociology of the Religion of Liberated Israel 1250–1050 B.C.E.* Maryknoll, N.Y.: Orbis.

———. 1985. *The Hebrew Bible: A Socio-Literary Introduction*. Philadelphia: Fortress.

Mayes, A. D. H. 1974. *Israel in the Period of the Judges*. SBT 2/29. Naperville, Ill.: Alec R. Allenson.

———. 1992. "Amphictyony." *ABD* 1:212–16.

Noth, Martin. 1960. *The History of Israel*. 2d English ed. London: A. & C. Black.

———. 1991. *The Deuteronomistic History*. JSOTSup 15. 2d ed. Sheffield: JSOT Press.

Rad, Gerhard von. 1962. *The Theology of Israel's Historical Traditions*. Vol. 1 of *Old Testament Theology*. Edinburgh: Oliver & Boyd.

Richter, Wolfgang. 1964. *Die Bearbeitungen des "Retterbuches" in der deuteronomischen Epoche*. BBB 21. Bonn: Peter Hanstein.

———. 1966. *Traditionsgeschichtliche Untersuchungen zum Richterbuch*. BBB 18. 2d ed. Bonn: Peter Hanstein.

Schwartz, Steven. 1987. *Pavlov's Heirs: Classic Psychology Experiments That Changed the Way We View Ourselves*. North Ryde, NSW: Angus & Robertson.

Trible, Phyllis. 1984. *Texts of Terror: Literary-Feminist Readings of Biblical Narratives*. OBT 13. Philadelphia: Fortress.

Vaux, Roland de. 1961. *Ancient Israel: Its Life and Institutions*. London: Darton, Longman & Todd.

Yee, Gale A., ed. 1995. *Judges and Method: New Approaches in Biblical Studies*. Minneapolis: Fortress.

3

The Book of Ruth

OVERVIEW

The book of Ruth is a fascinating and enigmatic story. Widely experienced as engaging, it cannot be pinned down to any one meaning or message.

In the Greek canon, followed by English-language Bibles, Ruth comes between Judges and Samuel. After all, it begins: "In the days when the judges ruled . . ." (Ruth 1:1). In the Hebrew canon, Ruth belongs with the Writings, located between Proverbs and Song of Songs. Given that the book of Ruth is telling its own story and not attempting to portray events from the time of the judges, there is a general consensus that it properly belongs with the Writings.

What I offer here is a brief outline of the book, pointing particularly to those places where the story escapes facile interpretation. Because it belongs with the Writings, full study of the book will not be attempted here.

The book begins with a man and his wife (Elimelech and Naomi) and their two sons (Mahlon and Chilion) leaving Bethlehem in Judah to live in Moab, because there was a famine in the land. First Elimelech dies, then after marriage and living in Moab some ten years, both sons die. Naomi decides to return from Moab because she had heard that the LORD had given his people food. No other reason is given—nothing about conditions in Moab and nothing about a desire to return to her own people.

In a powerful part of the story, Naomi (the widow) sends her two daughters-in-law back to the houses of their mothers; she can offer them no sons as husbands. Both grieve. Ultimately, one (Orpah) leaves her mother-in-law to return to her people; the other, Ruth, stays with Naomi and the two return to Bethlehem. There the whole town is said to be stirred because of them, and the women greet her as Naomi. She declines the name Naomi, opting for Mara—"for the Almighty has dealt bitterly with me." A final verse repeats the information about their return (1:22), as though the tradition has been expanded.

The narrator comments that Naomi has a kinsman on her husband's side, a prominent rich man named Boaz (2:1). Boaz will enter the story in a couple of verses (2:3); only considerably later will Naomi claim Boaz as a kinsman (2:20). In all of this, there is an enigma. We, the audience, are given significant background information that heightens our interest in the unfolding narrative, but the information is not disclosed to Ruth until she gives her mother-in-law a report on the day, twenty verses into the second chapter.

Naomi and Ruth have to eat, so Ruth goes gleaning, collecting leftover stalks of grain behind the reapers. According to the text, "as it happened," she came to the part of the field belonging to Boaz (2:3). The Hebrew is rather more emphatic about the "happened" than the NRSV; it uses a verb and a noun: "it chanced a chance." The text explicitly speaks of chance; implicitly, it is difficult not to see the text pointing to providence. The story is no superficial narrative.

Boaz comes on the scene and shows a particular interest in Ruth. He is concerned for her protection and her welfare, and he knows her background (2:11–12). He is solicitous of her at the mealtime and ensures that she gets ample grain. At the end of the day, Ruth tells all this to Naomi, who then reveals Boaz as a kinsman (2:20). (The narrator had noted this for us before the day had even begun [2:1]). At the end of the harvest time, Naomi speaks of the need for security and suggests that Ruth show a particular interest in Boaz. Specifically, she is to clean up, use some perfume, and put on her best clothes (3:3). After Boaz has had his meal at the threshing floor and has settled in for the night, Ruth is to "uncover his feet" and lie down. Interpreters differ on what is meant. There is an echo of a euphemism for sex, but only an echo and an uncertain echo at that. Despite what is close to a commitment to marriage, anything untoward is unlikely. As Boaz makes clear, there is a nearer relative who ranks ahead of Boaz in the line of precedence. "If he will act as next-of-kin for you, good: let him do it" (3:13).

The following morning, a group of elders is convened and the due legal processes are fulfilled. The nearer relative is willing to buy Elimelech's land, but taking Ruth into his family would damage his inheritance structure. So he renounces his right in favor of Boaz, who is ready to acquire both land and lady. The elders pronounce an elaborate blessing that involves comparisons with Rachel and Leah on the one hand and with Perez, son of Tamar and Judah, on the other.

Boaz marries Ruth and, with the LORD's blessing, she conceives and bears a son. That is the last we hear of either. The neighbor women take over, pronounce a blessing on Naomi, and then name the child. His name is Obed, to be the father of Jesse, the father of David.

A genealogy is appended, opening with the formal "these are the descendants of," and going back to start with Perez, then following through to achieve a total of ten males, ending with David. Elimelech, whose name was to be perpetuated, is absent from the list; so is Ruth.

The story is done and we are left wondering what its meaning or message might be. The link to David and his Moabite ancestry is brought in at the end; it has nothing to do with the plot of the story beyond Ruth's origins. Israel's association with Moab ignores the fidelity attributed to Ruth. Ruth invokes the LORD in her oath not to separate from Naomi (1:17; cf. v. 16: "your people shall be my people, and your God my God"). The LORD the God of Israel is invoked by Boaz to reward Ruth for her fidelity in seeking refuge under God's wings (2:12). The LORD is invoked by Naomi to bless Boaz (2:20). The LORD is again invoked by Boaz to bless Ruth for her fidelity in turning to him (3:10). Finally, it is said that the LORD made Ruth conceive (4:13). Ruth's fidelity to Naomi has brought her into the sustaining embrace of the community of Bethlehem. Naomi, who came home to Bethlehem bereaved and bitter ("Call me no longer Naomi, call me Mara," 1:20), ends the story wonderfully blessed (4:14–17). Those who depart in pain and return either in sadness or in fidelity find a home in God's community and are royally blessed. There may be more; there is at least this.

4

1 and 2 Samuel

with 1 Chronicles 1–22

OVERVIEW OF SAMUEL

The books of Samuel open with Samuel's birth; the books of Kings open with David's death. Between these two events, much happens for Israel. Monarchy gets off to a false start with Saul and is established with David; Samuel presides over its inauguration and anoints David to replace Saul. A radically new era is portrayed for Israel: Moses and Joshua presided over the people's beginnings; prophets and kings will take up the relay. Moses promised that "the LORD your God will raise up for you a prophet like me from among your own people" (Deut 18:15; cf. 18:18); in many ways, Samuel is portrayed as that prophet.

How much of 1–2 Samuel reflects spiritual insight and how much political process is difficult to determine. Samuel anoints Saul as "king-designate" (*nāgîd*), and he becomes king later; Samuel's anointing of David (16:1–13) is unmentioned in the subsequent stories of David's struggles. The primary task of 1–2 Samuel is to come to terms with the presence of a king in Israel and to assess the place of monarchy within the identity of Israel. Its basic claim is that, for Israel, monarchy is of God. David's success came because God was with him; disaster followed when David departed from God. The success is evident in David's rise to power and its establishment; God was with him. The disaster begins with Bathsheba and Uriah (cf. 2 Sam 12) and culminates in the story of David's census (2 Sam 24), both of which follow the report of Samuel's death but involve two other prophets, Nathan and Gad.

At the closing of the story of Ruth there was a benign invocation of Rachel and Leah. At the opening of 1 Samuel, Hannah and Peninnah's relationship is much closer to the Genesis portrayal of Rachel and Leah, with rivalry and bitterness. Hannah's barrenness harks back even further, to Sarah's barrenness at the start of Israel's story. The birth of Samuel promises a new beginning in the life of Israel. The spiritual leadership of the Elides will be terminated; as the section ends, Samuel is given exalted status: "All Israel from Dan to Beer-sheba knew that Samuel was a trustworthy prophet of the LORD" (3:20). With the passing of the power of the Elides, the ark of the covenant, the symbol of the LORD's presence and power, leaves Shiloh, never to return (chaps. 4–6).

The emergence of a radically new structure in a community is often a source of confusion. The transition to monarchy caused confusion in ancient Israel; the biblical texts faithfully mirror something of that confusion. The transition begins with the assurance that Israel was not under immediate threat: "The hand of the LORD was against the Philistines all the days of Samuel" (7:13). The problem arose with Samuel's sons, whom he had made judges and who "took bribes and perverted justice" (8:3). The elders came to Samuel and asked for "a king to govern us, like other nations" (8:5). This is where the confusion begins. The LORD's response is clear: "Listen to their voice and set a king over them" (8:22; cf. vv. 7a, 9a). However, the chapter also has a strong warning about the "ways of the king" that Samuel is instructed by God to give the people (8:11–17), and stronger still, kingship is portrayed as apostasy, the rejection of God (8:7b–8, 18). These various views of the monarchy existed in Israel: kingship as God's gift, to be accepted enthusiastically; kingship as a necessary institution, to be accepted cautiously; kingship as rejection of God, to be treated as rebellion and apostasy. The text holds them all.

Overlooking God's subduing of the Philistines for "all the days of Samuel," the text then has God bring Saul to Samuel to be anointed as the one "to save my people from the hand of the Philistines" (9:16). Other procedures too identify Saul, by oracle and by lot, leading to his acclamation as king (10:20–25). He rallies Israel to the relief of humiliated Jabesh-gilead and is crowned with full festivity before the LORD at the sanctuary of Gilgal. A speech by Samuel articulates the theological principles that integrate monarchy into the self-understanding of Israel. An obedient king and people will be loyal to the LORD; a disobedient king and people will find that God is against them (12:14–15).

Saul clearly rates in the text as a disobedient king. He lasts for three chapters, two of them about being rejected. The middle chapter, 1 Sam 14, features a stunning surprise victory by Jonathan, which Saul mismanages almost to the point of failure. The scenario is such that it might have been written by David's supporters. After the second prophetic rejection of Saul, David is brought on the scene to be anointed by Samuel (16:1–13), but Saul stays on the scene—because politics is not always run by religious rules—and the tension between the two heats up until David quits the country and the Philistines kill Saul. According to the text, gingerly—and including a long civil war—David centralizes power and becomes king over, first Judah, then Israel. He takes Jerusalem and builds a palace; he defeats the Philistines; his royal house is promised stability by God; "and David administered justice and equity to all his people" (2 Sam 8:15). Monarchy has made it into the constitutional mainstream of ancient Israel. David's obedience-disobedience rating is troubling, but the Bible seldom paints life in simple colors.

Second Samuel 11–20 depicts details of royal life in David's middle years (not mid-life; middle years of his reign). This material was once known as the Succession Narrative, but the issue of succession is largely peripheral to the text. It has also been called the Court History, which is misleading, for it is not history and the focus of some 60 percent of the action (2 Sam 15–20) is outside Jerusalem. It is, rather, a close narrative study of aspects of David's life and behavior—the sort of thing future royal advisors might cut their teeth on: When might David have sought advice? What advice might have been offered? What might have been the consequences?

First, there is a self-contained narrative of David's royal misbehavior: taking Bathsheba, the wife of another man, for sex; the murder of Uriah, her husband; the confrontation with Nathan, pointing to this as a baneful model for the house of David; finally, marriage with Bathsheba, the death of their first child, and the birth of Solomon. It is an extraordinary story, opening many windows and closing none. It is followed by stories of rape, murder, and estrangement in David's own house: Tamar is raped (13:1–22), Amnon is murdered (13:23–36), Absalom is estranged (13:37–14:33). Then the estrangement is intensified. Absalom organizes a rebellion and David takes flight across the Jordan (15:1–17:23); Absalom is killed and David is restored to power in Jerusalem (17:24–19:44 [NRSV, 19:43]). Finally, what has begun within the family is extended to the kingdom: Sheba ben Bichri calls the north into rebellion, a rebellion suppressed by Joab (20:1–22). It is a remarkable reflection on David's middle years as king. Within Jerusalem, David is portrayed at best as unwise in his own behavior and, in his behavior toward others, as incompetent (or perhaps as ruthless). Outside Jerusalem, he is portrayed as supremely competent (and again perhaps as ruthless). This double-edged aspect alone makes a postexilic date most unlikely. What manner of man is this king?

A collection of four chapters brings the book to a close. It has all the appearances of an independent collection, revealing to us among other things just how much about David's operations remains unknown to us. The collection has at its core two poems attributed to David. One is the near equivalent to Ps 18 (22:1–51); the other, shorter, is entitled "the last words of David" (23:1–7). Outside these are two sets of traditions about David's warriors. The first tells of four killings by David's men of descendants of the giants (21:15–22); the second lists the membership of the two top organizations in David's military command, the Three and the Thirty (23:8–39). The exploits and the organizations are otherwise unknown to us; equally, most of the warriors mentioned are unknown to us—even David's three top commanders (the Three). Framing all this are two sacral episodes involving David. In one, a famine is ended (21:1–14); in the other, a three-day pestilence is ended—with the location marked as the place of the future temple (24:1–25).

The structure of 1–2 Samuel is fundamentally tripartite: the preparation for David's emergence; the politics of David's establishment; the perplexities of David's middle years. This fundamental structure can be represented as shown on page 115.

THE BEGINNINGS OF STABLE MONARCHY IN ANCIENT ISRAEL   1–2 SAMUEL

Two aspects of this presentation may be surprising. One is the primary focus on David rather than Saul, Israel's first king with a claim to chronological priority. From a purely political point of view, Saul's kingship is of more than chronological significance. But this is not merely a political text. Its goal is David not Saul, for at least two reasons. First, the internal justice sought in 1 Sam 8 is not claimed for Saul but for David: "And David administered justice and equality to all his people" (2 Sam 8:15). Second, the external defense, above all against the Philistines (1 Sam 9:16), is credited to David not Saul: "David attacked the Philistines and subdued them" (2 Sam 8:1). David, not Saul, is seen as Israel's foundational king. Saul was hardly on the throne before God's prophet dismissed him for disobedience.

The other surprise is the description of David's middle years under the rubric of "modeling." The limiting of the text involved—excluding 2 Sam 9–10 and 1 Kgs 1–2—will be discussed in the appropriate place, but it will help to note here that in the self-contained story of 2 Sam 11–12 David is manifestly guilty of sexual violence (Bathsheba) and homicidal violence (Uriah). In what follows, David's eldest son, Amnon, rapes Tamar, a princess and his half-sister. Another of his sons, Absalom, murders Amnon. Absalom then moves into broader violence, heading a rebellion against his father's rule. He would have been happy to have David dead (cf. 2 Sam 17:1–4, esp. "the advice pleased Absalom"; also 16:11); instead he dies himself. The violence continues, with Sheba ben Bichri leading another rebellion and Joab suppressing it by having Sheba killed. Nathan's prophetic words to David are accurate: Because of what you have done with Uriah and his wife, "the sword shall never depart from your house" (2 Sam 12:10).

THE BOOK OF CHRONICLES: AN OVERVIEW

First and Second Chronicles must be allowed its own independence and integrity. For too long, it was regarded as a late and overly pious rehash of Samuel–Kings, historically unreliable and prone to reshaping reality in terms of its own interests. Relatively recently, biblical scholarship has resumed the task of taking Chronicles seriously. (Among others, see Hoglund 1997, 29: "Looking at Chronicles through the lens of the historiographic practices of the Hellenic world both rehabilitates Chr and raises new questions about the value of his narrative for contemporary historical understandings of Israel";

Rainey 1997, 72: "Is it not reasonable to suggest that a large measure of that insight derives from his main supplementary source, 'Chronicles of the Kings of Judah'?"; Kalimi 1997, 89: "The literary nature of Chronicles is historiography.")

A full study is not possible here; however, comparison of Chronicles with Samuel–Kings helps reveal the very different concerns that led to the composition of Chronicles. It is far from competing with the Deuteronomistic History. Its structure and its omissions and additions need to be understood in terms of its central concern for the story of Jerusalem's temple—its building, its destruction, and the decree for its rebuilding. Chronicles offers us insight into what the temple meant to certain circles in ancient Jerusalem. Rebuilding the temple was to be part of rebuilding the community (cf. Ezra–Nehemiah). The misrepresentation over Chronicles goes back at least to Jerome: "what we can more significantly call a *chronicle* of the whole of divine history" ("quod significantius χρονικόν totius divinae historiae possumus appellare," quoted in Rudolph, comm., iii). Rudolph himself describes the purpose of Chronicles as "a portrayal of the realization of theocracy on Israel's soil" (viii). To be brutally brief, Chronicles is certainly not a history of Israel (against, for example, Hooker: "an alternative history to that presented in the Samuel–Kings complex" and "this great retelling of the history of Israel" [comm., 2, 6]; Japhet: "a comprehensive parallel to the earlier biblical historiography from Genesis to Kings" [comm., 8]; see, similarly, Japhet 2000, 158–59). It is not even Noth's "history of the formation of the post-exilic community" (Noth, comm., 97). It is rather the story of the Jerusalem temple (De Vries: "the story not of a nation but of a congregation" [comm., 18]; Braun: "the author was interested above all in presenting the Jerusalem temple as the only legitimate temple of Yahweh" [comm., xxviii]; Nelson: "Chronicles is really a history of the Jerusalem Temple and those who are devoted to it" [1998, 152]). The kings of Judah had recurring impact on the temple—sometimes for better, more often for worse; at the end, the conduct and leadership of some of their number brought about its desecration and final destruction by fire (cf. 2 Chr 36:5–21, esp. vv. 7, 10, 14, 18–19). There is much to support the view that Chronicles is the story of the Jerusalem temple (see the thorough discussion in Kalimi 1997). With regard to dependence on existing material, Williamson cautions: "We should beware of attempts simplistically to reduce to a single category the nature of the Chronicler's composition or his use of sources" (Williamson, comm., 23).

Chronicles begins with Adam and the beginnings of the human race;

that is how important the Jerusalem temple was thought to be for humankind. Then some nine chapters of rather disconnected genealogical traditions are gathered together. Immediately following is the account of the fate of Saul and his sons on Mount Gilboa (10:1–12). Two verses dismiss Saul as an unfaithful king; "he [the LORD] put him to death and turned the kingdom over to David" (10:13–14). Then all Israel gathers at Hebron "and they anointed David king over Israel" (11:1–3). Samuel's involvement is reduced to a half-verse: "according to the word of the LORD by Samuel" (11:3b). None of this suggests the authors of Chronicles were not well informed about the traditions they passed over in silence (cf. 12:1); we are entitled to assume that they knew all we know—and probably more. It is, therefore, fair to assume that they chose not to use what distracted from their goal. David is to be the founder of the temple that Solomon will build, and their text rushes toward that goal.

Following the establishment of David as king, Chronicles moves to the capture of Jerusalem, and then to traditions about the military men involved with David. After a consultation with the leaders, David moves to bring the ark up to Jerusalem, but because of Uzzah's death it stops short at the house of Obed-edom. The Chronicles text then has David's palace built by workers from Hiram of Tyre, lists David's wives and children in Jerusalem, and recounts David's success against the Philistines, with the final comment that "the fame of David went out into all lands, and the LORD brought the fear of him on all nations" (14:17). With this achieved, the liturgy and participants are organized in great detail and the ark comes to Jerusalem. Nathan's promise of a dynasty for David and the assurance that David's son would build the temple comes after the installation of the ark. The text continues with David's international successes and the personnel of his administration, then the failed embassy to Hanun, son of Nahash, king of the Ammonites, and subsequent campaign, concluding with the capture of Rabbah. The traditions of the killing of the four descendants of the giants follow and then the account of David's census, leading to the decision by David about the pestilence and its stopping at what was eventually to be the place for the temple and the altar of the LORD (22:1). Chapter 22 has David report a word from the LORD to the effect that the bloodshed associated with the wars he had waged prevented him from building God's temple. Solomon, the man of peace, shall build it. David is credited with having prepared the finances, workers, and materials necessary. David's endorsement of the temple project is total. The theology is noteworthy: "You will prosper if you are careful to observe the statutes and the ordinances that the LORD commanded Moses for Israel" (22:13).

In 1 Chr 23:1, David makes Solomon king, so we can break off the story at this point. It is worth noting that David has been explicitly credited with commitment to the building of the temple in a way that is not the case in the Samuel text. The beginnings of the theological groundwork have been laid for the failure of the kingdom and the temple's future destruction (cf. 22:13). A more detailed comparative treatment of this part of Chronicles will be given after the text of Samuel has been discussed below. It is enough for now to recognize that the two quite different works—the Deuteronomistic History and the Chronicler's History—are both entitled to their independence and their integrity.

MAJOR TEXT SIGNALS
IN 1–2 SAMUEL

1. The first signal concerns the arrival of Samuel on the national scene and the realization that no figure in ancient Israel received the attention given Samuel's early origins—not the major prophets (Isaiah, Jeremiah, Ezekiel), not David, not Joshua; perhaps, to a lesser and different degree, Isaac, Moses, and Samson. The barren mother evokes the images from Israel's origins; the birth is the gift of God: "the LORD remembered her" (1 Sam 1:19). The spiritual leadership of Israel, traced back to Egypt, is disgraced and its future under sentence of death ("it was the will of the LORD to kill them," 2:25). Two interventions make this clear (2:27–36; 3:10–14). Samuel is repeatedly said to grow "both in stature and in favor with the LORD" (cf. 2:26). The final statement about Samuel is unparalleled: "And all Israel from Dan to Beersheba knew that Samuel was a trustworthy prophet of the LORD" (3:19).

2. The second signal concerns the departure of the ark from the national scene. In certain traditions, the ark of the covenant was a powerful symbol of God's presence and leadership in Israel. So it was for the leadership through the wilderness (Num 10:33–36; 14:44); it was central to the crossing of the Jordan and the capture of Jericho. Now it leaves Shiloh and it will not return there. The narrative points unmistakably to God's will: "Why has the LORD put us to rout today?" (4:3); "the glory has departed from Israel" (4:21, 22); the submission of the Philistine god (5:1–5); the outcome of the Philistine divination

(cf. 6:9, God or chance); the dispatch of the ark to Kiriath-jearim (6:20–7:1).

3. The third signal concerns the emergence of monarchy. Despite Samuel's lifelong protection of Israel (cf. 7:13) and despite the countervailing voices that even declared the demand for kingship to be apostasy (cf. 8:7b–8; 10:18–19), kingship is portrayed as both ordered and given by God—ordered by God in response to Israel's request, seeking internal justice; given by God in response to Israel's need for external defense. In the latter case, Samuel will anoint Saul as king-designate (*nāgîd*, cf. 9:1–10:16); he will do the same for David (16:1–13). Politics prevails over prophets; Saul remains on the throne until his death. Two traditions report Saul's becoming king (10:24–25; 11:14–15). A speech by Samuel establishes the constitutional understanding that integrates the monarchy into the structures of the people of God (12:6–25). Royal power is not absolute; there are checks and balances. Obedience to God assures loyalty; disobedience means apostasy with all its consequences (12:14–15). Saul's reign is given three chapters, two of them consecrated to his disobedience and rejection. Nonetheless, the monarchy has become an established fact within Israel.

4. The fourth signal concerns the political moves to establish David as king. With the anointing of David, Samuel's task is largely done (cf. 15:35), and his death is reported at 25:1. Prophetic designation is one thing; its political realization is another, however. Some thirty-five chapters are devoted to that realization. David's emergence on Israel's political scene, at the court of Saul, is narrated in association with the traditions of single combat with the Philistine champion, Goliath. At Saul's court, increasing tension between a rejected king and a favored substitute leads to open rupture. David lives as a guerrilla leader in the rugged deserts of Judah. Ultimately, afraid for his life, David leaves Judah for Philistine territory. Saul and his sons die in battle with the Philistines. David then fights a long civil war (cf. 2 Sam 3:1) to emerge as the sole king in Israel. A capital city, children, subjugation of the Philistines, the coming of the ark to Jerusalem, God's promise through Nathan of political (dynastic) security, and the general subjugation of potential surrounding enemies points to the long-term future of monarchy within Israel and the fact of David's establishment as Israel's king.

5. The fifth signal concerns the stories of David's middle years. The stories from 2 Sam 11–20—from the taking of Bathsheba to the rebellion of Sheba ben Bichri—are stamped with a quality that is rare in

Israelite narrative. Something akin to it is found in 2 Sam 2–4 and 1 Kgs 1–2, but the body of narrative from 2 Sam 11–20 is focused around a remarkable theme—what we might call the fragility of David. Juxtaposed against the immediately preceding portrayal of David as established king, the evident fragility of David's person and his kingdom comes as a surprise. Perhaps it should not, for as Lord Acton, Regius Professor of Modern History at the University of Cambridge, remarked, "Power tends to corrupt and absolute power corrupts absolutely," adding that "great men are almost always bad men." Nathan's intervention shows that David's power may have been absolute, but it was not uncontested. The stories often leave us torn between potential incompetence and potential ruthlessness. What manner of man is this king?

6. The sixth signal concerns the final appendix of independent traditions about David. As has been pointed out, the final four chapters (2 Sam 21–24) have a concentric structure suggesting an independent collection. Two episodes would otherwise be unknown to us in the book of Samuel: the elimination of Saul's descendants (21:1–14) and the census ordered by David (24:1–25). That should not be surprising. What is thoroughly surprising, however, is to realize that in an area where we are entitled to think that we were well informed, we did not possess the slightest hint of the core structural aspects of David's guerrilla organization. We are entitled to think that we are well informed about David's time as a guerrilla leader. We know the makeup of his band (see 1 Sam 22:1–2); we know the guidance he received from God (see, e.g., 22:6–14); we know how he lived off the land (see chap. 25). We are entitled to be surprised to find that his command structure comprised the Three and the Thirty (cf. 2 Sam 23:8–39), both of which we have never heard of. We are entitled to be surprised to find that the names of the Three are unknown to us (cf. 23:8–12). We are entitled to be surprised to find that we have only heard of five names among the Thirty: Abishai, Benaiah, Asahel, Eliam, and Uriah the Hittite (cf. 23:18–39; note: the three sons of Zeruiah are frequently known by their mother's name, not the father's). Uriah we did not hear of until 2 Sam 11; beyond the two lists of officials, we will not hear of Benaiah as a participant in the narrative until 1 Kgs 1; Joab, of course, we know but he is not mentioned, except as the brother of Abishai and Asahel and in conjunction with Naharai, his armor bearer (v. 37). It is a remarkable collection, and it sends a significant signal to us of how much in the world outside the text is unknown to us.

Reading the Sections

PREPARATIONS FOR DAVID'S EMERGENCE
AS KING-TO-BE
1 SAMUEL 1:1–16:13

Prophetic: arrival of Samuel on the national scene
1 Samuel 1:1–4:1a

The birth story of Moses brings Moses into the court of Pharaoh (Exod 2:1–10). The call story of Jeremiah brings God into the life of Jeremiah (Jer 1:4–10). Similarly, the birth story of Samuel brings Samuel into the sanctuary of God (1 Sam 1:1–28). The story begins with a pious man and a barren woman. He went on pilgrimage regularly from his town to Shiloh to worship; she was loved and barren and wept because of it. According to the MT, the barren wife was provoked by her fertile rival (a timeless scenario, cf. Gen 16:4; Prov 30:21–23). In the LXX version, there is no mention of a rival wife, and the later sacrifice is duly offered by the man (cf. Walters 1988). Interpreters need to be aware that more versions of some stories almost certainly circulated in ancient Israel than are preserved in any particular text tradition. Further clear examples will be found at 1 Sam 17–18 and 1 Kgs 12:24.

At the sanctuary, Hannah, the sorrowing wife, and Eli, the old priest of Shiloh, are brought together in the narrative. Her son will replace his family in the spiritual leadership of Israel. By and large, the narrative will treat Eli well. At the end, it is he who elicits God's disastrous word from Samuel and accepts it with dignity (3:17–18). Though he will bless Hannah (1:17), his initial reaction to her in the narrative is one of misjudgment and misunderstanding: "Put away your wine" (1:15).

There are strong emotions latent in this narrative. Eli's harshness wrings the cry of sorrow from Hannah: "I am a woman deeply troubled" (1:15), and her anguish brings out his compassion: "The God of Israel grant the petition you have made to him" (1:17). Hannah is symbolic of the anguish of Israel. In blessing her, Eli blesses the new force that will sweep away his family's role.

After Hannah returns from the place of pilgrimage, "the LORD remembered her" (1:19). A son is born and she names him Samuel, since "I have asked him from the LORD" (1:20). Popular etymologies for names are notoriously unreliable, tending to play on words or sounds rather than linguistic derivations. The name Saul ("asked") is much closer to "I have asked him from the LORD." Some find the etymological wordplay irresistible and postulate some underlying association with a birth story of Saul. There is no question that, as an etymology, verse 20 would work better for Saul than Samuel (cf. 1:27–28), but this is serendipitous and totally uncorroborated; there is no trace of any context for a birth story appropriate to Saul. The Saul story starts with 1 Sam 9:1, with Saul fully grown. The idea is no more than a pleasant flight of fancy and is best resisted. The sequence is appropriate: I prayed a vow > you heard my prayer > I keep my vow. It explains the origin of the son, but not his name.

In due course, after being weaned, the young Samuel is "given to the LORD" (1:28). According to the LXX and Qumran (at 1:11, 22), he is to be a Nazirite until the day of his death. (If such a tradition was authentic, there is no trace of it elsewhere in the Samuel traditions.) Nothing is said of Samuel's role or responsibilities at Shiloh; they are not what matters. The narrative will contrast the Elides and Samuel: They are in decline and he is on the rise.

But first there is the Song of Hannah. It is not exactly the sort of song an author might attribute to a woman who has just given up her only child. It opens with exultation and derision for "my enemies" (2:1); it is unlikely that that reference is to Peninnah. The reference to God's king is clearly from a later time (2:10). The song brings out what is only latent in the symbolism of the story: A prior situation has been reversed and Israel has been given life (2:6). The future lies with the monarchy.

The future does not lie with the house of Eli. In what follows, two passages focus on the evil of Eli's sons, and two pronouncements—a prophet's and God's—foretell the fall of the Elide house; interspersed are snippets favorable to Samuel. The last word is far-reaching in its impact, spoken by God, communicated unwillingly by the young Samuel, and received gracefully by the old Eli: "The iniquity of Eli's house shall not be expiated" (3:14). At the end, Samuel is beyond doubt God's instrument for the future, "a trustworthy prophet of the LORD" (3:20).

Traditional: departure of the ark from the national scene
1 Samuel 4:1b–7:1

The anti-Elide traditions of chapters 2–3 are unrelenting in their condemnation; nevertheless, the narrative does not associate the going of the ark with the sinning of the Elides—except that Hophni and Phinehas die in the defeat, a sign of the punishment yet to come (cf. 2:[31–33] 34; 4:11 [and 17]).

The departure of the ark from Shiloh is narrated as God's will; its failure to return there is equally the outcome of God's will. Something new is happening in Israel; the ark will come to Jerusalem when the change of epochs is achieved (cf. Ps 78:59–72). The opening passage in 1 Sam 4 is a good example of the difference between report and story. The elders of Israel ask a question: "Why has the LORD put us to rout today before the Philistines?" (4:3). In a report, the question features in the text because it was asked, even though the bringing of the ark will be followed by a more severe defeat—in short, reports reflect events. Stories, in contrast, interpret events. In a story, the question features because its significance is important to the understanding of the whole—especially because the storyteller knows what lies ahead. Commanders are not mentioned, just the Philistines and Israel. The tension is heightened by the Philistines' reaction to Israel's exultation (4:5–9). The slaughter is intensified more than sevenfold. This is more likely a story than a report.

Where the initiative in the campaign lies—whether Israel is portrayed as bringing the disaster on itself or not—depends on the text being followed. In the MT, Israel takes the initiative; in the LXX (followed by the NRSV), the initiative is with the Philistines. Justification can be found for both. According to the narrative, the God of Israel is responsible for the defeats and the departure of the ark (or of the God symbolized by it). First, the question asked is in 4:3: "Why?" not "Whether?" God defeated Israel. Second, the first defeat is followed by a worse one in 4:10–11, with the ark of the covenant captured. Third, the dying mother explains, "the glory has departed from Israel" (4:22). Fourth, the God of Israel defeats the Philistines, both their god in the Philistine temple and their people in three of the Philistine cities (5:1–12). Finally, in desperation, Philistine priests and diviners prove beyond question that the operative force in all this is the God of Israel (6:9). The cows drawing the wagon bearing the ark do the inexplicable and unbelievable: they take a straight line to Beth-shemesh. Yet there is no question of the ark returning to Shiloh; it is despatched to Kiriath-jearim, a backwater.

So the narrative unfolds, laying out a series of events as driven by God. First, a battle is lost without the ark; then, with the ark present, a second defeat is more serious and also definitive ("they fled . . . home"); then the ark is captured and Hophni and Phinehas are killed. At the culminating mention of the ark, Eli, the old priest, their father, dies. (The old man "trembled for the ark" [4:13]; a report would need an explanation, while a story simply heightens tension.) The wife of Phinehas gives birth, and, dying, gives her son a name that means, "the glory has departed from Israel" (4:21–22). In Dagon's temple at Ashdod, the Philistine god is submissive to the God of Israel; in the Philistine cities of Ashdod, Gath, and Ekron, the ark's presence inspires deathly panic. The solemn Philistine decision to send the ark back to Israel is accompanied with the appropriate offerings and involves a process of divination in order to determine whether the events were the doing of the God of Israel. They were. Safely home, the ark triggers a veritable bloodbath among its own. Like the Philistines, the people of Beth-shemesh want to send it elsewhere. (There is an ironic risk in hypothetically reconstructing this awful episode at Beth-shemesh. If the cause can be identified [e.g., X did not rejoice], the problem can be rectified [the wrongful behavior avoided]. If the cause remains mysterious, the deity remains dangerous—"Who is able to stand before … this holy God?" [6:20].) Surprise: the ark is not sent to Shiloh.

With the priestly family decommissioned and the ark apparently in mothballs, the narrative's coast is clear for Samuel.

In 1926, Leonhard Rost argued for four chapters constituting an Ark Narrative (basically 1 Sam 4–6; 2 Sam 6). The narrative celebrated the ark's movement from Shiloh to Jerusalem and the wonders that attended it, and would have been told to pilgrims visiting the ark sanctuary in Jerusalem (Rost 1982). In 1975, the reflective or theological implications of this narrative were explored more fully by A. F. Campbell (1975), who saw God's will expressed to reject the Israel of Shiloh and embrace the Israel of Jerusalem. In 1977, P. D. Miller and J. J. M. Roberts argued for an Ark Narrative beginning with the anti-Elide passages in chapter 2 and ending with 7:1. In their view, its purpose was to expound the power of Israel's God; its composition preceded the time of David's victories (Miller and Roberts 1977).

Prophetic: emergence of monarchy
1 Samuel 7:2–16:13

The biblical texts on the beginnings of monarchy in Israel focus first on the establishment of the institution and only then go on to narrate the actual exercise of kingship. Of course, the establishment of the institution does not happen in the abstract; it is worked out in the person of a particular king, Saul. It is worth observing that the text of 1 Sam 7–12 holds together a plurality of traditions about kingship and its origins and that there appears to be an attempt to reconcile these in the final discourse of 1 Sam 12. Under the conditions laid down in

12:14–15, Israel and monarchy can survive. It is only after this establishment of the institution that Saul's career as king is told, his failures—in the obedience required by 12:14–15—noted, and his replacement anointed. For our purposes, it is appropriate to treat the text in two stages: (1) the arrival of Saul and the monarchy and (2) the dismissal of Saul and the introduction of David.

1 Samuel 7:2–12:25   Arrival of Saul and the new institution of monarchy

The creation of a new institution as significant as monarchy has a substantial impact on its society. It is hardly surprising that there were several traditions preserved in Israel about how monarchy came on the scene; it is hardly surprising that not all of them were positive. Their preservation has been made possible by the skillful composition of the biblical text, beginning with traditions of an independent Samuel, then incorporating traditions of the origins of kingship, and concluding with a review and assessment in a major discourse by Samuel.

In 1 Sam 7, Samuel sets Israel in right relationship with God and has the Philistines defeated and outside Israel's borders "all the days of Samuel" (7:13). The phrase holds memories of the judges, either at the beginning (Judg 2:18) or in the forty-year "rest" with which the account of each judge ends. There is an irony in the memory: The pattern of Judges failed to provide Israel with stability. Samuel's appointment of his two sons as judges incurs the same failure (1 Sam 8:1–3), and moralizers see echoes of Eli's sons. The radically new is needed.

In chapters 8–11, the need is met by the monarchy. Two traditions are positive. First, responding to the need for justice, the elders of Israel ask Samuel to establish a king, and God instructs him to do so (8:1–22). Second, responding to the need for defense, God takes the initiative to bring Saul to Samuel to be anointed king-designate (*nāgîd*) to save God's people from the hand of the Philistines (9:1–10:16). The first tradition is completed by the selection and acclamation of Saul as king (10:17, 20–25); the second is completed by Saul's demonstration of his prowess and his subsequent coronation (11:1–11, 14–15). It is possible that the traditions relating to the need for justice were composed relatively early; however, it is unlikely that they became part of the biblical text before the revision of the Deuteronomistic History.

In chapters 8 and 10, traditions are expressed that are opposed to the notion of monarchy, and their inclusion within these chapters is appropriate. It would be disrespectful to oppose them to God's initiative; it is quite suitable to attach them, as a dissenting opinion, to Israel's request. Recognizing three basic stages of expression (given here without technical details) helps clarify a complex text:

Stage 1	8:1–6, 22: elders' request, Samuel's displeasure, God's command for a king
Stage 2	8:7a, 9b–10, 11–17, 19–21: God's warning about a king
Stage 3	8:7b–9a, 18; 10:18–19: kingship as apostasy and rejection of God

The warning (stage 2) is the major expression of dissent; then the opposition is more radically expressed (stage 3), claiming the establishment of monarchy to be apostasy from God.

Finally, in chapter 12, Samuel is presented articulating the condition under which a king is possible in Israel and assuring Israel that its existence as God's people can continue. The condition: obedience to God will guarantee loyalty to God (vv. 14–15).

The positive traditions are kept stylistically separate in the organizing of the composition. The tradition that a king was established by God for Israel's defense is narrated in story form (9:1–10:16 and 11:1–11, 14–15). The traditions associating the king with the elders' request, goaded by the need for relief from the perversion of justice by Samuel's sons, are grouped in accounts of assemblies at Ramah and Mizpah. Beyond these, Samuel's initial activity is located at Mizpah (chap. 7), and his final discourse is placed at Gilgal (chap. 12). Two brief traditions, 10:26–27 and 11:12–13, indicative of the change of epochs, require the combination of these traditions into a single composition (see McCarthy 1973).

Some details may be helpful in relation to this complex of traditions. The only trace of repentance recorded for the period of the Judges is within Judg 10:10–16. The repentance ceremony opening 1 Sam 7 is uncharacteristic for the Judges. Unlike the Judges, Samuel does not save Israel through some form of military valor; instead, he delivers Israel by interceding with YHWH, who duly routs the Philistines (7:7–11; for details, cf. Campbell and O'Brien 2000, 229–33). It is a serious distortion to view Samuel as the last of the Judges; his role is much more innovative. Any authority by which Samuel might have appointed his sons judges over Israel is unknown to us; their possible role in office and the significance of their being in Beer-sheba are equally unknown.

The story of God's initiative in preparing Saul for kingship is preserved in a complex text (9:1–10:16). At the least, it appears that an older story has been overwritten to give emphasis to the anointing by Samuel that, in the narrative sequence, prepares Saul to rally Israel and deliver Jabesh-gilead (chap. 11). Saul is portrayed as utterly unambitious; he is looking for his father's donkeys, not a crown. (A birth story in this context would be inappropriate.) The overwriting, with its emphasis on Samuel and the anointing, sharpens the focus on YHWH's initiative in bringing monarchy to Israel. It is unclear whether the story of the relief of Jabesh-gilead was originally linked with Saul's anointing; all we can say is that it is linked now. A fragment of text from Qumran has been included in the text of the NRSV, detailing Nahash's prior oppression of the Gadites and the Reubenites (NRSV, following 10:27). It is not in the MT, and there is debate whether it ever belonged there, with the balance of opinion moving toward "probably not."

The concluding chapter, 1 Sam 12, has long been viewed as the great attempt within deuteronomistic circles to review and reconcile the preceding traditions. It is clear that, to some degree, it performs this function. However, the chapter is something of an enigma: It is close to the deuteronomistic traditions, but it is not of characteristic deuteronomistic composition (cf. Campbell and O'Brien 2000, 245–49). In terms of the history of the growth of the text, it is without doubt a puzzle. In terms of the present biblical text, it brings the institution of the monarchy to a close, while claiming how Israel under the monarchy can be a loyal people of God.

1 Samuel 13:1–16:13   Dismissal of Saul and beginning of David's arrival

The first two chapters of this section are a clearly delineated account of Saul's reign and, for precisely that reason, are strangely puzzling. They open with the initial accession formula for his reign (13:1)—but the formula is notoriously incomplete. They close with an all too evidently adequate summary of Saul's reign (14:47–52)—but his reign is all too evidently incomplete. He will die as king in 1 Sam 31. What exactly is the text's attitude toward Saul's reign?

As far as a summary goes, 14:47–52 appears to look back on Saul's reign from at least near its end. Verses 47–48 paint a picture that hardly fits with the rest of the tradition we possess. According to these two verses, Saul fought against Moab, Ammon, Edom, Zobah, the Philistines, and the Ammonites; he defeated them, did valiantly, and "rescued Israel out of the hands of those who plundered them" (14:48). His family—sons, daughters, and wife—are listed, with his army general and the fathers of the two men. A concluding verse (14:52) refers to "hard fighting" against the Philistines, hardly congruent with verse

47; it includes the phrase, "all the days of Saul," suggesting an observation point around the end of Saul's life (cf. 1 Sam 7:13, 15; 1 Kgs 5:1, 5 [NRSV, 4:21, 25]). The close parallel is with the summary of David's reign in 2 Sam 8:1–15 (16–18). Both passages have in common that they occur in the texts well before the reigns of the respective kings come to an end. The Davidic passage differs in not containing anything that necessarily situates it around the end of David's life. Second Samuel 8 brings a narrative focus to an end. Is a similar force at work in 1 Sam 14:47–52?

The history of the growth of these chapters is complex and uncertain and need not concern us here. For example, the rejection of Saul in 13:7b–15a is prepared for by the command in 10:8, where it appears to be secondary in the context. What appears to be clear is that 14:47–52 brings something to a close; the verses look on Saul's reign as though it were over. This stops looking like an aberration when we recognize that Saul is definitively rejected in 15:1–35 and David is anointed as his replacement in 16:1–13. Saul's formal reign has been ignominiously dumped off into a couple of chapters, which include a first rejection (13:7b–15a) and a near mess-up of his son's valorous escapade (14:1–46). While Saul may remain on the throne until his death, as this narrative has been put together, a discredited Saul is summarily dismissed as king in 15:1–35, and in 16:1–13 David is anointed to replace him.

The only material here that is positive toward Saul are the traditions of 14:47–52. If verses 47–48 are authentic rather than sheer fiction, they are surprising evidence of just how much we do not know. Beyond this material, the rest is unremittingly negative toward Israel's first king. If 14:47–52 came from sources favorable to Saul, the rest did not. This in itself is cause for reflection: What is the function of the little collection? Is its function to establish Saul's rejection and replacement in order to move him aside as legitimate king and focus on the figure of David, sought out by the LORD as "a man after his own heart" (13:14)?

The overall impression from 1 Sam 13 is overwhelmingly negative. It opens with the organization of a small force and a minor victory (won by the impetuous Jonathan). The downside of victory follows at once, with the Philistines mustering against Israel (v. 5). Israel either hides or deserts (vv. 6–7)—not a positive picture for the opening of a royal reign.

To many, it seems most unfair that in the first account of Saul's rejection (13:7b–15a) Samuel sets the deadline ("seven days you shall wait," 10:8), Samuel does not observe the deadline, and Saul suffers for it. The

passage gives some insight into the absoluteness of prophetic demand
and the nature of the condition in 1 Sam 12:14–15. Failure in obedience has cost Saul his crown: "because you have not kept what the
LORD commanded you" (13:14). The same theme returns in 15:1–35:
"To obey is better than sacrifice" (15:22); "You have rejected the word
of the LORD, and the LORD has rejected you from being king over
Israel" (15:26). Saul features as the paradigm of the condition expressed
in 12:14–15, as far as kings are concerned.

There is no report of a battle or outcome after the massive Philistine
muster of 13:5. The people with Saul number about six hundred (13:15;
14:2), the same number that will be reported later for David's band of
guerrillas (cf. 1 Sam 23:13; 27:2; 30:9). The Philistines send out three
companies of raiders; it would seem that King Saul was not worth
more. The final verses, 13:19–22, spell out in blunt terms the dire
straits and military inferiority of Israel at the time, totally dependent
on the technical superiority of the Philistines.

The Michmash story is not complimentary to Saul. It is Jonathan's
victory, nearly spoiled by the folly of Saul (cf. 14:29–30); the story
might well have come from David's supporters, aware of his commitment to Jonathan.

The second account of the rejection of Saul is a more formal story
(15:1–35). The text appears to have been reworked, in much the same
way as was 1 Sam 9:1–10:16. In this case, a rebuke (see esp. vv. 14–25)
was reworked into a rejection (see esp. vv. 26–30). As it stands now,
Saul's divinely authorized kingship is at a definitive end: "Samuel did
not see Saul again" (15:35). Instead, Samuel is sent by God to anoint
one of Jesse's sons in Bethlehem, "for I have provided for myself a king
among his sons" (16:1). The mention of "a king" is explicit here; later
in the same passage, not even the more discrete "king-designate"
(nāgîd) is used (cf. 16:13). Samuel's work is done. According to the
prophets, God's will has been expressed. Now it is time for politics to
take its course.

At this point, it is helpful to reflect a little on one of the potential
sources for traditions about Saul and David, namely, the so-called Story
of David's Rise. The adjective "so-called" is appropriate not because
there is any doubt about the existence of traditions attributed to such a
source; they constitute a substantial part of the early biblical text of 1–2
Samuel. Despite evidence that such traditions existed, however, we do
not have compelling evidence that such a source existed in documen-
tary shape. It is probable that it did; in fact, it is probable that there were
several versions at various times. The nature of the traditions is such

that most of them are either largely independent stories or form part of smaller collections that could be largely independent. In these circumstances, it is imprudent to speak of "the Story of David's Rise" as if there were a single one. Although we may speak of traditions appropriate to such a narrative, we cannot specify that particular traditions were combined to constitute this specific and identifiable text, the Story of David's Rise. Its beginning has often been sought in 1 Sam 16; it is possible that some versions may have begun as far back as the early levels of text for 1 Sam 9. Its conclusion has traditionally been located in 2 Sam 5; again, it is possible that some versions extended further, perhaps to 2 Sam 8. Once we are aware of the uncertainty that the independence of the traditions forces on us, we can undertake the interpretation of the present text with more caution.

This same quality of independence allows a semblance of pseudoplausibility to attempts to distribute part of the Samuel material across sources, insisting that doublets reflect sources, putting together what might be left separate, indulging the interpreter's imagination, and advocating arbitrary conclusions (e.g., Halpern 1981, 149–74; 2001, 263–79 and passim).

POLITICAL MOVES TO ESTABLISH DAVID AS KING
1 SAMUEL 16:14–2 SAMUEL 8:18

So far, the text has been careful not to have God's will obtrude on the political process. In 1 Sam 9:1–10:16, Samuel anointed Saul as "king-designate" (*nāgîd*), not king. In this tradition, Saul's anointing as king occurs in 1 Sam 11; Samuel's role there, if original, is minimal (cf. 11:15). In 1 Sam 16:1–13, although Saul is said to have been rejected by God as king and a king is provided by God among Jesse's sons (16:1), no mention is made of the kingship when it comes to the actual anointing (16:13).

The political achievement of what the prophet has decreed on God's behalf will, in the case of Saul and David, take time and a lot of action. First, there will be tension between Saul and David themselves. Then, after the death of Saul and three of his sons in battle with the Philistines, there will be a long civil war between David's forces and those of the house of Saul. Finally, David will achieve the royal power in Israel for which he was anointed and his kingship will be established—with a capital city and a palace, the coming of the ark, God's promise of a dynasty, and military security.

Extensive traditions narrate the initial tension between Saul and David. First, tensions simmer while David is present at Saul's court. Then, open rupture becomes inevitable and David becomes a guerrilla chief in the wilderness of Judah, on the run from Saul, ending in his flight to the Philistine Achish. Finally, a major campaign erupts pitting the Philistines against Saul and resulting in Saul's death in battle. Surprisingly, after it, we hear no more of the Philistines until they move against David and are twice defeated (2 Sam 5:17–25). As regards the Philistines, what Samuel set in motion with Saul is achieved with David.

Tension between Saul as king and David as anointed
1 Samuel 16:14–31:13

1 Samuel 16:14–21:1 (NRSV, 20:42)   David at the court of Saul

A balefully ominous sentence opens the text here: "The spirit of the LORD departed from Saul, and an evil spirit from the LORD tormented him" (16:14). It reads like an interpretative comment. The narrative has Saul's servants say: "an evil spirit from God is tormenting you" (16:15). This can and probably should be understood as denoting an episodic phenomenon. Its interpretation in the preceding verse almost certainly cannot be. "The spirit of the LORD departed from Saul" reflects a tradition of divine rejection, not a matter of episodic ill-health. For the ill-health, a musician is sought to soothe Saul. Jesse's son is mentioned, and David is sent for. He joins the court as lyre player and armor bearer to Saul. Irony of ironies, God's designated replacement is brought in to be Saul's needed healer. (The armor bearer's job alone should rule out any idea that David was a little chap; kings, especially the more primitive, do not usually hire the physically diminutive for their royal guard or the role of royal armor bearer.)

At this point in its history, Israel may well have had wealthy farmers (such as Nabal, 1 Sam 25), but the traditions do not speak of great houses or aristocratic families from whom kings might come. Saul is looking for his father's asses; David is keeping his father's sheep; Moses was keeping his father-in-law's flock (Exod 3:1). Of course, shepherd was a literary metaphor for the ancient Near Eastern king, but it is likely that David's shepherding task (not his permanent livelihood) was preserved in the tradition. Kings shepherded their people from their thrones, not the woolly beasts on their father's farms (despite McKenzie 2000, 47–51). It is not so much that Israel's earliest kings stemmed from simple beginnings but that there were no other beginnings to stem from.

In the early stages of monarchy, the power of the king was largely dependent on the power and energy of that person himself. Naturally, there would have been interest in the beginnings of such achievers. For David, as for Saul, there were two traditions that have survived. The one beginning here leads into the story to come; the other has its beginning within the story to come and leads out of it. Both traditions are compatible with each other, but the text does not attempt any serious harmonization. By and large, one tradition is found alone in the LXX, while both are interwoven in the MT (for fuller discussion, see Campbell, comm. [2003]; for a visually helpful layout, see Campbell and O'Brien 2000, 258–65).

There is no question that in the traditions we have, David comes to prominence in Israel through the killing of a Philistine champion, Goliath. Saul's death, at the end of 1 Samuel, comes at the hands of the Philistines. The major defeats of the Philistines are achieved by David once he has come to power in Jerusalem. The symmetry is superb: Defeat of the Philistines brings David to prominence; defeat by the Philistines brings Saul to his death; defeat of the Philistines is David's achievement, once brought to power. The symmetry may be a little too good to be true. It is a reminder to the interpreter that the structures are here reflecting a carefully crafted narrative, and carefully crafted narratives may reflect more accurately what their narrators wanted than what actually was. We do not know; we cannot be sure. We can only be cautious.

In one portrayal, David is introduced into Saul's court as lyre player, enjoys Saul's favor, and is commissioned as Saul's armor bearer. The following episode has the Philistines mass their forces against Israel and a Philistine champion, Goliath, utter a menacing challenge to the Israelite army. As the king's armor bearer, David stands at Saul's side and offers himself to meet the Philistine challenge. He uses a sling to find the invincible Philistine's weak point and kill him, initiating a great Israelite victory. This leads to his posting as a commander among Saul's troops and his continued success against Israel's foes (cf. 1 Sam 18:13–16).

Two factors, above all, have led to widespread misunderstanding of this story. First is the belief that David is portrayed as too young and too small to have any chance against the Philistine veteran. Second is the conviction that the sling was not an appropriate weapon for military combat of this kind. David's victory, therefore, must have been entirely God's doing. This is beautiful, devotional, pious—and utter rubbish.

David is not portrayed as too young. He is described as a *na'ar*, usually translated "youth," or "young man." A *na'ar* is someone who is in some way dependent, usually either remaining still in the family or being in service—for example, Samuel as an infant in arms or Jeroboam as a senior public servant (cf. Stähli 1978). David's brothers are described as *na'ar* (16:11, Hebrew), and the three eldest are in Saul's army; the courtier who recommended David to Saul is described as a *na'ar* (16:18). David is not "too young"; he is a recent recruit facing a grizzled veteran (cf. Stoebe, comm., 1.335; Gooding 1986, 56). David is not portrayed as too small. He has the stature to be Saul's armor bearer (and that means standing tall); the offer of Saul's armor is not laughable (and Saul was a big man); he exchanges gear with Jonathan (and Jonathan was hardly the runt of the family). David describes himself as fast enough to catch a predatory lion or bear, with courage enough to rescue its prey, and with quick enough reflexes to kill the predator if it turned on him—one very tough young man (cf. 17:34–36).

Finally, David's sling was a most appropriate weapon for the circumstances. The ancient sling is not to be confused with the modern slingshot; slingshots are for kids, but slings were for killing. The sling was a standard military weapon in the ancient world (cf. Judg 20:16; 2 Chr 26:14). Against an otherwise invincible infantryman, the sling was brilliant lateral thinking, as devastating against Goliath as the Welsh longbow against French cavalry at Crecy and Agincourt or the Molotov cocktail against German tanks in World War II.

The story illustrates perfectly the narrative drift so far: Saul has been rejected by God and David chosen to replace him. On the battlefield, Saul is "dismayed and greatly afraid" (17:11)—most unkingly behavior. David emerges as a most kingly candidate. His words to Saul, especially 17:37, and his words to the Philistine (17:45–47) are all that might be expected of one who would loyally follow the LORD as king.

The second tradition, found only in the MT, tells of the same single combat but paints a quite different picture of David. He has not been nominated to Saul's court but comes to the battlefield from the farm. It is not where he comes from but what he is portrayed doing when he gets there that gives this tradition its edge and its difference. David shows raw ambition: "What shall be done for the man who kills this Philistine?" (17:26). As David goes out to the combat, he is unknown (17:55–58); when he comes back from the combat, he is conscripted into Saul's court, befriended by Jonathan, given a command in the military, and promised Saul's elder daughter (Merab) as wife (18:1–5, 17–18).

Both traditions have David catapulted into public prominence by his victory over the Philistine (the name Goliath is used only twice in the story [17:4, 23], once for each tradition; it may have migrated from 2 Sam 21:19). In one tradition, David is on the battlefield as a member of Saul's court; in the other, David's performance on the battlefield introduces him to Saul's court. In the first, faith and loyalty are at the fore; in the second, ambition is the driving force. Any observer of human nature knows that these two characteristics are compatible: Faith may support ambition; ambition may fuel faith. The text juxtaposes the two traditions; it does not develop the issue of their interrelationship. The second tradition (ambition, the MT only) is not given in its entirety. Three major segments are told: the scene on the battlefield (17:12–30), the introduction to Saul's court (17:55–18:5), and the offer of Saul's daughter (18:17–19); the interstices are easily filled in. In this tradition, the Philistine's death is given a verse (17:50), as is David's success (18:30). All that is needed is available. The present MT offers possibilities for integrating the two traditions (cf. 17:15–16, 31); storytellers would need to draw on their experience and skill.

No follow-up to this major victory over the Philistines is noted. The defeated Philistines were chased home (Gath and Ekron); no more is said. The stories to come are about internal politics, not the history of peoples. While Saul will, of course, feature in these stories, their focus is on David. Interpreters should be aware of the bias implied by this focus.

In both traditions, David is at the court of Saul by Saul's invitation (16:22; 18:5). It is portrayed as an uneasy coexistence: "Saul eyed David from that day on" (18:9). The text from this time at the court refers to three things: Saul's hidden moves to kill David through his daughters Merab and Michal (18:17, 25), Saul's open moves either through his entourage or with his own spear (19:1, 9–10), and, finally, the moves to save David, made by Saul's daughter Michal, the prophet Samuel, and Saul's son Jonathan (19:11–17; 19:18–24; 20:1–21:1 [NRSV, 20:42]). David has support where it counts and Saul fails, even with his own spear. But Saul is king and so David leaves court.

1 Samuel 21:2 (NRSV, 21:1)–27:12   *Open rupture between David and Saul*

David is driven from Saul and ends up with Achish. While his time with Achish is specified, "one year and four months" (27:7), we are not told the length of time he was in Judah on the run from Saul. The accounts of David's flight from Saul and its consequences, along with an account of the flight to Achish, form an envelope around the traditions of

David, chief of the guerrilla band in the wilderness. It is helpful to take a bird's-eye view before looking more closely.

The text has two accounts of flight. In one, David stays in Judah, encountering Ahimelech at Nob, on the way to the wilderness; the tensions have consequences for David's family and the priests with Ahimelech. In the other, David leaves Judah for Achish at Gath; if used, this would require considerable reshaping of the text we have. The texts of flight occupy chapter 21; those of the consequences occupy chapter 22.

With the beginning of chapter 23, David and Saul are sharply contrasted as deliverers in Israel. The town Keilah's food supply is being pillaged by Philistines; David, after inquiring of the LORD, defeats the Philistines and delivers the town. Saul is told that David has entered a walled town and believes, mistakenly, that David has been delivered into his power. David works for Keilah's deliverance; Saul schemes for David's downfall.

With chapters 24–26, a trio of stories is told that redound to David's credit; he spares the lives of Saul in a cave, Nabal on a farm, and Saul again, this time in his camp. Far more remarkable than David's respect or restraint are the commendations of David attributed to Saul, Abigail, and Saul again. Saul of David: "You are more righteous than I. . . . Now I know that you shall surely be king" (24:17–21). Abigail of David: "For the LORD will certainly make my lord a sure house. . . . When the LORD . . . has appointed you prince over Israel . . ." (25:28–31). Finally, Saul again of David: "I have done wrong; come back, my son David, for I will never harm you again"; and "Blessed be you, my son David! You will do many things and will succeed in them" (26:21, 25). No future king of Israel could wish for a better set of endorsements. Practically speaking, this is about all we are told of this hugely significant and largely undisclosed period of time.

Despite the endorsements, the narrative proceeds as though it all had never happened: "David said in his heart, 'I shall now perish one day by the hand of Saul; there is nothing better for me than to escape to the land of the Philistines; then Saul will despair of seeking me any longer within the borders of Israel, and I shall escape out of his hand'" (27:1). Has the reconciliation been left too late, as will be the case with Absalom? Does David know from bitter experience the instability of Saul's commitments? Are different traditions juxtaposed? Is the narrative overly selective and unfairly favorable to David?

The sequence of the narrative in the present text is perfectly possible; it is not perfectly troublefree. As it stands, David left Jonathan and went to the priest Ahimelech at Nob, from whom he obtained food and a sword. Thus provisioned, he fled to the Philistine, King Achish of Gath. Recognized there as dangerous, he escaped to the cave of Adullam, near the Philistine frontier. On the prophet Gad's advice, he moved his base of operations further into the interior of Judah. There are two awkwardnesses here, one quite minor, the other not-so-minor but not insurmountable either. First, 21:11 (NRSV, 21:10)—"David rose and fled that day from Saul"—would be perfectly suitable before the meeting with Ahimelech (e.g., "And David rose and fled that day from Saul and came to Nob"). At the end of the episode with Ahimelech, it is slightly awkward. It can be accommodated by rendering the "and" as "so," with the following understanding: "So David escaped that day from Saul, having acquired food and a sword." Second, David would be most unwise to show up at Gath with Goliath's sword. If it was exceptional enough to be kept in the sanctuary at Nob, it was exceptional enough to be recognized in Gath. This is awkward, but not at all insurmountable. A storyteller could have David discard or conceal the sword almost immediately; what he needed was food. Alternatively, a storyteller could have David discard the sword once near Gath; he certainly was not going to fight his way into the town. The text does not point to either easy solution; it does not even mention the sword. At Gath, it is not the recognition of Goliath's sword but the recognition of David himself that creates a problem. It is far from certain how the episode with Ahimelech and that with Achish are to be handled.

It is possible that the episode with Achish at Gath was one way that a tradition began the narrative of David's flight. David fled from Saul to Achish. The sequence can then continue in one of two ways. First, David's presence at Gath is dangerous (beyond the song, he is described as "the king of the land"); he escapes back into Judah and the narrative sequence continues. To allow for this, a storyteller would need to make some adjustment to the account of David's second arrival at the court of Achish (cf. chap. 27). The easiest way might have been a word to Achish from a counselor, advising caution since this David was a cunning dissembler and had deceived them before. Second, David remains with Achish at Gath and the traditions now in chapters 22–26 are passed over. To allow for this, a storyteller would need to account for David's having eventually won the trust and confidence of Achish. David's brutal tactics while at Ziklag (cf. 27:8–12) are a pointer in this direction.

It is possible that the episode with Ahimelech at Nob was one way that a tradition began the narrative of David's flight, with David leaving Nob and escaping to the cave of Adullam (cf. 22:1). The presence of the Achish episode in the text is then simply a reminder of another way that the narrative can be begun. Most commentaries take the equivalent of this approach, by declaring 21:11–16 (NRSV, 21:10–15) a later incompatible addition, although they do not pause to explain why such an episode should have been added later.

It is probably most straightforward to accept that the tradition maintained at least two accounts of the start of David's flight and that the present text employs the Ahimelech episode as its beginning, but places the Achish episode within reach as an alternative.

The basic geography is independent of these choices. David first heads west, either to the court of Achish or to the cave of Adullam. Advised by Gad, in due course he moves back into the interior of Judah, in the "forest of Hereth" (22:5). Traditions speak of his activity in that area, as well as at Carmel in Maon and at En-gedi—in other words, toward the east of Judah.

The traditions are clear enough, but some aspects are worth highlighting. David's "brothers and all his father's house" join him at Adullam (22:1; hardly consonant with the image of the young shepherd of no consequence)—and we hear no more of them. David's four hundred followers are described in disreputable terms (unless these terms obliquely reflect classes of people in need of deliverance): "Everyone who was in distress, and everyone who was in debt, and everyone who was discontented gathered to him" (22:2). David's mother and father are left with the king of Moab for safekeeping, "until I know what God will do for me" (22:3). The implication is clear: The trouble will not go away; David will not yield before Saul. Note the high level at which negotiations are conducted. Mother and father stay with the king of Moab while David is "in the stronghold" (22:4)—and we hear no more of them. Gad's advice, not described as a prophetic word from God, may reflect fear of the neighboring Philistines; David's own fighters will later rate them as more dangerous than Saul (23:3).

In the report of David's exchange with Ahimelech no attempt is made to account for the fact that David lied. He was not on a mission from the king; he had no rendezvous planned (cf. 21:3; NRSV, 21:2). The narrative does not offer the lie as an excuse, nor is it used as such by Ahimelech. It is on a par with Abraham's lie in Egypt about his wife (cf. Gen 12:11–19). It does not flatter David, and Saul's reaction certainly does not flatter Saul. Eighty-five priests and an entire city are wiped out. The blood of a priestly family is on Saul's hands; God's ephod is in David's. What Israelite soldiers would not do, Doeg does for Saul (22:17–19). Saul is burdened with sacrilege and murder.

The Keilah episode draws a sharp contrast: David the deliverer of oppressed Israelites over against Saul the would-be destroyer of the town and its deliverer. What follows, however, is unexpected: The people of Keilah are ready to surrender David to Saul; Jonathan covenants to surrender the succession to David; the people of Ziph are ready to surrender David to Saul. One individual, the crown prince, is reported as favorable to David; two groups of people are hostile to him. This fits with the note of a long civil war following Saul's death (2 Sam 3:1).

The next trio of stories is more than unexpected; all three are extra-ordinary. In them, David spares Saul's life twice, once by day and once by night, and Nabal's just once. God gets Nabal, which is not a good omen for Saul. In the cave, the "by day" story, David's speech against killing Saul comes too late (24:6–7); he has already cut the corner off Saul's cloak. Waving the corner of the cloak in broad daylight before a search party of some three thousand of Saul's troops requires explanation, especially with Saul asking, "Is this your voice, my son David" (24:16). A "daytime" version of the "nighttime" story of chapter 26 is likely (for the reverse view, see particularly Koch 1969, 132–48).

What is clear about all three stories is that they enhance David's claim to be one who did not kill his way to power. A number of people who stood between David and the throne were killed. Saul's support-ers were under no illusions: "Murderer! Scoundrel! The LORD has avenged on you all the blood of the house of Saul" (2 Sam 16:7–8 [Heb.; not NRSV]). These three traditions lean in the other direction. They were to David's benefit in more ways than one. After all, he was very soon to be the LORD's anointed himself. What is quite extraordinary, however, is the commendation of David offered in each, as we noted above. The commendations are about as high-flown as the nominating speeches at party conventions. They are part of that strange mixture of the unreal and the all-too-real in the Davidic traditions.

The all-too-real surfaces when the narrative takes David into Philis-tine territory, as Achish's vassal. David annihilates enemies and tells Achish he has raided allies (27:8–10). He leaves absolutely no survivors, lest someone might blow his cover (27:11). In the traditions of David's middle years, further ahead, the question will recur several times: Was David indulgent toward his children or ruthless in his politics? The question must be asked about Amnon's death, perhaps too about the sending of Tamar unaccompanied to her fate, probably about the rec-onciliation with Absalom, and certainly about the killing of Absalom. This tradition here favors the answer: ruthless. A caveat has to be entered: Consistency is not a quality that interpreters can count on. Napoleon Bonaparte, for example, could destroy recalcitrant villages and villagers at the drop of a hat and could equally be very tender with some of his own family.

1 Samuel 28–31   Ultimate failure of Saul

The sequence of these four chapters need not be rearranged; it is rhetorical or schematic, certainly not chronological. The question that had to worry all David's supporters was: Could David and his warriors perhaps have saved Saul from defeat? Saul died fighting Philistines while David and his band were absent, chasing Amalekites. Did David, a Philistine vassal at the time, deliberately withhold support from Saul? Could David and his six hundred have made a difference?

The narrative's answer *from the outset* is a resounding No. God had decreed Saul's death (chap. 28); there was nothing that David could have done. The Philistine commanders ordered David dismissed from the battle force and sent back to Ziklag (chap. 29); David's absence was not of his choosing.

There were two possibilities. David and his force might have returned to Saul's side as the storm with the Philistines began brewing, or David and his force might have turned sides and supported Saul in the middle of the battle. Saul's implacable hostility toward David, evidenced in the preceding chapters, might have been felt to exclude the first possibility (cf. 27:1). The Philistine commanders are portrayed anticipating the real danger of the second (cf. 29:4), hence their order: "Send the man back . . . ; he shall not go down with us to battle."

In Israelite narrative, God outranks the Philistine commanders. The story of the consultation with Samuel therefore precedes the story of the decision on the part of the Philistine commanders. According to the first, God has decreed Saul's death; according to the second, David will not be present at the battle.

The scene is set in 28:1–2. The coming conflict is noted (28:1a); the coming problem is signaled in Achish's statement to David (28:1b). The realities are hinted at in the ambiguity of the response attributed to David (28:2).

The consultation with Samuel follows (28:3–25). The problem has been signaled; the solution to it is provided. There will be war; Saul will die, because God has decreed his death (28:16–19). The stage is set for the consultation story by the absence of mediums and wizards, the presence of the Philistines, and the silence of God. The Philistines are at Shunem and all Israel at Gilboa; the story is situated on the eve of the decisive battle (cf. 28:19). Saul has expelled "the mediums and the wizards from the land" (28:3). By orthodox standards this is unquestionably a good deed, worthy of one of the great reforming kings. It is noteworthy that we have heard nothing of it. The LORD does not respond to Saul's inquiries—echoes of 16:14.

As the consultation unfolds, puzzling issues multiply. Central to them is why the text should have the medium see Samuel and recognize Saul. How did it happen? What are the implications? Does the text need improvement? Various suggestions have been made; in my judgment, they do not help and the reality is that we do not know. The text leaves challenges to storytellers that they probably rose to; all we know for sure is that we cannot.

Samuel's message for Saul was scarcely cheerful. At its barest, it reduces to: "The LORD has turned from you and become your enemy. . . . Tomorrow you and your sons shall be with me; the LORD will also give the army of Israel into the hands of the Philistines" (28:16, 19aßb). This in itself is a death sentence. The prophetic reworking visible in 1 Sam 15, especially verses 26–30, is drawn on in the middle here to heighten the intensity of the death sentence. Almost at the beginning, Samuel had pronounced God's rejection of Saul and election of David; now it is about to take effect. The die has long been cast.

The dismissal of David's forces from the Philistine ranks is treated in a flashback. The Philistines, on their way north, are at Aphek (most probably on the coastal plain); the Israelites are in Jezreel. The note of gathering for war against Israel does not need to be repeated from 28:1. The dismissal is effective in 29:11, with David heading south to Ziklag and beyond and the Philistines north to Jezreel. When the story of David's raid on the Amalekites has been told (chap. 30; note: There were not supposed to be any Amalekites after 1 Sam 15, but after this slaughter four hundred escaped [30:17]—the story of 1 Sam 15 was a cautionary tale), the narrative turns to the final battle with no preliminary details (cf. 31:1); these have already been told. The outcome is extensive, especially if verse 7 is drawn on, added to verses 1–6. Saul and his sons are dead and Israel defeated, towns are forsaken, and there is generalized flight, involving even those beyond the Jordan—unmentioned in this campaign until now. As to the forsaken towns, "the Philistines came and occupied them" (31:7), but there is no follow-up in the narrative. The Philistines desecrate the body of Saul; the people of Jabesh-gilead give the three bodies honorable burial. The reign of Saul is at an end.

Civil war in Israel
2 Samuel 1–4

Relatively early in the piece, David is anointed king of Judah at Hebron (2 Sam 2:1–4a). David's rule over Judah at Hebron is reported as lasting seven years and six months. From that time, we have episodes occupying perhaps a little more than four days—roughly a day or so each for: (1) the execution of the Amalekite and lament over Saul and Jonathan; (2) the battle of Gibeon and death of Asahel; (3) the death of Abner (although the preliminaries demand more time); (4) the assassination of Ishbaal. The chronology suggests that the focus is exclusively on a limited aspect of David's rise to power. At base, it is the claim of David's innocence in relation to three key killings—those of Saul, of Abner, and of Ishbaal.

The obvious discrepancy between a seven- to eight-year period of time and text occupying some four days of that time provides a valuable opportunity to reflect on the meaning and function of much biblical narrative. Of course, the seven years and six months is probably schematic or symbolic; a forty-year period of rule for both David (2 Sam 5:4; 1 Kgs 2:11) and Solomon (1 Kgs 11:42) is unlikely to be chronological. It may mirror generations. Similarly, the four days is not precise chronology, but it is an accurate characterization of the texts. What then is their meaning and function? In many modern Western democracies, political leaders hold office for three- or four-year terms. If, for example, a text is composed of material occupying some four days in the course of a U.S. president's two terms in office (eight years), then automatically the question is raised of the meaning or function of that text. So here—and often elsewhere in biblical narrative.

Such a text may be valuable to a historian, a political scientist, a sociologist, and so on. Still, the central question remains: What is the meaning or function of the text? In the case of 2 Sam 1–4, in my judgment, neither history nor sociology is the answer to that central question—although the text may provide valuable information in such areas. In my judgment, the meaning and function of the text of 2 Sam 1–4 is to make the claim of David's innocence in relation to the killings of Saul, Abner, and Ishbaal. It is less a question of how David rose to power than of how David did not rise to power. His rise to power was certainly facilitated by the deaths of two of these three men. According to the text, he did not rise to power by having them killed. The question whether the text reflects the reality of the events is a separate issue from the question whether this interpretation reflects the reality of the text. The task of textual interpretation is to explore the reality of the text. The task of history or sociology etc. can be to explore the reality hinted at within the text. The two tasks are not the same.

The present composition—our biblical text that has been composed from a number of traditions—relates the first episode before moving to material about David's being installed as king over Judah. The second episode comes next, setting up hostility between Joab and Abner, before the statement of civil war and the list of David's sons born in this period. Finally, the third and fourth episodes (associated rather than independent) bring the issue of David's rise to power to a close. The rise is over; all that remains is to take the power. So, in the first episode as David's rise draws to a close, the narrative reflects on his attitude toward the death of Saul. Only after that does David accept being anointed "king over the house of Judah" (2:4). The battle that begins with two groups of twelve "young men" spreads to the two armies under Abner and Joab. In the heat of battle and flight, Abner kills Asahel, Joab's brother. We are told that this is why, in due course, Joab killed Abner (3:27, 30). So episode number two provides the motive for the death of Abner—a blood feud over the killing of a brother. There are other possibilities. Political rivalry could have had Joab eliminate Abner before Abner could take Joab's place as the power behind David's throne. At its most shadowy, David might have manipulated the deaths of both Abner and Ishbaal (so Halpern 2001, 81–84); but unlikely for Abner. The text has made its claim (3:27, 30); skeptics may harbor their suspicions. However, the text goes on to note that there was a long civil war and beyond this lists the sons born to David at Hebron—six of them. The sons of six wives, they could have all been born within a week or two; nevertheless, the list suggests the passage of time. The final two episodes tell of the elimination of Abner and the assassination of Ishbaal. According to the text, Joab killed Abner and two traitors killed Ishbaal—David had no part in either death. Of the long civil war, the reasons for it and the loyalties involved, the text tells us nothing. Why, with David at Hebron, Abner should have moved Ishbaal to Transjordan we are not told. Revealingly though, the lead role is given to Abner; we are told that Abner took Ishbaal to Mahanaim and made Ishbaal king over his dominions (2:8–9). Ishbaal's dominions are listed as Gilead, the Ashurites, Jezreel, Ephraim, Benjamin, and Israel, all of it (2:9). The list is a little odd, with a series of parts and then a claim of the whole. To read the final claim as "that is to say, all Israel" would make sense but does not reflect the structure of the verse. It is clear that Abner was in command of Ishbaal's kingdom; it is not clear exactly what that kingdom was. It is clear that toward the end, the kingdom crumbled. And the text has David there to pick up the pieces.

To go back a little, with Saul dead and David out of the country, how should the narrative address David's role in picking up the pieces of Saul's kingdom? Everyone associated with Israel knew that David became Israel's king after Saul. Given that awareness, it will be rewarding to explore at this point the narrative's focus of interest.

The first story picks up the action a few days after Saul's death (2 Sam 1:1–27). The chronological linkage is not precise; it is "after the death of Saul" and on the third day after "David had returned from defeating the Amalekites," but there is no precise correlation of the two events. The text itself is structurally balanced. First, Saul's fate is reported (vv. 2–10), then David's mourning until evening (vv. 11–12); second, the Amalekite's fate is reported (vv. 13–16), then comes David's lament for Saul and Jonathan (vv. 17–27).

The details of Saul's death do not tally with 1 Sam 31. For example, in 31:4, "Saul took his own sword and fell upon it"; but the Amalekite claims, "So I stood over him, and killed him" (1:10). The divergences are hardly surprising and should not be given importance. Saul's crown and armlet are equally devoid of broader significance; we do not hear of them again. Their function in the narrative is to symbolize what is left unsaid: The Amalekite is certainly bringing David the news of Saul's death, and the crown and armlet symbolize that he believed he was bringing David Saul's kingship—for which he surely expected a reward. In due course he will receive his reward: his death.

First, however, the narrative attends to David's reaction to the deaths of Saul and Jonathan. The verse is comprehensive: "They mourned and wept, and fasted until evening for Saul and for his son Jonathan, and for the army of the LORD and for the house of Israel, because they had fallen by the sword" (1:12). Three verbs for the grief, four objects for the focus of that grief—but not Abinadab and Malchishua, mentioned in chapter 31. The traditions are independent. The fourth phrase, "the house of Israel," does not feature in the preceding; the designation is surprisingly rare in Deuteronomy–Kings and may not be original here.

From the general the narrative turns to the particular. The situation of defeat and death has been reported, along with the reaction to it of David and all those with him. The narrative focuses on the individual who brought the news—the Amalekite. It casts the death of Saul in a different light. In the Amalekite's version, he had done Saul a kindness (1:10). In David's version, the Amalekite had destroyed YHWH's king (1:14–16). The Amalekite is executed. The focus remains particular:

David intoned a lament over Saul and Jonathan—a single poet (David) and a personal focus (Saul and Jonathan) in relation to the image of national defeat. The historical significance of the Philistine victory is unclear. Just as with the defeat of the Philistine champion earlier (chap. 17), there is no follow-up here to what is portrayed as a major campaign. What the narrative claims to make clear is that there was no joy for David in Israel's defeat and Saul's death.

David's move to Hebron is portrayed as his response to divine guidance. David's anointing as king over the house of Judah is portrayed as the action of the people of Judah. In between these two statements is the political reality that David and his entire establishment, a potent military force, relocated to the vicinity of Hebron. Was David invited as a powerful protector or did David impose his presence through his power? The text attributes the episode to God's decision and the people's action. So we are told, but perhaps still we do not know.

It is appropriate at this point to reflect briefly on the assessment or evaluation of traditions in the biblical text. In some cases, biblical text can be evaluated against extrabiblical evidence, whether archaeological or textual. Such is the case for aspects of the book of Joshua. In other cases, the biblical text itself holds divergent traditions. Such is the case for the origins of kingship in 1 Sam 7–12 (two positive but different; one negative). Sometimes evaluation may be assisted by situating particular traditions within a wider horizon. Sometimes wider horizons are not helpful or available. In David's case, the claim to be innocent of bloodshed is widely expressed. From Saul's camp, it is flatly contradicted by Shimei ben Gera's "You are a man of blood" (2 Sam 16:8). The two figures belong on opposite sides of the political divide; there is no independent witness to verify their claims. The text here says that "David inquired of the LORD" and was told to go up to Hebron (2 Sam 2:1). Divine oracles have an unenviable reputation for uncertainty or ambiguity (e.g., "delphic"), even downright dissembling, dishonesty, and error. The story in 1 Kgs 22 explores something of Israel's experience of this, as do Jer 28 and other texts. In our present case, David's kingship over Judah is based at Hebron; Abner has established Ishbaal as king over most of the rest based at Mahanaim, east of the Jordan (2:8–9). The political movements have been considerable, and we know precious little about them. For David, however, Hebron was a very sound base. So the question has to be asked: Did God tell David or did David tell God? The text answers clearly: God told David (2:1). Skeptics may harbor their suspicions. To the best of my knowledge, there are no independent witnesses to assess this or similar claims. Neither the assertions of the text nor the suspicions of the skeptics can attain to certainty. That is the nature of the beast. (Regrettably, Halpern overplays his hand all too often in this area—for example, "We know that Samuel is accurate because it is nothing but lies" [2001, 100]; earlier, he repeatedly sides with Shimei—for example, "Chances are, David commissioned the hit" [82].)

Only twice in these four chapters does the narrative take a longer view of events than the four episodes of some twenty-four hours each. The first is 2 Sam 2:4b–11 (overview of the two kingdoms); the second, 3:1–5 (overview of civil war and sons). The broad focus of these two moments in the narrative underscores the narrow focus of the other passages. The second is essentially 3:1; there was a long civil war and David's forces gradually got the upper hand. That says bluntly what could otherwise only be surmised. The first, 2:4b–11, is appropriately situated chronologically before 3:1, gives some valuable details, raises some fascinating questions, and offers no answers.

The opening in v. 4b (literally, "and it was told to David") creates a break in the narrative sequence. Although associated with David's anointing as king (cf. v. 7b), the break distances the passage from the move to Hebron; it also establishes an independence from 1 Sam 31, where the actions of the inhabitants of Jabesh-gilead are recounted. David sends messengers to express his thanks to the people of Jabesh-gilead and to promise to deal favorably with them. There is a diplomatic invitation to rally to David's cause (v. 7). The report of David's gratitude serves to distance him from any involvement in Saul's death; the invitation suggests that there is more running here than meets the eye.

The text immediately moves to Abner's actions, establishing Saul's son, Ishbaal, in Mahanaim and making him king over much that was not Judah (including Gilead, Jezreel, Ephraim, and Benjamin). The text adds that "the house of Judah followed David" (2:10b); it is apparently but not necessarily independent of 2:4a. Ishbaal's reign is noted as two years; David's at Hebron is given as seven years and six months.

Three questions are unanswered. First, what is the point of a report of David's embassy to the people of Jabesh-gilead, in northern Transjordan, well to the north of Mahanaim? Second, what lies behind Abner's establishment of Ishbaal in Mahanaim, well to the east of the Jordan, with a claim to kingship over extensive territory west of the Jordan? Third, whatever the accuracy of the dates given, what is the chronological picture underlying the two reigns, with David's period at Hebron given as more than three times the length of Ishbaal's reign?

Any answers have to be speculative; the text gives none. We do not know how much time passed between Saul's death and David's move to Hebron. The assassination of Ishbaal appears in the text to follow closely on the death of Abner. This need not have been so; time may be allowed for Ishbaal's weakness to become apparent and his two assassins emboldened. Equally, time may be allowed between Ishbaal's death and the offer to David of Israel's crown. Although the chronological statements suggest a prompt transfer of David's seat of government from Hebron to Jerusalem, they may be more schematic than fine-tuned. An immediate move is unlikely without the time for prior preparations. There are possibilities in plenty and certainty in none. Chronicles, of course, presents a totally different picture of the whole period (1 Chr 11:1–3; 12:23, 38–40).

One thing is clear in all this, and it is surprising. The Samuel narrative quite openly reports the tradition that there was a long war between the house of Saul and the house of David (3:1). At the same time, the narrative reports extensively the traditions claiming that David in Judah fled before Saul, his persecutor, and that David was in no way involved in the deaths of Saul or his sons or his general. Civil war is acceptable; assassination is unacceptable. It is surprising.

The chronological uncertainty is exacerbated by the second major episode. The geography is clear; the timing is not. The two generals and their mercenary troops, Abner and the servants of Ishbaal and Joab and the servants of David, meet at the pool of Gibeon. While Abner's troops are referred to initially as Ishbaal's mercenaries and while they depart from and return to Mahanaim, in the body of the narrative they are referred to as Benjaminites. Saul's power base was, of course, Benjamin, so harmonization is perfectly possible. At the same time, a blending of traditions is not out of the question. This is also the first direct mention of Joab (indirect in 1 Sam 26:6); his status is taken for granted. The combat of the twelve young champions from each side suggests a set-piece battle rather than a random encounter; it does not affect the subsequent narrative. The outcome of the combat was indecisive. The maneuver is known from a relief at Tell Halaf; it may be intended literally or it may symbolize that neither side gained the victory (cf. de Vaux 1959 and references there). The reality of the link between this combat and the following battle is unclear; nothing is said. However, a fierce battle resulted (2:17).

In the rout, Joab's brother Asahel pursues Abner. The narrative has Abner fail to dissuade him from his pursuit and so kills him with a backward blow from his spear. (Despite contrary views, the old fox had probably sharpened the spear's rear end.) This pits the remaining two brothers, Joab and Abishai, against Abner. Fratricidal extermination of the two forces is prevented by a truce; night marches see both groups back at their bases, Mahanaim and Hebron. The hatred of Joab and Abishai for Abner will recur in the next episode. The focus of the narrative appears to be accounting for that hatred.

We have looked at the notice of the long civil war; there is no need to revisit it. There is time and probably need to pause again in puzzlement at a text that goes to such lengths to avoid even the hint that David might have shed royal blood and then blithely notes that "there was a long war between the house of Saul and the house of David" (3:1). Perhaps it is an omen of things to come: Joab and Abner will fight out the war and David will embrace the winner—and the throne. If so, the next episode will not be the last. We have also noted that the birth of six sons to six wives does not necessarily determine the time that has passed. It does, however, have a sense of establishment and of David's growing right to the role of king.

In what follows (3:6–39), Joab and Abishai are assigned guilt for Abner's murder (v. 30). It is repeated on David's lips at the end of the passage: "These men, the sons of Zeruiah, are too violent for me" (v. 39). Yet only Joab does the killing and only Joab is mentioned in the body of the narrative. David is declared innocent: "So all the people and all Israel understood that day that the king had no part in the killing of Abner son of Ner" (v. 37). Three levels in the text are exposed: David may be innocent of murder, Joab may be guilty of political ambition, and Joab and Abishai may be guilty of blood vengeance over the death of their brother in war. It is hardly likely that these three levels are innocently or accidentally intermingled.

The levels and possibilities within this text are complex and densely woven; the politics and rivalries of human competition are seldom less. The story proper opens with a reference to the war (3:6). David's side may be winning the war, but Abner was winning the power struggle on his side of the war. So the narrative plays on at least three sets of sensitivities. We may assume that David wanted kingship over Israel as well as Judah. We may assume that Joab's power within David's kingdom was threatened by the increasing power of Abner on the other side. We may assume that both Joab and Abishai wanted Abner dead because of their brother Asahel. The narrative maneuvers in and out of all three levels and leaves us unequivocally uncertain. David is the least likely to be actively involved (despite Halpern); he has the least to lose or gain— the kingdom is coming to him anyway. Joab has the most to lose. If

Abner succeeds in bringing all Israel over to David (cf. 3:12), then at the very least Joab will have a powerful rival to compete with. Later experience makes us think of "Israel" as the senior partner to less powerful Judah. But in this case, the house of David is winning the war (3:1). The relative strengths of Abner and Joab are unknown to us, but, under David, they would be rivals. The hatred of Joab and Abishai for the man who killed their brother is a real enough element within a narrative, but a skeptic has to wonder whether it is something of a cover for a more politically motivated killing. It is used to justify Joab's murder by Solomon's henchman (cf. 1 Kgs 2:5); interestingly enough, it is used there only of Joab—nothing is said of Abishai. Politically, Joab died for backing Adonijah (cf. 1 Kgs 2:22, 28).

It is not certain that Abner's affair with Rizpah, Saul's concubine, signaled a move on Ishbaal's crown. The expostulation we find in 1 Sam 18:8 or 1 Kgs 2:22 would make the matter clear, but the narrative has nothing of the kind. Sexual rivalry has always been a good source of rifts. Abner's "military theology" may not be as naive as it sounds; it also speaks of "what the LORD has sworn to David" (3:9–10), which is unknown to us. If Ishbaal "could not answer Abner . . . because he feared him" (3:11), we know who held the power in that kingdom at that point. Not for the first time a woman is brought into the narrative as a pawn in a bigger political game. Abner has just promised "all Israel" to David. David is entitled to test Abner's ability to deliver on his deal. Michal is probably the test. The test applies to Abner's power (v. 13); the demand is served on Ishbaal (v. 14). At the end of the vignette, if there was ever any doubt, we see Abner calling the shots (v. 16b).

Abner comes with an embassy to negotiate terms with David. Joab would be naive if he did not realize his power was threatened; he does not hesitate, but assassinates Abner promptly. Asahel's death is recalled (v. 27b). More fuss is made over David's innocence here than in any comparable scene (cf. vv. 28–29 and 31–39). One phrase sheds light on both elements: "All Israel understood that day" (v. 37). Shortly, "all Israel" was to come under David's rule and Joab's authority. Joab might be more easily forgiven a vengeance killing than a political killing. David could not be seen to be responsible for the killing of Abner if he was to acquire the allegiance of those who held Abner as a leader (cf. vv. 17–19). So David had to be totally free of blame, Joab had to be excused because of his brother's death, and Abner had to be praised as "a prince and a great man" (v. 38).

In many ways, the fourth episode is a replay of the first. The Amalekite brought David Saul's crown and paid for it with his life;

Baanah and Rechab bring David Ishbaal's head and pay for it with their lives. Their speech is an elegant summary of many of the Davidic traditions in 1 Samuel; nevertheless, the right words at the wrong time cost them their lives. Again: if David was to win the allegiance of Ishbaal's subjects, referred to as "all Israel" (cf. 4:1b), he had to avoid any suspicion of assassination—unless he was ready to seize power by force.

Establishment of David as king: completion of David's arrival
2 Samuel 5–8

Arches have their keystones and roofs have their coping or capstones; with rulers, the trick is, having gotten to the top, how to stay there. The narrative has taken us through David's trajectory to the top; now it spends four chapters on how he stayed there. In fact, he stayed there so well that his dynasty ruled in Jerusalem until the end.

Political establishment: arrival of David in Jerusalem (5:1–16)

As for the kingdom of Judah, so for the kingdom of Israel: The people offer it to David (5:1–3). For the third time, we hear of a direct divine promise to David (2 Sam 5:1; cf. 3:9–10, 18) which previously had only been known to us obliquely, also three times (1 Sam 13:14; 15:28; 16:1). The formulation of 2 Sam 3:18 encapsulates what is to come: "Through my servant David I will save my people Israel from the hand of the Philistines, and from all their enemies." So, at Hebron, David is anointed king over Israel and adds the throne of Israel to that of Judah (where he was also anointed). It should be noted that these, and the many other anointings of kings, are often unspecified, usually by people or priests. Only three times is an anointing specifically described as the action of a prophet: Samuel of Saul (as *nāgîd*, 1 Sam 10:1), Samuel of David (as king-to-be, 1 Sam 16:1), and Elisha's disciple of Jehu (as king, 2 Kgs 9:6).

Having been anointed king and given the throne over both Judah and now Israel, David must take steps to see that the power he has acquired is retained. First, he captures a city to be his capital—Jerusalem, the "city of David." Then he has a palace built for himself. Finally, he expands his royal establishment.

Security of the kingdom I: external—from the Philistines (5:17–25)

The danger posed by the Philistines has already been mentioned, before Saul's anointing (1 Sam 9:16) and just before David's (2 Sam 3:18). When the people had gathered at Mizpah under Samuel, the

Philistines heard about it and went up against Israel (1 Sam 7:7); now at Jerusalem under David, the Philistines hear about it again and all move against David (2 Sam 5:17). Two signals alert us to the schematic and symbolic rather than chronological nature of this material. First, while it is associated with David's anointing, it is located in the sequence of the narrative after the capture of Jerusalem, the construction of a palace, and the birth of eleven sons. Second, when David hears of the Philistine move, he goes down "to the stronghold" (v. 17). Explicable but puzzling; either where did he go or where did he come from? David and his troops carried off the Philistine idols (5:21), but it is not said what they did with them. No territorial reorganization is noted. "From Geba all the way to Gezer" (5:25) is from the hilly spine to the coastal plain, but it is a line to the north of the Philistine pentapolis (cluster of five cities: Ashdod, Ashkelon, Ekron, Gath, and Gaza). Historians sometimes are not great with symbols, so we may not find out just what happened; but we have a strong sense that David was believed to be bad news for the Philistines. With David in power, the Philistines apparently ceased to be a life-threatening menace to Israel.

Traditional establishment: arrival of the ark in Jerusalem (6:1–23)

Reputedly almost impregnable, Jerusalem had no place in Israel's foundational traditions. This involved benefits and dangers for David. Benefits: the city was not tied to any particular group or tribe—it was the "city of David." Dangers: a capital perceived as alien could alienate David's governance from the goodwill of those he needed to govern. The ark of the LORD had been sidelined for a generation or more, mothballed in Kiriath-jearim. It would be a brilliant political move to bring to Jerusalem this traditional symbol of Israel's relationship with its God. It would be a far more brilliant theological move to have this traditional symbol make its own choice to move to Jerusalem. It would bind the Israel of the past (focus: Shiloh) to the Israel of the future (focus: Jerusalem). This is precisely what 2 Sam 6 as text achieves.

According to past texts, the ark had a habit of determining its own moves. In Philistine territory, it made itself obnoxious enough to be moved from Ashdod to Gath to Ekron and finally back to Israel (1 Sam 5–6). At Beth-shemesh, it made itself obnoxious enough to be moved to Kiriath-jearim, safely out of the way. The text of 2 Sam 6 has the ark make itself obnoxious enough once again not to be moved to Jerusalem until the signal came from the LORD. The traditional symbol of God's relationship with Israel had been sidelined for a generation or so; with David in power in Jerusalem, the ark returns to Israel's mainstream—

the ark makes Jerusalem Israel's mainstream. It is a political and religious coup of the first order. The text of 2 Sam 6 portrays it as God's doing rather than David's.

The relationship between the text of 2 Sam 6 and 1 Sam 4–6 is disputed; the debate need not delay us here (see Campbell 1979). If a single text once existed, the junction can be recovered, reading the MT. If two texts are postulated—1 Sam 4–6 and 2 Sam 6—the necessary minor emendation is widely accepted (i.e., from "citizens of Judah" [MT] to "Baale- or Baalat-judah" [= town name, i.e., Kiriath-jearim]).

The text of 2 Sam 6 opens with an initiative under David's control. A group, led by David, set out to bring the ark of God up to Jerusalem. With the death of Uzzah, the move stops. Two aspects of the narrative are to be noted. First, it is pious and anachronistic nonsense to suggest that Uzzah should not have touched the ark. The two sons of Abinadab have been the guardians of the ark at Kiriath-jearim; they first and foremost in Israel have the duty of caring for it. The Hebrew of verse 7 in the MT is appropriately unintelligible, as it is in 1 Sam 6:19; both incidents are mysterious. Mystery should not be resolved by textual emendation. Second, the focus of the text is on David's reaction, expressed in three sentences: He is angry (v. 8), he is afraid of the LORD (v. 9), and he is unwilling to take the ark into his city (v. 10). So the ark was shunted off to the house of Obed-edom, the Gittite—a foreigner.

The text could stop here and the ark stay with Obed-edom, as it had with Abinadab. But the text goes on. The ark is three months with Obed-edom, and the LORD blesses Obed-edom and all his household. Of itself, this information might be intriguing and the subject for theological reflection. Coupled with the report given David ("because of the ark," v. 12a) and David's reaction (v. 12b), it becomes something else. YHWH's blessing becomes YHWH's green light for the continuation of the ark's move to Jerusalem. The second stage of the journey is under YHWH's control. The signal is given by YHWH's blessing; without it, we are left to assume that David would have remained angry, afraid, and unwilling.

It was a brilliant move on David's part to attempt the transfer of the ark to Jerusalem. With the death of Uzzah, it failed. The text achieves the far more brilliant move of having God choose to transfer the ark, this traditional symbol of Israel's relationship with its God, to David's new capital of Jerusalem. God blessed Obed-edom; ultimately, in this narrative, God blesses David. Hence the extensive celebrations when the ark is duly set in its place inside the city of Jerusalem.

There is a little coda added to the narrative. A sharp exchange between David and Michal, daughter of Saul, is narrated and accounts for an estrangement that leaves her childless until the day of her death (6:16, 20–23). The earlier demand for her return to David (4:13–16) looks clearly to have been politics rather than passion. Now a future heir unifying both houses is out of the question.

Prophetic establishment: dynasty of David in Jerusalem (7:1–29)

Traditions can attach a present to the roots in its past; therefore, the ark could lock Jerusalem into Israel's past. Prophets tend to look to the future, which Nathan does for David. Nathan's prophecy with its promise of David's dynasty has been the object of incredibly intensive study; the bibliography is boundless (see Campbell 1986, 72). As all interpreters know, God cannot be bound by human words. The prophecy ends with an emphatic statement: "Your house and your kingdom shall be made sure forever before you [MT; NRSV: "before me"]; your throne shall be established forever" (7:16). Alas, not so. In 1 Kgs 9:4–5, the promise to David is reported as unconditional, but the condition of Solomon's good behavior is introduced for the continuation of this dynastic commitment to future generations. In 1 Kgs 2:4 and 8:25, the condition is introduced into the promise made to David and is applicable to David's heirs, both Solomon and future generations (cf. Campbell and O'Brien 2000, 332–33, 353, 359–61). The expression of the tradition embodying straightforwardly an unconditional commitment to the Davidic dynasty in Jerusalem is formulated in terms of David's *nîr* (lamp or dominion; cf. 1 Kgs 11:36; 15:4; 2 Kgs 8:19). In some of these cases, at least, experience has been allowed to have its way with theology; texts have been modified to mirror the reality of later experience.

Attention to editorial activity in 2 Sam 7 has been intense. There is widespread agreement on two areas in the development of the text, one early in the piece regarding the promise of a dynasty to David and the other from the deuteronomistic period regarding Solomon's building of a temple for God's name. Central to the first stage is the rejection of David's proposal to build a temple (house) for YHWH and YHWH's promise to build a dynasty (house) for David. From this comes the conclusion in 7:16, quoted above. The key sentence here is: "The LORD declares to you that the LORD will make you a house" (v. 11b). Central to the second stage is the promise that a temple will be built for God's name by Solomon. The key sentence here is: "He shall build a house for my name" (v. 13a). The reference to the house being built "for my name" establishes the origin of the phrase in deuteronomistic theology (for more detail, see Campbell and O'Brien 2000, 290–91).

The reason alleged later why David could not build the temple—because of his warfare (cf. 1 Kgs 5:17 [Heb.; NRSV, 5:3]; Chronicles passim)—does not appear in 2 Sam 7. The reason there is that so far there has been no demand for it from God (cf. 2 Sam 7:7; it recurs in 1 Kgs 8:16).

David's prayer of thanksgiving which follows (vv. 18–29) has a fulsome style that distances it from the preceding verses 1–17. A focus on the dynasty is visible in David's expression of gratitude, and expansion from Jerusalem circles is not unlikely. Understandably, the issue of Solomon's iniquity is not taken up.

Security of the kingdom II: external relations generally (8:1–18)

Two aspects need to be kept separate in interpreting 2 Sam 8. One is the role of the text in its context. The other is the historical detail that can be derived from this text. The two are not the same. Our concern here will be with the role of text. For an example of the daunting task of the historian, see Halpern (2001, 107–226).

So far, the narrative has seen David established as king over Judah and Israel, with a capital, a palace, and further children in Jerusalem. The Philistine threat has been removed, the move of the ark of the LORD has brought Jerusalem within the religious ambit of Israel, and Nathan, the prophet, has given David God's promise of a lasting dynasty. One thing is lacking to the security of David's establishment: his hegemony over the surrounding peoples who might otherwise upset his rule. For Saul, it was claimed in relation to Moab, Ammon, Edom, Zobah, and the Philistines (1 Sam 14:47)—whatever we may think of the historicity of the claim. For David, it is claimed in 2 Sam 8. The Davidic summary adds Amalek to Saul's list (8:12). The Davidic notes include garrisons among the Arameans of Damascus (vv. 5–6; in modern southern Syria); the Ammonites do not feature among these notes, but they have a prominent part in chapter 10 and are part of the framing of chapters 11–12. The notes that have been brought together in verses 1–14 do not constitute anything like a standardized list, staking a formal claim to the extent of David's power. They can be vague (e.g., v. 1 on the Philistines; v. 3 on the river), they can take quite different forms, they can make quite different claims. All in all, they communicate the sense of David as political master of his surroundings.

As such, 8:1–14 is the crowning summary of David's rise to power and establishment as king. He was anointed king, he acquired all the trappings of kingship, and he dominated the peoples around his nation. With such a record, a loose narrative beginning perhaps with Saul's anointing in 1 Sam 9 or with David's anointing in 1 Sam 16 can come to a satisfactory close: "So David reigned over all Israel; and David administered justice and equity to all his people" (2 Sam 8:15).

There follows a brief list of David's officials: Joab in charge of the people's army, Jehoshaphat responsible for the records, Zadok and Ahimelech the priests, Seraiah the secretary, Benaiah in charge of the mercenaries; David's sons were priests—whatever that may mean. In a similar place, the list of Saul's officials is limited to one, Abner the commander of Saul's army (1 Sam 14:50). A second list of David's officials, at the end of the stories of David's middle years, records a few changes (2 Sam 20:23–26). Joab remains in charge of the people's army and Benaiah in charge of the mercenaries; Adoram is a new figure, in charge of forced labor; Jehoshaphat remains the recorder, while Sheva replaces Seraiah as secretary and Abiathar replaces his son Ahimelech as priest with Zadok; Ira was David's priest—and again we do not know what this office involved. A similar list is given for Solomon (1 Kgs 4:1–6). Jehoshaphat, Benaiah, and the priests Zadok and Abiathar hold their jobs; seven names are new, as well as three of the jobs.

Appendix I

TRADITIONS ASSOCIATED WITH
DAVID'S MIDDLE YEARS
2 SAMUEL 9–10

In my judgment, neither the Mephibosheth tradition in 2 Sam 9 nor the traditions of the Ammonite wars in 2 Sam 10 belong within the great narrative work whose core is 2 Sam 11–20. Since Leonhard Rost's study in 1926, this was for a long time called the Succession Narrative and delineated as 2 Sam 9–20 and 1 Kgs 1–2. More recently, a tendency has emerged to refer to it as the Court History. A more neutral and more accurate term would be the Stories of David's Middle Years, and its extent should be limited to 2 Sam 11–20. (For a fuller discussion of recent research in this area, see the final chapter, "Diachronic Dimension," in Campbell, comm. [in press].)

There are four main reasons for excluding 2 Sam 9–10 from what follows: (1) literary style, (2) the recognition that succession as the theme of what follows is an illusion, (3) for 2 Sam 9, there is positive tension with what follows, and (4) for 2 Sam 10, there is no need for the text in what follows.

1. Literary style—or whatever the combination of elements is that we find characteristic of particular literary pieces—is a most elusive criterion. When Doris Lessing, for example, wrote under the pseudonym of Jane Somers, the "redoubtable" Bob Gottlieb of Knopf in New York said, "Who do you think you are kidding?" but almost no one else noticed. This raises the question: What is it that the perspicacious recognize, when they do? (cf. Lessing 1984, 7). *Something* is widely recognized as peculiar to 2 Sam 11–20, and perhaps it is a matter of style. Or perhaps it is concern with the ordinary aspects of everyday life that can shape major events of political life. There are passages that come close to it in style; for example, 2 Sam 2:12–4:12 and 1 Kgs 1–2 have been noted. While one could debate whether part of 1 Kgs 1–2 might belong with 2 Sam 11–20, a strong case cannot be made for 2 Sam 9 or 10.

2. If succession were the central issue of the larger narrative, 2 Sam 9 might have a place within it; but the larger narrative, even with 1 Kgs 1–2, is not centered on succession. Royal courts are always interested in the issue of succession (cf. Saul's comment in 1 Sam 20:30–31), and any stories of royalty impinge on issues of succession. The deaths of Amnon and Absalom certainly affect succession. Nevertheless, it is increasingly recognized that the key focus of 2 Sam 11–20 is not succession. Second Samuel 9–10 and 1 Kgs 1–2 can be cut loose from the core. While, however, the traditions in 1 Kgs 1–2 can be seen as an independent account of how Solomon came to succeed to David's throne, the case of 2 Sam 9–10 is different. Both chapters preserve traditions that relate to episodes within 2 Sam 11–20, and neither chapter can really be located anywhere else. For 2 Sam 9, a later location would clash with 2 Sam 21:1–14; for 2 Sam 10, any later location would be too far from the siege of Rabbah which frames 2 Sam 11–12. Earlier locations are out of the question.

3. Second Samuel 9 rehearses a tradition concerning Jonathan's son that is preserved in three different places in 2 Samuel (9:1–13; 19:25–31 [Heb.; NRSV, 24–30]; 21:1–14). As is evident, the first and third of these are outside 2 Sam 11–20. More significant is the fact that the version within 2 Sam 11–20 is coherent with 21:1–14 but does not agree with 9:1–13. At their meeting on the Jordan bank, Mephibosheth describes all his father's house as "doomed to death," and he alone was spared to eat at the king's table (19:29 [Heb.; NRSV, 28]). The descendants of Saul are alive and Mephibosheth alone is spared. This is the situation portrayed in 21:1–14; seven descendants of Saul are to be impaled, but Mephibosheth is spared (vv. 6–7). The situation portrayed in 9:1–13 is quite different. David asks, "Is there still anyone left of the house of

Saul?" (v. 1) and Mephibosheth alone is found. We can conclude that the other descendants of Saul are dead. This chapter cannot belong in the narrative of 2 Sam 11–20. It can be preserved, but as an (anticipatory) appendix to the major narrative. Historicity is not the issue; the various versions each have their particular interest.

The contribution made by 2 Sam 9 is to provide the background to (1) Mephibosheth's relationship to David and (2) Ziba's relationship to Mephibosheth. It also offers an alternative account of David's role in the affair. Second Samuel 9 is not explicit about David's part in the deaths of Saul's descendants; 2 Sam 19 implicates David; 2 Sam 21 lays the charge explicitly at David's door. Mephibosheth's place at David's table is absent from chapter 21 but present in chapter 19; the extent of the lands bestowed on Mephibosheth is only given in chapter 9. Of course, whether Mephibosheth's presence at David's table was a mark of David's benevolence, or of his surveillance, or both, escapes any interpreter—as is the case later for Jehoiachin (2 Kgs 25:27–30). It is noteworthy that when David has fled to Mahanaim, at the time of Absalom's rebellion, one of the three notables to meet him with support is Machir ben Ammiel from Lo-debar, who had been host to Mephibosheth (cf. 2 Sam 17:27). No further mention is made of Mephibosheth's young son, Mica (9:12).

4. The traditions in 2 Sam 10 concern campaigns against the Ammonites, leading up to the besieging of Rabbah. It may help to note the account of this siege of Rabbah in chapters 11–12; the verses reporting the siege—11:1 and 12:26–31—frame the story of Bathsheba and David. The story involves events covering a couple of years; it includes a first pregnancy, a murder, a period of mourning, a marriage, the birth and death of a son, a second pregnancy, birth, and prophetic visitation. The frame is complete in itself. David sends out Joab and the troops (11:1). Joab sends for David to preside over the capture of the city (12:26–29). There is a complete absence of any need for 2 Sam 10.

What 2 Sam 10 offers is an account of two campaigns that precede and lead up to this siege of Rabbah. Technically, 2 Sam 10 consists of a notice concerning David's embassy in response to a new situation (10:1–5), two battle reports covering the two campaigns (10:6–14, 15–18), and a notice giving the outcome (10:19). These have been put together to constitute a text accounting for the Davidic attack on Rabbah. A change in the king of the Ammonites led to provocation and a change in relationships between Israel and Ammon; the earlier relationship we can surmise but are not informed about. Aramean forces are defeated and, when reinforced, are defeated again. As a result, the

Ammonites are bottled up in their capital city (v. 14) and cannot expect help from their allies. The field is clear for David's forces to besiege Rabbah. Historical reconstruction may be uncertain. The association with chapters 11–12 is appropriate; chapter 10 leaves the Ammonites in their capital (v. 14) and bereft of any help from their allies (v. 19). It is a classic case: 2 Sam 10 prepares for 2 Sam 11–12; 2 Sam 11–12 does not require 2 Sam 10.

On the other hand, 2 Sam 10 preserves some helpful incidental insights. First, when the Ammonites team up with the Arameans, David sends out Joab and all the army (v. 7); when the Arameans seek allied reinforcements, David gathers all Israel and crosses the Jordan (v. 17). This parallels what is related in 2 Sam 11–12; David sends out Joab for the initial engagement (11:1) and comes out himself at the end (12:29). As far as the story itself is concerned, any moralizing over David's remaining in Jerusalem is out of place. Second, there is no mention of the presence of the ark in either campaign. The word of a Hittite is not to be built on in matters of Israelite tradition (cf. 11:11; note also 1 Sam 4:3). Third, Joab achieves victory while fighting a battle on two fronts, a strategist's nightmare (vv. 9–14). Either Joab was a brilliant military leader or the enemy coalition was weak—or perhaps both.

STORIES OF DAVID'S MIDDLE YEARS: INTERNAL SECURITY THREATENED
2 SAMUEL 11–20

"Stories of David's Middle Years" is an objective and neutral title for a narrative that is scarcely about succession and hardly a history. In terms of "middle years," Amnon, David's eldest, has grown up enough to be a rapist; Solomon, born in chapter 12, has to grow up enough to be king. "Middle years" is about right.

The style, insight, and interest that raise so many questions and answer so few begin with the story of Bathsheba and David (2 Sam 11–12) and end with Sheba's rebellion and Joab's return to Jerusalem (2 Sam 20). Nathan's words contain a pretty good analysis of the plot and is a close observation of human nature at the top: The king fouls up, and his foul-up impacts on his family and his kingdom.

This narrative, or series of stories, would be of great interest to those whose future involved giving counsel to kings. At many points, the question can be asked: What would it be wise to do here? There are multiple answers, multiple possibilities to explore. It is unlikely that anything exposing David so thoroughly would have seen the light of day at the court of either David or Solomon. At the same time, it is unlikely that something so thoroughly detailed was put together at much distance from Israel's early monarchy. The division of the kingdom, after Solomon (cf. 1 Kgs 11–12), meant a new royal court and a new monarchy under Jeroboam, with the accompanying need for new royal counselors—and nobody particularly well disposed to the southern kingdom. A narrative such as these Stories of David's Middle Years might have functioned very well at the court of Jeroboam in northern Israel. The stories reveal David at his worst and also at his best; they show the fragility as well as the sureness of his hold on power. They celebrate counselors (Ahithophel and Hushai) and give enormous insight into the significance of wise decision making.

At all times, interpreters need to remember that this is literary text. History is not its focus. What happened may be of interest, but it cannot be allowed to dominate. The focus must be on what is told as story and the implications of its being told just this way.

2 Samuel 11–12   David: the modeling of a king

Within the framework of the siege of Rabbah, the David and Bathsheba story is remarkably dense and complex. Within the story, Bathsheba has two husbands: Uriah, whom David murders, and David, who marries her. Bathsheba has two sons, both fathered by David; the first dies and the second will be king. Nathan's confrontation with David focuses on homicidal violence and sexual violence. One issue raised by the text is straightforward: Why is this story told and told in this way? A clear answer is not given.

Among the many factors that militate against seeing this story as part of a narrative focused on Solomon's succession to the throne is the fact that, at the crucial moment, Nathan and Bathsheba are not portrayed appealing to the story. In 1 Kgs 1, Nathan and Bathsheba appeal to an oath sworn by David (vv. 13, 17, 30); whatever may be the truth about the oath, they do not appeal to YHWH's favor, expressed in 2 Sam 12:24–25. Instead, the question remains outstanding: Why was this story told in such detail and in precisely this way? Although David's actions have often been construed as a crime of royal passion, which imprisoned him inextricably in its trammels, such construals are almost certainly inadequate, if not downright misleading. The text resists any simple interpretation.

David is unquestionably responsible for serious wrongdoing. But to see as a delinquency his remaining in Jerusalem while sending Joab and

the army into the field is probably unjustified and wrongful misinter-
pretation. It runs against 2 Sam 18:3 and 21:17, to say nothing of the
paradigm offered in 2 Sam 10. It should also be noted that the MT
begins the story as follows: "In the spring of the year, the time when
messengers go out . . ." (11:1). Given the role of messengers in the story,
this is not inappropriate.

The nature of the encounter between David and Bathsheba has often
been seriously misinterpreted; the text actually reflects badly on David
alone. First, David was walking on the palace roof; nothing is said about
where Bathsheba was. Second, the verb translated "bathing" can mean
to wash or bathe. Regrettably, it is probably prejudice rather than a
quirk of translation that has ten of the eleven occurrences of the verb
in Deuteronomy–Kings translated by "wash" and only this one by
"bathe." Given what we know of Davidic Jerusalem, Bathsheba was
more likely washing with a basin than in a bath. Third, since she was
purifying herself after her period (v. 4), washing, quite limited washing,
would have been more than adequate. Interpreters need to be careful
not to read the laws and customs of a later time back into stories of the
early monarchy. Nothing in the text suggests that the woman's actions
were unduly revealing, much less seductive. "The woman was very
beautiful" (v. 2). Any connoisseur of fashion will be aware of the beauty
of a wrist, an ankle, or the nape of a neck; exposure is not needed.
Fourth, David did not know her; he had to inquire about her identity.
In modern terms, it was a one-night stand. Fifth, some restraint was in
order and should have been recommended. Morals apart, Bathsheba's
husband was one of David's troops (rank unknown); her father, Eliam,
may well have been the son of David's top counselor, whose word was
like the word of God (cf. 2 Sam 16:23; 23:34).

One further point needs discussion. David is usually referred to as
an adulterer; rape is not commonly used to describe the sexual affairs
of royalty. Is it always assumed that sex with royalty is consensual? Or
is royal rape in a category of its own? As a rule, of course, royals do not
marry their mistresses or their conquests. Bathsheba was a married
woman, and the term "adultery" implies consent. The Hebrew gives no
indication of consent whatsoever. To speak of adultery is to charge
Bathsheba with a consent that is not given in the text. There are four
verbs in the relevant verse: He *sent*, he *took*, she *came* to him, and he *slept*
with her (11:4). The Greek applies all four verbs to him: He sent, he
took, he came to her, and he slept with her. In either version, as in
Nathan's condemnation, responsibility in the affair is David's. Biblical
Hebrew is not strong on the language of courtship and wooing—

whether as a matter of language, culture, or the limited nature of biblical texts. At 1 Sam 25:39, for example, the NRSV has "David sent and wooed Abigail, to make her his wife"; more literally, the Hebrew has "David sent and spoke to Abigail, to take her to him for wife." There is no mention in 11:4 of anything being "said" to Bathsheba. To speak of adultery is to charge Bathsheba with a consent that is not given in the text. In so careful a text as this, interpreters must be on their guard. Where this text is concerned, the term "adultery" and its derivatives cannot be used, out of simple justice to the woman.

The text uses descriptive language: He sent, he took, he slept with (11:4); you "have taken his wife to be your wife" (12:9). It does not at any point characterize the action with language such as adultery or rape. In fact, on this issue, the text is silent. Rather than "adulterer," which has implications for the woman, David is more objectively described as one who took another's wife and had her husband murdered. Rather than language that characterizes David as rapist/adulterer and murderer, there is the descriptive language that names David as the man who took Uriah's wife and had Uriah murdered—wife-taker and murderer. The text does not say that Bathsheba resisted or was unwilling; it does not say that she was willing or did not resist. It is silent. The contrary is the case for Tamar in the following story; there the text is eloquent (13:12–14). For whatever reasons, the text is silent about Bathsheba's feelings and emotions; it is not concerned with her inner disposition. In modern thought, however, she is innocent unless proven guilty. The language of interpreters should not violate that innocence.

It may be that the language of violation is the most appropriate to the situation. Beyond doubt in the story, the initiative is taken throughout by David, the king; the one exception is Bathsheba's sending of her message: "I am pregnant." Whether Bathsheba was willing or not, David's initiative violated the bond of Uriah's marriage—whether we see the bond as one of intimacy or property. In terms of Bathsheba's person, whether she was willing or not, David's initiative was a violation of her. In Israelite law, she had no right to give herself to David and he had no right to take her. His initiative violated the law; it also violated her. David can rightly be described as violator and murderer. The nature of the violation may need to be spelled out; in this, it is faithful to the uncertainty of the narrative.

"She was purifying herself after her period" (v. 4). This statement involves three minor points. First, the observation confirms the narrative sequence: He slept with her; she conceived (vv. 4–5). The child was David's. Second, she was probably at peak fertility, so conception was likely. Yet there is no mention of children with Uriah. Third, in this context she would have known within a couple of weeks that she was pregnant.

"She sent and told David, 'I am pregnant.'" This is one of the more baffling points in the story. Why did she tell him? Had ambition awakened? How should we complete the sentence? "I am pregnant, my darling"? "I am pregnant, you bastard"? If the former—for it had been a wonderful night and she had seen a loving tenderness in his eyes—why David's attempts to get Uriah in bed with her? If the latter—for it had not been consensual sex and she felt overwhelmed—why risk telling him? David's simplest response would have been to have her killed; it could have been easily arranged. After all, the storyteller knows David will have her husband killed; why would he have scrupled at killing her? In the next story (2 Sam 13), Tamar, victim of a brutal rape, tears her robe and cries aloud (13:19); her brother Absalom counsels silence (13:20). The text here has Bathsheba tell David. Why? A case can be made in the story for her love; a case can be made in the story for her hate. A case can be made for her ambition. It is the brilliance of the story to leave interpreters uncertain. Hers will not be the only case where both storyteller and plot leave uncertainty unresolved as to the state of mind of a figure in the story. In what is to come, that will be the case for both David and Uriah.

In Jerusalem, David's strategy with Uriah is puzzling. Underlying the puzzle is our uncertainty about what David wants. Is he committed to Bathsheba, in love with her? Then what does he hope to gain by having Uriah sleep with her? It is, at best, a short-term maneuver. Or is he committed to extricating himself from an affair that has turned embarrassing? We do not know and the subsequent marriage does not decide the matter. A further possibility has to be entertained: that David is portrayed as unsettled and casting around for short-term solutions.

Uriah's dealings with David are also tinged by uncertainty. The basic question is: Did he know or did he not? Too many others have been involved for Uriah's innocent ignorance to be taken for granted. Was he a righteous soldier, who was committed to his principles despite the wishes of his commander-in-chief? Or was he an angry husband, who would not cooperate in an attempted cover-up by the man who cuckolded him? As a righteous soldier, he could have gone to his home, slept on the floor, and sent the present back to the palace. To sleep with the guard at the palace entrance—as if no other place was available and with the result that David is promptly told of it—smacks of the angry husband.

David has Uriah murdered, after sending him back to the front. We are not told why. Did David want Bathsheba for himself? Did David want to be free from potential scandal? Did David want an angry Uriah silenced, to prevent any possible blackmail? Did David want a cuck- olded Uriah silenced, rather than returning from the front to a preg- nant wife or a wife and child? We are not told.

Joab changes David's orders. "Then draw back from him" (v. 15) most likely would have involved a number of soldiers being given orders that are not given Uriah. Putting Uriah where "there were valiant warriors" (v. 16) did not require secret orders for his comrades. Two possibilities seem to be offered for telling of Uriah's death. In one, "the men of the city came out and fought" (v. 17); in the other, the defenders shot from the wall (v. 20). The latter version may help to introduce David's anger. The episode of David's anger serves to empha- size his ruthlessness: "Do not let this matter trouble you, for the sword devours now one and now another" (v. 25). The possibility of a ruth- less side to David, portrayed here, will recur in the stories ahead.

The king is to be a source of justice. More than once, when the king becomes responsible for injustice, it is a prophet of God who calls him to account. This is a remarkable phenomenon in ancient Israel. It is radical here, with Nathan the prophet trapping David into his outburst, "The man who has done this deserves to die," and countering it with his own famous charge, "You are the man!" (12:5–7). Two aspects stand out: the modeling involved in David's actions and the immediacy of David's forgiveness.

Nathan speaks of the sword that shall never depart from David's house as though it is a matter of natural consequence, of cause and effect (v. 10a); the action against David's wives is attributed directly to God (v. 11). Nothing is said explicitly of punishment; it is obvious. Nothing is said explicitly of modeling; it too is obvious. Whatever of the theology in Nathan's speech (consequence or punishment), the dif- ference between sin and its consequences is clear, even if not always dis- tinguished in Hebrew language. If one parent culpably loses the children's education money, in due time the other may forgive, but the money is gone. David may be pronounced forgiven, but the conse- quences of what he has done emerge in due time.

David's response to Nathan is unequivocally direct: "I have sinned against the LORD" (v. 13a). Nathan's reply is surprisingly immediate: "Now the Lord has put away your sin; you shall not die" (v. 13b). Whether this exchange once followed directly on Nathan's "You are the man!" (v. 7a) is not of great importance. What is crucial is that the admission of sin is followed immediately by the assertion of forgiveness. This too is a remarkable phenomenon in ancient Israel.

The next sentence, however, causes many moderns grave problems: "Nevertheless . . . the child that is born to you shall die" (v. 15). The claim of cause and effect is made unpleasantly clear. "Because by this deed" (v. 14), "the LORD struck the child" (v. 15). A first comment must be made. Stories are told after the event. We may assume the child died; that cannot be changed. What many a modern will find unacceptable is the attribution of this death to God's action because of David's sin. Ezekiel 18 lies in the future. Ancient Israel attributed illness to God's action. Today many must conclude that the child's death is cause for sorrow, but the text's theology explaining it is unspeakable.

In modern eyes, David's pleading with God for the child (v. 16) may be admirable; in ancient eyes, it was cause for surprise and wonder (v. 21). As text, it reveals a facet of the image of David. There is an inexorable pragmatism to his faith. Ask for the possible; accept the real. Pray with passion; leave nothing to chance. Psychologically, such prayer is equivalent to anticipatory grieving and need not be unhealthy. What seems almost callous need not be.

A second son is born and is named Solomon. The narrator notes that the LORD loved him and, through Nathan the prophet, named him Jedidiah. The name is never referred to again.

2 Samuel 13–19   The modeling within David's family

In Nathan's words, the sword would never depart from David's house and what David did secretly would be done before the sun. In the stories to come, Amnon and Absalom will die by the sword; David's concubines will be violated in full view. As David had his way with another man's wife, David's eldest son Amnon will have his way with his half-sister Tamar. The text does not explicitly say that it understands these actions as the impact of David's behavior on his children. Nathan claims cause and effect; cause and effect can be understood as modeling. David's son Adonijah is described as a spoiled brat (1 Kgs 1:6). Modeling is not far from the thinking here. The sequence of the narrative allows for it.

The question that has to be asked throughout these stories of David's middle years concerns the degree of David's direct responsibility. Was he overindulgent or was he ruthless? The narrative does not ask the question and does not answer it. But the question is there and cannot be ignored. Amnon raped Tamar; Absalom killed him for it; David kept Absalom at bay for five years; Absalom rebelled against David; Joab killed Absalom. Did all this happen with David totally uninvolved, apart from the bad example of 2 Sam 11–12? Or was David more intimately involved than we might like to admit? As with Bathsheba's message, "I am pregnant," the text does not address motivation. The interpreter cannot avoid it.

2 Samuel 13–14   Internal impact: without threat to David's rule

The story of Amnon's rape of Tamar is told in 2 Sam 13:1–22 and need not be retold here. Some salient points may be made. The principal characters are: Amnon, David's eldest son; Tamar, a beautiful woman and Absalom's sister (v. 4) and Amnon's half-sister (Amnon was the son of David and Ahinoam; Absalom was the son of David and Maacah); Absalom; and Jonadab, David's nephew (v. 3). Jonadab is characterized as "a very wise man" (v. 3, 'îš ḥākām mĕ'ōd; the NRSV's "a very crafty man" is most misleading. Only once and only here does the NRSV use "crafty" to translate ḥākām. Otherwise, "crafty" translates 'ārûm. What is clear here and elsewhere is that wisdom can be used for good and bad ends).

Amnon is visibly sick with love for Tamar. Jonadab provides him with a way to have access to her. Jonadab's strategy involves David, so at this point questions have to be asked about David. The first question is whether David was aware enough of Amnon's sickness—"so haggard morning after morning" (v. 4)—that he could/should have asked questions about it when it was reported to him. Jonadab, in the story, asked the question; Absalom, in the story, knew the answer (v. 20). What might David have known? The second question is whether David was prudent, within the context of an ancient Near Eastern court, to send an unmarried princess to one of the princes without an escort (cf. v. 2, where Tamar is deemed inaccessible). The story assumes separate houses for David, Amnon, and Absalom (cf. vv. 7–8, 20). The frightening question one would rather not ask is whether David knew all that Absalom knew and whether rather than imprudent he was utterly ruthless. A strong kingdom needs a strong king. It is horrendously unpalatable but not wholly unthinkable that David might have wanted bad blood between his two potential heirs in order for the stronger successor to emerge. Tamar, in that case, would be a sacrifice to political opportunity. (The MT tradition does not have the comment in v. 21 that David "would not punish his son Amnon, because he loved him, for he was his first-born.") Something of the kind is found at Qumran and in the LXX, i.e., other traditions (cf. 1 Kgs 1:6). So there are questions to be raised here. We cannot totally dismiss the possibility that

Jonadab was acting on David's orders—that is, that he was David's provocateur (cf. Halpern 2001, 87–88). Was David's anger feigned? Was Absalom's hatred wanted? We may hope such questions can be innocently answered; we must accept the possibility of political ruthlessness. The alternative, of course, is David's grave imprudence. David's confession of sin in 12:13 might have been thought to preclude further scheming, but the personal realm is often dissociated from the political.

Two more observations concern this story. First, Amnon ordered everybody out of his presence (v. 9). They left. With them, any hope for Tamar's safety left too. One burly soldier with orders from his king not to leave the princess would have kept her safe. A couple of Amnon's associates who demurred would have kept her safe. The security of the community has been denied her; she might just as well have been in the open country (cf. Deut 22:25–27).

Second, Tamar is the only figure in the story portrayed as noble. Just as well, since she is also a pawn in the narrative. After verses 20 and 32, she is not mentioned again. In the two verses where she speaks (vv. 12–13), she situates what Amnon wants ("lie with me, my sister") within their culture ("such a thing is not done in Israel") and in itself ("so vile"), she speaks of the impact on her ("as for me") and on him ("as for you"), and she offers him an alternative ("speak to the king")—but she is overwhelmed by brute force ("he forced her and lay with her").

Amnon rapes her and then rejects her, Absalom silences her, and David does nothing. Absalom's anger will fester and the scene is set for more trouble.

For two years, trouble brews. Suspicion again will fall on David, this time more squarely. Absalom invites the king and his court to a sheep-shearing party. The king demurs: "We will be burdensome to you" (v. 25). Absalom then asks for Amnon at least. Again the king demurs: "Why should he go with you?" (v. 26). Absalom insists and the king gives in; Amnon and all the king's sons can go. It is the signing of Amnon's death warrant. After the invitation is reported in verse 23, the actual exchange between David and Absalom is given four full verses. It would be remarkable if David were unaware over two years of Absalom's hatred for Amnon. It would be ruthless if David absented himself to allow his sons to settle the issue of succession between them. But, in the event, that is what happens.

When the incautious Amnon is killed on Absalom's orders and the party abandoned, David is told that all his sons had been slaughtered by Absalom (v. 30). It is Jonadab again who informs him that "Amnon alone is dead" (v. 32). Observant instinct or inside knowledge? We are not told.

Absalom flees to his mother's father, Talmai, king of Geshur, across the Jordan east of Galilee. In due course, David is ready to move on from the death of Amnon and yearns for Absalom (13:37–39; partial duplication apparent). What follows is strange. Absalom has been in exile for three years; Joab observes David's change of mind; he moves to force David's hand, staging some brilliant storytelling by a woman from Tekoa. David recognizes Joab's role; nevertheless, he orders Absalom's return—but excludes him from his presence (14:24). Another two years pass, it takes arson to get Absalom an interview with Joab, and finally reconciliation with David is achieved: "The king kissed Absalom" (14:33).

As the next verses show, it is too late. Why the five years—exile for three years and exclusion for two years more? Was David overindulgent, nursing his grief and not exercising his anger? Was David ruthless, testing his son for something? The text does not say. What would have been the point of such testing? There again, the text does not say. The outcome is Absalom's revolt.

2 Samuel 15–19   External impact: with grave threat to David's rule

These five chapters constitute the core of the Stories of David's Middle Years. As they stand, they cannot be broken up into smaller stories; the beginnings and endings are not there, although they could be created easily enough. In addition, what is there is not easily characterized. The narrative rehearses a series of incidents that extend from David's departure from Jerusalem through David's return there. Approximately one and a half chapters are devoted to the departure from Jerusalem and the decisions made along the way over the Mount of Olives. Approximately one and a half chapters are devoted to Absalom's planning within Jerusalem. The battle and the death of Absalom receive a chapter. David's return to Jerusalem receives a chapter. Succession to the throne is scarcely central; Absalom's rebellion is suppressed and Absalom killed. For a court history, the selection of incidents is remarkable. The story of each incident is a reflection on human decisions. What is the function of the storytelling?

It is not a matter of political analysis. It is not a matter of historical remembering. Too much is left aside for that. Absalom's strategies and support for his rebellion are missing. The whys and wherefores of fighting in Transjordan and the nature of the armies and the support on both sides are passed over. The special interests and the special deals that got David back in power in Jerusalem are only hinted at. What is the function of the storytelling?

Another aspect of the storytelling needs mention. The preceding stories are intimately linked to chapters 15–19; they provide something of the motivation without which chapters 15–19 would be rootless. A surprising aspect, however, is that David is portrayed as gravely deficient within the city, while outside it he is supremely efficient. Within Jerusalem, David has taken another man's wife and had her husband murdered, has at best been imprudent in exposing his daughter Tamar to a rapist's lust and has failed to act on her behalf, may have contributed to the murder of his son Amnon, and has finally dithered for five years over how to deal with the murderer, Absalom. Outside Jerusalem, his decisions are prompt and judicious; on campaign, he is skilled and successful. Only one major area is subject to suspicion, that is, the death of Absalom. On return to Jerusalem, once again he is not in control; the power lies with Joab.

Good storytelling serves more than one purpose. It is suggested here that one function such storytelling could have served was as a training ground for royal counselors—for example, at the northern Israelite court of Jeroboam—to test their ingenuity, increase their capacity for reflection, and stretch their imaginations. The stories need no retelling; some comments, however, may help open up aspects of their power and subtlety—for example, the skillful creation of narrative around what is left unsaid, or the alternation of motives (e.g., faith and fatalism balanced with planning and strategy), or the unsaid political significance of David's decisions.

15:1–12. The opening episode focuses on Absalom: how he "stole the hearts of the people of Israel" on his way to rebellion against his father. There is an irony in the opening verses. The issue is justice and how Absalom would see to it that people received justice, were he in charge. It is, however, precisely the failure of Samuel's sons to dispense justice that was one of the reasons alleged for the need for a king (cf. 1 Sam 8:1–5). Nothing is said of where David failed or how Absalom made his promises plausible.

This episode relates the actual onset of Absalom's coup. It culminates a four-year period (the MT has "forty" and the ancient translations have "four"; the figure therefore may be symbolic.). The text leaves a lot to the imagination. Absalom claims he wants to worship at Hebron in order to fulfill a vow made years ago in exile in Geshur. David gives the permission. Two hundred men from Jerusalem go as invited guests, knowing nothing about the coup; when it happens, we assume they stay: "The conspiracy grew in strength, and the people with Absalom kept increasing" (15:12). No names are given beyond Ahithophel, no tribes are named, no indication given of the organization that allows secret messengers to spread the word throughout all the tribes of Israel (v. 10). This is a major operation and we cry out for more detail—which is not given us. Why is David not aware? How could two hundred notables not be aware? What is amiss in David's kingdom that rallies people to Absalom's cause? What sort of support makes Absalom's coup possible?

15:13–16:14. David's departure from Jerusalem is the initial focus of the narrative. It follows David to the outskirts of the city, up the Mount of Olives to its summit, and beyond the summit to Bahurim. The word is brought to David of Absalom's rebellion, and the immediate result is a hasty departure: "Hurry, or he will soon overtake us, and bring disaster down upon us" (v. 14). The king's officials concur in the royal decision (v. 15). So the royal household departs, leaving only ten concubines to look after the palace (v. 16). Courtiers and military—including the traditional mercenary force and a contingent of six hundred Gittites from Gath—all leave the city (v. 18). There is no mention of any council of war, no input from David's advisers. The decision is David's, and the officials simply go along with it (v. 15). Without a fight, why abandon the apparently impregnable city (cf. 2 Sam 5:6)? No answer is given.

Ittai the Gittite is a military commander equal to David's best; when the decisive battle comes, the army will be divided between Joab, Abishai, and Ittai (2 Sam 18:2). David offers him his freedom, on the grounds of his recent arrival; he is urged to return to his king. Ittai refuses, committing himself to David: "Wherever my lord the king may be, whether for death or for life, there also your servant will be" (v. 21). Is this deep personal loyalty or the perception of a shrewd observer that David will emerge the winner?

A third episode closes the narrative of David's departure from Jerusalem. It may explain something of Ittai's behavior, and it casts a fascinating light on the image of David. The ark of the covenant is brought along to accompany David; David sends it back into Jerusalem. With faith or fatalism, David comments that he will be brought back to Jerusalem if YHWH favors him, and if YHWH does not his fate will be sealed (vv. 25–26). There is apparent total trust in the power of God to dispose. This is promptly followed by strategic planning, involving the two priests of the ark and their sons, establishing a communications network. This is a classic example of what might be called "Davidic theology": Leave absolutely nothing to God except total trust.

The procession of David's entourage goes on, up the slope of the Mount of Olives. The alternation of prayer and planning goes on too. Told of Ahithophel's defection to Absalom, David prays, "Turn the counsel of Ahithophel into foolishness" (v. 31; more literally: "fool the counsel of Ahithophel"). The prayer will be heard. The strategy to make it happen follows in the next episode. The attribution of Ahithophel's defeat to the LORD's determination is noted in 17:14, but without explicit reference to David's prayer.

At the summit of the Mount of Olives, Hushai meets David. David instructs Hushai to be his double agent among Absalom's counselors to defeat the counsel of Ahithophel—just a moment ago, the object of David's prayer. Hushai is initiated into the communications network established a little earlier. "So Hushai . . . came into the city, just as Absalom was entering Jerusalem" (15:37). In this narrative, nothing happens by chance.

The narrative follows David a little longer before switching focus to Absalom in Jerusalem. There is reason for staying a little longer with David. The role of the house of Saul has to be assessed before switching to the next generation of the house of David. First Ziba, the steward responsible for the affairs of Mephibosheth, Jonathan's crippled son, comes on the scene with supplies for David's entourage. Where is Mephibosheth? According to Ziba, waiting in Jerusalem for Saul's kingdom to be handed back to him. True or false, realistic or illusory? The text does not say. The house of Saul is on the scene; support for Mephibosheth is plausible. Shimei ben Gera is a different kettle of fish. His abuse of David probably found a place in the text because of the fatalistic piety of David's response (16:10–12). What Shimei reveals to us is how Saul's supporters and David's opponents viewed David's rise to power (16:7–8). Shimei has given up on the house of Saul; the future lies with Absalom. His verdict on David is clear: "Murderer . . . man of blood."

16:15–17:23. The narrative now turns to Absalom. Of "all the people, the men of Israel" with Absalom, only Ahithophel is named (16:15). Hushai lists Absalom's supporters as "the LORD and this people and all the Israelites" (16:18). Details are not given.

On Ahithophel's advice, Absalom's first action in the city is to violate his father's "concubines" (harem wives, secondary wives). When Nathan spoke of this, it was couched in the language of YHWH's instigation: "Thus says the LORD: . . . I will take your wives before your eyes, and give them to your neighbor. . . . I will do this thing before all Israel" (12:11–12). Here, it is Ahithophel who suggests it. A little later on, the comment is made that "the LORD had ordained to defeat the good counsel of Ahithophel" (17:14). It may be unwise to contrast the sacral atmosphere of the stories of David's rise to power with the secular atmosphere of the stories of David's middle years. The level of expression may differ; the thinking appears to be much the same.

It should also be noticed that the violation of these women is Absalom's first action on entering Jerusalem. In the narrative, David's first action on returning to Jerusalem is to attend to their isolation. Narratively, their treatment forms a structuring marker around this episode in the history of Jerusalem—the forced absence of its king. Leading up to Absalom's action, the focus is on David's moves, his plans and strategies as he flees the city. Leading up to David's action, the focus is on the outcome of David's moves, those plans and strategies bearing fruit in preparing his royal return. Absalom's violation of these ten women marks his seizure of power in the city; David's isolation of these women marks his recapture of power and return to the city.

The counsel of war over the course to follow against David is central to these chapters. The narrative has its complexities. Ahithophel's advice sounds good, but it is not certain that it would have worked. David's experience as a guerrilla leader in the Judean desert would have alerted him to basic strategies of keeping watch and keeping concealed. Hushai's advice seemed promising to Absalom, but events showed it was not. From Hushai's point of view, of course, it gained David some breathing space. What probably won the day for Hushai and lost it for Ahithophel would have been a combination of politics and pride. The rapid commando raid that night would have brought immediate credit to Ahithophel (cf. Joab and David, 2 Sam 12:28), and Absalom would not have liked that. The massed army, mustered from Dan to Beersheba with Absalom at its head ("you go to battle in person," 17:11), would have flattered Absalom's sense of royal dignity and military honor. So Hushai's advice prevails. Of course, the narrative has its own interpretation: It was the LORD's doing, "so that the LORD might bring ruin on Absalom" (v. 14).

Three aspects of the story, as written, arouse interest. First, the message Hushai sends David would be identical if the decision had gone the other way and Ahithophel's advice had been accepted (cf. 17:16). Did Hushai fear a double-cross, or was he asked to leave before the decision was taken? The text says nothing. Second, a servant girl is introduced into the message system. The Hebrew has "the servant girl"; she is known. The NRSV has a frequentative for the verb, she "used to go," which correctly reflects the Hebrew but cannot correctly reflect the situation for this, the first message. Other versions of the story may be impacting here. Third, the two boys were spotted, then hid in a well at Bahurim with grain spread over the mouth of the well, and the searchers missed them entirely (17:18–20). Some questions beg to be answered: How did the spotter recognize the two? How did they know they had been spotted? When was the hiding place organized? How did the searchers know to ask at this house for these two boys by name? How is it that David and his troops had not crossed the Jordan and now took the risks of a night crossing? A lot is left to the storyteller.

Ahithophel took his life when he saw that his counsel was not followed. Perhaps the rejection of his advice was felt as a loss of prestige and standing. Perhaps he knew that if David and his men got across the Jordan, Absalom's cause was lost. We are not told.

17:24–19:9 (Heb.; NRSV, 17:24–19:8). This passage opens with the gathering of the armies and closes with David joining his troops. In between, the climactic battle between the two forces gets almost no attention; the narrative's primary focus is on the killing of Absalom and David's reaction to it.

David's forces come to Mahanaim (on the Jabbok), which is where Abner established Ishmael's kingdom (2 Sam 2:8); it will later be one of the administrative centers for Solomon's kingdom (1 Kgs 4:14). Why David chose it as his base we are not told. Absalom's forces—"all the men of Israel" (to be understood as civilian soldiers rather than professional troops)—encamp in Gilead (a more general term for the district, probably to the north of Mahanaim). In place of Joab, Absalom's civilian army is placed under the command of Amasa, Joab's cousin.

Strategies for battle are at a minimum in the text. For Absalom, none are given; for David, three army groups are formed, under Joab, Abishai, and Ittai respectively. David is not with the fighting force, and orders are given to deal gently with Absalom (18:1–5). That is all. The focus of the passage is on the killing of Absalom and David's reaction to it.

Three verses note the support and supplies given David by three notables from east-of-Jordan, of whom we know nothing (17:27–29). Shobi son of Nahash was from Rabbah of the Ammonites. This is the only reference to him in the Hebrew Bible. Nahash is not unknown as a personal name (cf. 2 Sam 17:25). Shobi may have been of the royal house of Rabbah, but it is far from sure; a survey of the ten texts with the name Nahash does not support the identification. Machir son of Ammiel was from Lo-debar; Mephibosheth had lodged with him (2 Sam 9:4–5); he is not mentioned again. Barzillai the Gileadite was from Rogelim and is described as "a very wealthy man" (19:33; NRSV, v. 32). He is mentioned later as declining to reside in Jerusalem and as remembered in David's testament to be rewarded for his loyalty (19:32–40 [NRSV, vv. 31–39]; 1 Kgs 2:7; cf. also Ezra 2:61; Neh 7:63). Significant as they obviously are, the text tells us nothing of these three nor why they should have supported David.

The account of the battle between David and Absalom dismisses the defeat in, at most, three verses (18:6–8). The focus is on Absalom's death, the two runners bearing the news of it, and David's reaction to it. The text does not raise the question that has to be asked: Was David indulgent or ruthless? Did he secretly order Absalom's death, or did he really desire his survival?

It must be said from the outset that the text itself is unequivocally clear: David wanted Absalom spared. The text offers no evidence to suggest the contrary. It is only the failure to address an obvious issue and the text's unabashed assertion of David's desire for Absalom's survival—"Would I had died instead of you, O Absalom, my son, my son!"—that raises the unpalatable question.

David's indulgence of his children is openly expressed in the narratives. When Amnon raped Tamar, David is reported as "very angry," but he did nothing (13:21). Adonijah's preemptive move to take David's place as king is given its primary explanation in the text as due to David's indulgence of his son (1 Kgs 1:6). David's indulgence is on record; so is his ruthlessness (2 Sam 11:25).

Absalom's history would have to give the most doting father pause. He was, without question, a first-rate hater and had had time in plenty for his hatred to fester. For two years he hated Amnon before he had him murdered (13:22). For three years he was in exile; for a further two years in Jerusalem he was banned from the royal presence. For another four years or so he actively fomented rebellion against David. His readiness to have his father killed was known to David (16:11). Ahithophel's proposal to kill only David pleased Absalom (17:4). Politically, there can be little doubt: For David's rule to be secure, the danger posed by Absalom's emotions and ambitions had to be neutralized. Of the options available, killed in action was probably the most acceptable. Permanent exile, if at all possible, would have been risky. Close surveillance, such as Mephibosheth's (2 Sam 9), would have been impractical and unseemly. House arrest and disablement, such as Adoni-bezek's (Judg 1:6–7), might have seemed unduly cruel and dishonorable.

If indeed David opted for Absalom's death, he played a ruthless game according to the text's portrayal. He would have had to have instructed

Joab to kill Absalom, while alerting Joab to David's own need to present a totally different persona in public. This would, however, go some
way to accounting for Joab's portrayed harshness in rebuking his king
for the display of royal grief (cf. 19:6–8; NRSV, vv. 5–7). Noteworthy in
this connection is the absence of Absalom from the list of those Joab
murdered, in the words given David as advice to Solomon (1 Kgs 2:5).
Was a hint of David's responsibility known in the tradition?

19:10–44 (Heb.; NRSV, 19:9–43). The narrative of David's return to
Jerusalem casts surprising light on the fragility of David's rule. It opens
with discussion of David's future, first "throughout all the tribes of
Israel" (19:10–11; NRSV, vv. 9–10), then with an attempt to woo the
support of Judah (19:12–16; NRSV, vv. 11–15). The two Saul supporters who figured in the earlier part of the narrative, Shimei and Mephibosheth, are both at the Jordan to pledge their support to David.
David's megarich supporter, Barzillai, is there to decline a royal offer
of residence in Jerusalem. Finally, there is an account of fierce political
rivalry between representatives of Israel and Judah. The surprise: the
hostility to David is deep enough that Israel and even Judah are sure
they want him back. The energy that fueled Absalom's rebellion is not
named; 2 Sam 15:1–8 suggests it may have been injustice (which fueled
the resistance to Samuel's sons, 1 Sam 8:1–5). It is clear that the text
portrays David's control as balanced on a knife edge.

In northern Israel, the text portrays it as "all the people . . . throughout all the tribes" who were arguing over commitment to David. No
information is provided about who or how. There is nothing about the
cause of the revolt, but the benefits attributed to David are in the realm
of defense ("the king delivered us from the hand of our enemies")—the
reason given for Samuel's anointing Saul (1 Sam 9:1–10:16).

A little more information is given about Judah. Zadok and Abiathar
are representatives for David; they are to make a pitch to "the elders of
Judah" and a job offer to Amasa. Absalom's rebellion had been inaugu-
rated in Hebron; Judah was not solid for David. The offer to Amasa to
become general of the army in Joab's place is puzzling. David's dismissal of Joab for the murder of Absalom would be most understandable, but the text says nothing and Joab returns "to Jerusalem to the
king" at the end of the narrative (20:22). On the other hand, a secret
word or two to Joab would have easily secured his understanding; Joab
would have been certain of equally easily finding an appropriate opportunity for assassinating Amasa. The text does not say and we do not
know. For would-be counselors of a king, the opportunity to exercise
wisdom in hindsight is unparalleled.

It is remarkable that the two Saulide contenders are portrayed committing their support to David. Shimei has troops with him and claims he is the first of the house of Joseph to commit to David—probably shrewd political judgment on Shimei's part. Mephibosheth claims Ziba was a treacherous liar, and David divides the estate between the two—probably another case of shrewd political judgment, but on David's part. He did not know the truth; nor do we. The place of Barzillai is puzzling. If the issue is one of reward for loyalty, why no mention of the other two, Shobi and Machir? Has the offer something to do with retaining the loyalty of those east of the Jordan? Again, we do not know. The concluding sentence is ominous; with the king were "all the people of Judah" and "half the people of Israel" (19:41; NRSV, v. 40).

The political debate is rekindled between Israel and Judah. Judah prevails for the moment (19:42–44; NRSV, vv. 41–43). Issues raised are kinship, patronage, and numbers. Light is not shed on the overall political situation. But all appears more than ready for Sheba's rebellion.

2 Samuel 20   The modeling within David's kingdom

The modeling here is of the "might is right" variety. What David wanted, he took; if it cost a husband his life, no matter. The rights of others—Bathsheba, Uriah—mattered little; the rights of others in the community may not have mattered more. Sheba ben Bichri took what he wanted, probably what his community wanted. He failed for lack of enough might. Joab took back what he wanted. He apparently succeeded; he had might enough not to be ignored.

One may wonder how serious Sheba's rebellion was. In the text, David fears it will be more harmful than Absalom's (20:6), so it was serious. This reality, in its turn, reveals something of the stability of David's "kingdom." It was sufficiently unstable that a single individual could trigger a rebellion—whether with active sedition over several years (as in Absalom's case), or with a single rallying cry (as in Sheba's case). More significant still, power appears to have been personal to the individual. Absalom's revolt wanted David dead; Absalom's revolt died with Absalom's death. Sheba's revolt ended the same way. Monarchy may have been established; dynasties were not, and monarchs could be overthrown—their hold on power was tenuous.

Amasa's case invites reflection. Was he set an impossible task, or did his delay point to treachery? Was Joab bringing justice to the traitor, or revenging himself on his replacement? Was Joab thwarting David, or was there collusion between them? The soldier's cry (v. 11: for Joab and for David), the naming of the troops (v. 16: the army with Joab), and the lead role in the negotiations (vv. 16–22: "Are you Joab?") all point to both Joab's personal power and his collusion with David.

Finally, the role of the wise woman raises questions for our understanding of urban organization at the time. She is described as a "wise woman," she negotiates directly with Joab, she takes her proposal to "all the people" (v. 22), and her wisdom is acted on. The elders are not mentioned, nor is any town council. Her saying from the old days throws no light on the situation.

"Joab returned to Jerusalem to the king" (v. 22). We are back where we were in chapters 11–12. The narrative has, for the time being, reached equilibrium. The list of royal officials appended here (vv. 23–26; discussed at 1 Sam 8:16–19) reinforces the sense of closure.

Appendix II

INDEPENDENT TRADITIONS ABOUT DAVID
2 SAMUEL 21–24

Both their arrangement and their content suggest that these four chapters formed a separate collection of Davidic traditions, with an independence all of its own. It begins and ends with two texts of sacral ritual (perhaps better: sacral outrage). Within these are two sets of military traditions, most probably from David's early guerrilla days, which reveal organizations and episodes otherwise completely unknown to us. At the core of the collection are two songs or poems attributed to David. The concentric arrangement suggests an independent collection. The fact that the contents are otherwise unknown to us and include military command structures we would expect to know about is a further pointer to the independence of the collection.

The first ritual report (2 Sam 21:1–14) involves two incidents and implies a third. In the first, David is given the occasion to eliminate any remaining descendants of Saul. In the second, Rizpah, daughter of Saul's concubine, does honor to her kin, and David is given the occasion to secure honorable burial for Saul and his dead descendants. The third, the incident that is implied, relates to Saul's execution of Gibeonites (described as Amorites, hardly priests of YHWH); details are not provided. The first military report (21:15–22) consists of four fragments of tradition from the Philistine wars. In each, one of the "descendants of the giants" is killed by one of David's men. The first song (22:1–51) is almost identical with Ps 68. The second song

(23:1–7) is described as "the last words of David." The fact that two more sets of traditions follow is indicative of the formalized structure of the collection.

It is the second report of military traditions (23:8–39) that holds some stunning surprises. It lists two military structures, the Three and the Thirty, that we have not heard of in all the traditions of David's military exploits. The names of the Three—Josheb-basshebeth, Eleazar ben Dodo, Shammah ben Agee—are otherwise totally unknown to us. Of the names listed under the Thirty, five are known to us—Abishai and Asahel, brothers of Joab; Benaiah; Eliam son of Ahithophel; and Uriah the Hittite. Abishai was chief of the Thirty, and Benaiah was a renowned warrior; neither man made it to the Three. Joab's name is mentioned three times, but he is not listed as a member of either group. Asahel is listed (v. 24), who was killed by Abner in battle (2 Sam 2:23). Some of the exploits noted belong within the context of the Philistine wars; for them, a setting early in the Davidic traditions is likely. As with the first report of military traditions, these exploits are completely unknown to us. It is a stark reminder that where the text appears to have revealed so much it in fact reveals so little. Concern for literary genre recurs: What kinds of literature are these various texts in 1–2 Samuel and what functions did they serve? It is unlikely that most of them were written primarily to provide information of use to historians.

The final element in this collection returns to the sacral sphere (24:1–23). As told here, it is a puzzling story. For starters, YHWH, the God of Israel, incites David, the king of Israel, against the people of Israel. Chronicles' version could not cope and said it was Satan who did the inciting (1 Chr 21:1). In Chronicles, the site duly bought becomes the location of the future temple (22:1); in Samuel, the link to the temple is not explicitly made. David orders a census, apparently of able-bodied fighting men (24:9); Joab and the military oppose it, and we are not told why. After it is all over, David is conscience-stricken, although in the Samuel version YHWH had incited it. For his sin, David's land is to be punished by pestilence. The plague stops at "the threshing floor of Araunah the Jebusite," on the threshold of Jerusalem. So David builds an altar there. On the same place, "the threshing floor of *Ornan* the Jebusite," Chronicles foretells the building of the Jerusalem temple (22:1)—because David was afraid to go to Gibeon, because of the sword of the angel of the LORD. This is very strange. The text could end with verse 16, and the sparing of Jerusalem would be an act of spontaneous divine mercy. Or verse 17 could follow on verse 15, with God's mercy won by David's confession and intercession. Or, as in the present text, both can be combined; after all, in the Samuel text, both God and David are to some degree responsible. That the place of the temple should commemorate the place of the plague's stopping before Jerusalem is understandable enough. That so dense a story should be told of the memorial is an invitation to respectful reflection.

READING THE WHOLE

The present Hebrew text of 1–2 Samuel follows the refrain, "There was no king in Israel"; the anarchy revealed the need for one. The earlier text assumed for the Deuteronomistic History follows the note of Israel's being given into "the hands of the Philistines forty years"—the longest such period by far (Judg 13:1). The text assumed for the Prophetic Record begins with the emergence of the prophet Samuel; its focus is on the prophetic endorsement of kingship, with a view to legitimating Jehu's seizure of Israel's crown (cf. the final chapter here [241] and Campbell 1986; also Campbell, comm. [2003], and Campbell and O'Brien 2000).

With Israel in need of a king, the entire structure of the people's existence will change. Kingship will come through the prophets, so Samuel emerges on the national scene. Few roles escape him, but his role as prophet is at the core of the narratives. The priestly family at Shiloh is dismissed; the LORD's promise is withdrawn. If it were simply a case of immoral priests, replacements could have been found. The change will be more radical than that, and the ark, the figurative symbol of unity in faith, must be withdrawn too (1 Sam 4–6).

The regime of the deliverer-judges, as portrayed, failed among other things to provide permanence and stability. With the death of a judge, the cycle of failure started again. Deliverance for the lifetime of Samuel is portrayed as assured (1 Sam 7), but his sons do not carry it on (8:1–5). The request by the elders of Israel for a king is based on this failure of justice. Samuel's sons "turned aside after gain; they took bribes and perverted justice" (8:3). God instructs Samuel to issue a warning and then to "set a king over them" (8:22). Before this order is implemented, God takes the initiative to begin the process of providing Israel with a king for the purposes of defense: "He shall save my people from the hand of the Philistines; for I have seen (the suffering of) my people, because their outcry has come to me" (9:16). The process proceeds with the "justice" king installed in 10:17 (18–19), 20–25 (26–27), and the "defense" king installed in chapter 11. To understand the nature of the text, it is important to note the claim that the story in 9:1–10:16 has been edited for the Prophetic Record, emphasizing Samuel's role; this editing is assumed to be from around the late ninth century. The traditions in chapter 8 have also been edited to express a view of monarchy as apostasy and rejection of God; this editing is assumed to be from around the sixth century. The text preserves, in a remarkably skilled composition, four traditions associated with the emergence of the monarchy in ancient Israel. The views put forward in chapter 12 could be considered a fifth.

The position advocated in 1 Sam 12 places stress on the king's obedience to the God of Israel. The brief reign given Saul preserves an example of this view. The Samuel who anointed him dismisses him twice for disobedience. Obedience to God is portrayed as an essential element for the successful exercise of kingship. David, a man after God's own heart (1 Sam 13:14), is anointed in place of Saul (1 Sam 16:1–13). It is typical of the theology in these narratives that some twenty chapters elapse between David's anointing and his coming to the throne of both Judah and Israel. It is also of theological interest, given Saul's dismissal for disobedience, that David sins on at least two occasions (2 Sam 11–12 and 2 Sam 24) and twice promptly confesses his sin. What was not allowed for Saul is allowed for David. Obedience is demanded, yet experience has found a place for fragility.

The issues of justice and defense remain crucial. Absalom's revolt is predicated on David's failure to ensure justice (2 Sam 15:1–6). The approval of David among Israel's tribes is based on his successful defense of the people (2 Sam 19:10; NRSV, v. 9). Despite the instability of David's kingdom (two rebellions), its permanence is assumed. Joab returns "to Jerusalem to the king"; David's altar is built on the threshing floor of Araunah the Jebusite, the site of the future temple.

A lengthy block of narrative has been associated with David's rise to monarchy. Almost as lengthy a block has been associated with David's exercise of monarchy in the middle years of his reign. In both, while success is portrayed as YHWH's gift in various ways, success is also portrayed as the outcome of careful planning and skilled strategy on David's part. At the end of the book, a collection is appended that is clearly independent of earlier Davidic traditions (2 Sam 21–24). The narrative tradition of the Hebrew Bible tends to amalgamate rather than adjudicate. Many sorts of texts have been integrated into the composition of the book; they serve many functions. One of these is not primarily to be of use to historians.

REVIEW ISSUES

1. What understandings are offered of Samuel's function, and how are the political and religious realms reconciled?
2. What might have changed and what might have remained if Shimei ben Gera (cf. 2 Sam 16:5–8) had composed the book of Samuel?
3. What insights does the book of Samuel offer into the function of kingship in ancient Israel?

A COMPARISON WITH CHRONICLES

From the point of view of interpretative method, it would be a major mistake to assume that we already know what 1–2 Chronicles is about. It would be a gross methodological error to assume that it is pursuing the same goal as the books from Deuteronomy through Kings (the Deuteronomistic History). Five steps are involved, if we are to avoid illusions. The first is to inventory the books: where they begin, where they end, what they cover. The second is to examine what they contain: what is included, what is excluded. The third is assessment of the nature of these contents: prose or poetry, fact or fiction, old or new, and so on. The fourth step is to identify the major blocks within the books and reflect on how these blocks are related to each other for the purposes of the books' communication. The final task is to pull together these aspects to formulate a proposal about the nature of Chronicles and its function. The assessment has been made, for example, that Chronicles "provides a survey of Israel's total history and prior events from the creation of the world to the time of Ezra and Nehemiah," a comment which—despite coming from a respected scholar of remarkably balanced judgment—is quite ridiculous (Fohrer 1968, 238). The "relatively scant attention" paid to Chronicles in Jewish writings is detailed by Kalimi (1998). The shifting stances of scholarship, past and present, on the historical reliability of Chronicles have been explored by Sara Japhet, who concluded that the jury was still out on the issue (Japhet 1985; for the nineteenth century, see Graham 1990). The verdict will necessarily vary from passage to passage.

The issues cannot be addressed in adequate detail here, but even an initial exploration is revealing. Chronicles begins with the beginning of the human race: "Adam, Seth, Enosh" (1 Chr 1:1); Cain and Abel were not part of the genealogical line. Chronicles ends with Cyrus's decree on building the temple at Jerusalem and returning there. Chronicles ignores the story of Israel until the death of Saul and the transition to David: "He [the LORD] put him [Saul] to death and turned the kingdom over to David son of Jesse" (1 Chr 10:14); Chronicles ignores anything between the destruction of the temple (2 Chr 36:19) and the decree of Cyrus (2 Chr 36:22–23). The story of northern Israel, unconnected with the temple in Jerusalem, is ignored. This coverage in itself is remarkable.

By way of global comparison, the Deuteronomistic History begins with Moses in Moab and ends with Jehoiachin in exile. It includes the traditions of Deuteronomy, Joshua, Judges, and 1 Samuel—omitted by Chronicles, along with most of the Tetrateuch. It accounts for the northern kingdom from start to finish. It says nothing about a rebuilding of the temple; its last word on the Jerusalem temple is the account of its thorough destruction and despoliation (2 Kgs 25:8–17).

Moving in to focus on the books of Samuel creates insight into the interests of Chronicles. Emphasis is laid on the unity of Israel and on the temple in Jerusalem. Samuel has a long war between David and Ishbaal and four chapters on the innocence of David in the deaths of Saul, Abner, and Ishbaal. Chronicles moves directly from Saul's death to David's anointing as king of Israel at Hebron and the capture of Jerusalem. Put differently, where Samuel speaks of David's seven years and six months at Hebron, filled by one sentence about war (2 Sam 3:1) and traditions occupying no more than four days, Chronicles has nothing at all. Disunity is passed over. Can we presume which scenario comes closer to what happened—if one of them does? For Samuel, David's resources at Ziklag were relatively few, and pitted against him were Saul and then, after his death, Saul's supporters. For Chronicles, David is joined at either Ziklag or the stronghold by significant warriors, including "Benjaminites, Saul's kindred," some Gadites, Judahites, and Manassites; these are joined by many more for the coronation at Hebron. The picture is one of steadily increasing support for David (cf. 1 Chr 12:23; NRSV, v. 22) from all the sections of the people (1 Chr 12). The issues of power and conflict are downplayed and left between the lines; the overall unity of Israel is to the fore, with some 350,000 troops committed to supporting David as king at Hebron over all Israel. The unified support for David—even among those Benjaminites "of whom the majority had continued to keep their allegiance to the house of Saul" (1 Chr 12:30; NRSV, v. 29)—is clearly emphasized. For Samuel, David is forbidden the building of a temple; Solomon will do it. For Chronicles, a vastly greater responsibility is given David in the preparation for the temple that Solomon will build.

Solomon was too young and inexperienced for so magnificent a task as the building of the LORD's temple, "so David provided materials in great quantity before his death" (1 Chr 22:5).

There is something to be learned here. All Israel must be behind David. The great king David must be behind the building of the temple. The centrality of the Jerusalem temple is of great importance to the book of Chronicles.

The question of the sources used by Chronicles needs to be addressed at this point. Much scholarship gives the impression that 1–2 Chronicles is largely dependent on and abbreviated from the narrative of Samuel–Kings. The situation is not so simple. Genesis 5:3–31, for example, lists ten names for the period between Adam and Noah; 1 Chr 1:1–4 lists the same ten. Second Samuel 23:24–39 lists names of warriors who were among the Thirty, in the command structure of David's guerrilla forces. First Chronicles 11:26–47 has most of these in much the same order, but with sixteen more names added at the end (cf. 11:41–47). Even more surprising, among the soldiers joining David are two said to have led the Thirty: Ishmaiah of Gibeon and Amasai (1 Chr 12:4 and 12:19 [NRSV, v. 18]). Neither is to be found among the names elsewhere in Chronicles or in Samuel. Just from this evidence it is clear that the issue is complex and unlikely to be susceptible of a single wide-ranging judgment; the sources utilized by Chronicles are manifold and not to be taken lightly. For an initial approach to this area, it may be helpful to consult Rudolph's listing of what he considers original to the Chronicler and what are to be seen as additions (Rudolph, comm., 1–5), but balanced by Japhet's view that "it is one work, composed essentially by a single author, with a very distinct and peculiar literary method" (Japhet, comm., 7), with both evaluated against the listing in Myers (comm., xlix–lxii).

The evaluation of the material from these sources is delicate and difficult. One thing is clear: We cannot view the Deuteronomistic History as authoritative and authentic and simultaneously view Chronicles as subsidiary and dependent. The two works are both from late in the story of ancient Israel, and the basic stages of composition occurred little more than a century or two apart. One may assume that sources from earlier periods were available to both. The compatibility of Chronicles' material with the picture portrayed in Samuel–Kings is an invalid criterion. Both works are advancing a point of view; neither need be objective. Coherence with what is known from outside sources would be helpful; alas, not much is known from outside sources. Coherence within either work might be considered valuable, but multiple sources have been used and both works follow the biblical tradition of amalgamating rather than adjudicating. The task of evaluation, passage by passage, must be approached with care. It has been begun in various studies; it is nowhere near an end.

Genealogies, beginning with Adam, occupy 1 Chr 1–9, with the Philistines and the battle of Mount Gilboa appearing in chapter 10. Of the three great modern sources for comparative studies (see p. 249), Vannutelli gives only a synoptic presentation of the genealogies (1931, para. 1–18), Bendavid provides the Hebrew of all parallel texts, with differences identified in red, and Endres et al. provide an English text of Chronicles, with appropriate parallels for the genealogies.

Vannutelli classifies the genealogies into three groups: Adam to Jacob (1 Chr 1:1–2:2), the tribes descended from Jacob (2:3–7:40), and additions (8:1–9:44), that is, concerning some who returned from the Babylonian exile and two snippets of Saul's genealogies (8:29–40 and 9:35–44), both giving Saul a Gibeonite pedigree. Within the Judah genealogies, for example, are included the descendants of David and Solomon, kings of Judah (1 Chr 3). Parallels alleged are drawn from a wide variety of sources; among the biblical books, Vannutelli notes Genesis, Exodus, Numbers, Samuel, Kings, and Ruth.

Two features stand out clearly. First, the genealogies in Chronicles are mainly no more than a list of names, devoid of details or patterning (e.g., compare 1 Chr 1:1–4 with Gen 5:1–32). Second, there are significant genealogical lists in Chronicles that have no parallel in other biblical texts (e.g., 1 Chr 2:18–55; 3:10–24; 4:1–23; 6:16–33 [NRSV, 6:31–48]; 8:12–28). All of this raises the question of Chronicles' sources. The "fact and fiction" brigade will have no trouble; for them, what Chronicles did not know was made up. Unfortunately for these, much of the extra material in Chronicles does not look as if it had to be made up; it could have been done without. The possibility of temple registries and other sources cannot be ignored. However, a closer study of the genealogies in Chronicles must begin, for example, with both Noth, comm., 36–42, and Japhet, comm., 8–10.

After the report of Saul's death, Chronicles has all the elders of Israel anoint David "king over Israel, according to the word of the LORD by Samuel" (1 Chr 11:3)—of course, Chronicles has no earlier report of Samuel at all. This is promptly followed, in Chronicles, by David and all Israel's march on Jerusalem and its capture. At this point, traditions of David's warriors are gathered, much as in 2 Sam 23:8–38, with differences that are not insignificant. First Chronicles 12 lists all those warriors who joined David, from Ziklag to the coronation at Hebron.

This aspect is not mentioned in Samuel. All Israel is reported to have joined David to bring the ark of God from Kiriath-jearim toward Jerusalem—but with its diversion to the house of Obed-edom (1 Chr 13). With the ark on hold at Obed-edom's, 1 Chr 14 takes space to establish David in Jerusalem and repulse the Philistines, much as in 2 Sam 5:11–25. The next two chapters report the final leg of the ark's journey in great detail. Whereas 2 Sam 6 gives it at most a dozen verses, 1 Chr 15–16 allots it some seventy-two verses, including twenty-eight verses of song.

Nathan's discourse to David, with its prohibition (no temple) and promise (sure dynasty), follows as in 2 Samuel. Reference to Solomon's future iniquity is passed over; the builder of the temple should hardly end his days in lust-driven apostasy. With Nathan's promise having put the Davidic dynasty on a secure footing, Chronicles moves on to the establishment of David's rule (1 Chr 18; cf. 2 Sam 8), then dealings with the Ammonites that end in the capture of Rabbah, and traditions from wars with the Philistines (1 Chr 19–20; cf. 2 Sam 10; 11:1; 12:30–31; 21:18–22). Chronicles does not have the Stories of David's Middle Years (2 Sam 11–20; i.e., the David and Bathsheba story and all that follows it).

With this, the narrative of 1 Chronicles has finished with the political side of David's kingship and turns toward the temple. The story of David's census and the ensuing three-day plague provides a rationale for the temple site (1 Chr 21; cf. 2 Sam 24). The rest of the account of David, to the end of 1 Chronicles, will be concerned with David's preparations for the building of the temple by Solomon. The charge to Solomon "to build a house for the LORD, the God of Israel" (22:6) is the theme of chapter 22. David hands over the monarchy to Solomon at the start of 1 Chr 23. For our present purposes, we can leave the matter there.

Chronicles begins with remarkably extensive genealogies (not merely culled from extant biblical text). It shifts to David's kingship over all Israel, his move to Jerusalem, and the move of the ark there, followed by Nathan's promise. In between it recounts traditions of David's warrior heroes and their exploits as well as traditions of David's foreign wars—the sorts of things that were said to have prevented David building the temple. There is a strong impression that 1–2 Chronicles is focused on the story of the temple in Jerusalem. It has as much resemblance to the Deuteronomistic History as *Jack and the Beanstalk* has to *Alice in Wonderland*. It must be evaluated in its own right.

REVIEW ISSUES

1. What significance can be given to the fact that Chronicles begins with creation (Adam, Seth, Enosh), then passes over Genesis, Exodus, Leviticus, Numbers, Deuteronomy, Joshua, Judges, and the first thirty chapters of 1 Samuel?

2. What might be made of the fact that considerable attention is given to David's preparations in his lifetime for the building of the temple and that these preparations are hardly referred to in the account of Solomon's temple building?

3. The portrayal of David in 1 Chronicles shows some significant differences with the portrayal in Samuel. What implications might this have for our thinking about some of the historical issues in both books?

Bibliography other than commentaries

Barthélemy, D., D. W. Gooding, J. Lust, and E. Tov. 1986. *The Story of David and Goliath: Textual and Literary Criticism.* OBO 73. Fribourg: Editions Universitaires.

Campbell, Antony F. 1975. *The Ark Narrative (1 Sam 4–6; 2 Sam 6): A Form-Critical and Tradition-Historical Study.* SBLDS 16. Missoula, Mont.: Scholars Press.

———. 1979. "Yahweh and the Ark: A Case Study in Narrative." *JBL* 98:31–43.

———. 1986. *Of Prophets and Kings: A Late Ninth-Century Document (1 Samuel 1–2 Kings 10).* CBQMS 17. Washington, D.C.: Catholic Biblical Association of America.

Campbell, Antony F., and Mark A. O'Brien. 2000. *Unfolding the Deuteronomistic History: Origins, Upgrades, Present Text.* Minneapolis: Fortress.

Fohrer, Georg. 1968. *Introduction to the Old Testament.* Initiated by E. Sellin. Completely rev. and rewritten by G. Fohrer. Translated by D. Green. Nashville: Abingdon.

Gooding, D. W. 1986. Contributions in *The Story of David and Goliath*, above under D. Barthélemy.

Graham, Matt Patrick. 1990. *The Utilization of 1 and 2 Chronicles in the Reconstruction of Israelite History in the Nineteenth Century.* SBLDS 116. Atlanta: Scholars Press.

Graham, Matt Patrick, Kenneth G. Hoglund, and Steven L. McKenzie, eds. 1997. *The Chronicler as Historian.* JSOTSup 238. Sheffield: Sheffield Academic Press.

Halpern, Baruch. 1981. *The Constitution of the Monarchy in Israel.* HSM 25. Chico, Calif.: Scholars Press.

———. 2001. *David's Secret Demons: Messiah, Murderer, Traitor, King.* Grand Rapids: Eerdmans.

Hoglund, Kenneth G. 1997. "The Chronicler as Historian: A Comparativist Perspective." Pages 19–29 in Graham et al., eds. *The Chronicler as Historian*, see above.

Japhet, Sara. 1985. "The Historical Reliability of Chronicles: The History of the Problem and Its Place in Biblical Research." *JSOT* 33:83–107.

———. 2000. "Postexilic Historiography: How and Why?" Pages 144–73 in *Israel Constructs Its History: Deuteronomistic Historiography in Recent Research.* Edited by A. de Pury et al. JSOTSup 306. Sheffield: Sheffield Academic Press.

Kalimi, Isaac. 1997. "Was the Chronicler a Historian?" Pages 73–89 in Graham et al., eds. *The Chronicler as Historian*, see above.

———. 1998. "History of Interpretation: The Book of Chronicles in Jewish Tradition from Daniel to Spinoza." *RB* 105:5–41.

Koch, Klaus. 1969. *The Growth of the Biblical Tradition: The Form-Critical Method.* New York: Charles Scribner's Sons.

Lessing, Doris. 1984. *The Diaries of Jane Somers.* Harmondsworth, Eng.: Penguin.

McCarthy, Dennis J. 1973. "The Inauguration of Monarchy in Israel: A Form-Critical Study of I Samuel 8–12." *Interpretation* 27:17–22.

McKenzie, Steven L. 2000. *King David: A Biography.* Oxford: Oxford Univ. Press.

Miller, Patrick D., Jr., and J. J. M. Roberts. 1997. *The Hand of the Lord: A Reassessment of the "Ark Narrative" of 1 Samuel.* Baltimore: Johns Hopkins Univ. Press.

Nelson, Richard D. 1998. *The Historical Books.* Nashville: Abingdon.

Rainey, Anson F. 1997. "The Chronicler and His Sources—Historical and Geographical." Pages 30–72 in Graham et al., eds. *The Chronicler as Historian*, see above.

Rost, Leonhard. 1982. *The Succession to the Throne of David.* Sheffield: Almond. German original, 1926.

Stähli, Hans-Peter. 1978. *Knabe-Jüngling-Knecht: Untersuchungen zum Begriff נַעַר im Alten Testament.* Frankfurt: Peter Lang.

Vaux, Roland de. 1959. "Les combats singuliers dans l'Ancien Testament." *Bib* 40:495–508.

Walters, Stanley D. 1988. "Hanna and Anna: The Greek and Hebrew Texts of 1 Samuel 1." *JBL* 107:385–412.

5

1 and 2 Kings

with 1 Chronicles 23–2 Chronicles 36

OVERVIEW OF KINGS

The first book of Kings opens with the note that David "was old and advanced in years" and the discreet comment that even with the most beautiful young woman in the territory the king was sexually past it. When the same phrase was used of Joshua's age, nothing was added indicative of his sexual vigor. Health and sexuality were required of an ancient Near Eastern king. With David, there may well be a link between that and what follows.

Adonijah, David's oldest surviving son, makes a play for the crown and organizes a coronation party at En-rogel. Solomon, with help from Bathsheba and Nathan, makes an end run around his elder brother and wins the backing of David and the king's own warriors; his coronation is held at Gihon, further up the Kidron valley nearer the city. David's role is sometimes dismissed as that of a befuddled and senile old man, yet his word appears to have decisive weight. Supporters' heads are counted among those who exercised power (1 Kgs 1:7–8); discreet pressure is brought to bear among the king's intimates. The precise balance is not given us. Solomon emerges a king and the succession is momentarily bloodless.

Solomon begins with great wisdom (3:3–14), his temple is consecrated with great promise, but with threat as well (9:1–9), and his reign ends with great disaster (11:9–13). It is almost forgotten that this fabled king, following his famous father, sets his kingdom on a downhill path that will lead to desolation and horror.

Two other features mark Solomon's reign: his administrative organization of the kingdom (4:1–5:14; NRSV, chap. 4) and the visit of the Queen of Sheba (chap. 10). The report of the latter is ambivalent; it may reflect unmitigated admiration for Solomon's wealth and wisdom, or it may conceal veiled criticism of his unmitigated excess.

The division of Solomon's kingdom into north and south comes immediately on his death. Its presentation in the text reflects the theology of Samuel–Kings. The prophet Ahijah announces the event to Jeroboam, having God say, "I am about to tear the kingdom from the hand of Solomon" (11:31). A popular election on taxation policy divides the kingdom (12:1–16). The narrator emphasizes that God's action is to be recognized in this political outcome: "It was a turn of affairs brought about by the LORD" (12:15). It is surprising, then, how some modern interpreters can speak of the biblical view of the wickedness of the northern rebels and totally overlook that, in the biblical view, the initiative for the northern kingdom comes directly from God.

From this point, until 2 Kgs 17, the narrative in Kings has the story of two kingdoms to follow: the northern kingdom ("Israel went away to their tents . . . and made him [Jeroboam] king over all Israel" [1 Kgs 12:16b, 20a]) and the southern kingdom ("there was no one who followed the house of David, except the tribe of Judah alone" [12:20b]). It achieves this by a certain synchronicity. Each king is dated in relation to his colleague in the other kingdom. The king in one kingdom is followed through until the end of his reign, at which point the narrative backtracks to deal with those who meantime have become king in the other kingdom. By switching back and forth, the narrative progresses simply enough. Prophetic stories are set within the reigns of kings: Ahijah and the anonymous prophet of 1 Kgs 13, both within the reign of Jeroboam; Elijah (1 Kgs 17—2 Kgs 2) within the reign of Ahab; Elisha (2 Kgs 2–9 [+ 13:14–21]) within the reign of Joram; Isaiah (2 Kgs 19:20–20:19) within the reign of Hezekiah; and Huldah (2 Kgs 22:14–20) within the reign of Josiah. At the time of Rehoboam and the split, Shemaiah's words may have prevented civil war; however, they are not set within a prophetic story (1 Kgs 12:21–24).

Jeroboam's primary achievement noted in the text is the establishment of objects and centers for worship in Bethel and Dan. Jeroboam's religious policies need careful evaluation; worship in Jerusalem would have been political suicide for him. The final word is written by his enemies; an earlier view can only be surmised. Clearly, for seventh-century Deuteronomists, Jeroboam's establishment was damned on two grounds: (1) it was not in Jerusalem, and (2) the worship of the golden calves was at least idolatry, probably apostasy. Behind those parts of the text marked by strongly southern thought, a concern is visible about the indiscriminate consecration of priests (13:33); early on, this may have bulked larger as a cause for the destruction of Jeroboam's house (e.g., "so as to cut it off and to destroy it from the face of the earth," 13:34). However, the report that Jeroboam was rejected by the prophet Ahijah who had designated him uses an unusual phrase that seems to point to apostasy, but may have had wider meaning (you have "thrust me behind your back . . . ," 14:9).

After Jeroboam, the narrative backtracks to Rehoboam, to the thoroughgoing evil attributed to the people of Judah, and to the raid by Shishak, pharaoh of Egypt. The parade of kings moves inexorably on until Omri and Ahab put their stamp on the northern kingdom. Ahab, in particular, marries a Phoenician princess and establishes the worship of Baal in Samaria, the city his father Omri had made his capital. At this point, the Elijah cycle is introduced—appropriately, given the hostility between king and prophet. Elijah opposes the menace of Ahab's apostasy to Baal with an extended drought. Elijah wins. Reading between the lines, it is clear that Jezebel at least has been indulging in prophet killing. Elijah runs. He is portrayed heading for Mount Horeb, where he encounters God and has his commission strengthened. Elijah's next confrontation with Ahab is over Naboth's vineyard; Ahab is roundly condemned for murder and theft. The next chapter, a Micaiah story, has Ahab die in battle. Ahab's son, Ahaziah, injures himself falling out of an upstairs chamber. He sends to inquire of the god of Ekron about his recovery—and his messengers ran into Elijah. Elijah's message to Ahaziah is terse: "You shall surely die" (2 Kgs 1:16). He did. Finally, in a study of the prophetic spirit, Elijah passes out of sight and his mantle is inherited by Elisha. Seven chapters or so are taken up with stories of Elisha, many involving kings and the like.

As the figure of Elisha fades from the narrative, the last act in a drama is played out, a drama that has been running through Samuel–Kings. The prophet Samuel anointed Saul and then rejected him; Samuel next anointed David. The prophet Ahijah designated Jeroboam and later rejected him. The prophet Elijah rejected Ahab; a disciple of the prophet Elisha is reported anointing Jehu king in place of Ahab's son. These five episodes in the story of monarchy in Israel are held together by a pattern of significant elements (cf. Campbell 1986; comm. [2003]; Campbell and O'Brien 2000); the whole expresses a theology of prophetic authority over kings that is unparalleled elsewhere. Jehu's coup is a brutal bloodbath, but it has its admirers, and a four-generation dynasty is claimed as its reward (cf. 2 Kgs 10:30).

King Ahaziah of Judah is one of the victims of Jehu's bloodbath. His mother, Queen Athaliah, organizes a bloodbath of her own, which includes her own grandchildren; she rules Judah in her own right for six years. One grandchild, Joash son of Ahaziah, is hidden by his aunt, Jehosheba, Ahaziah's sister; after six years, Jehoiada the priest, her husband (cf. 2 Chr 22:11), organizes a coup with the help of the royal guard. Queen Athaliah is assassinated and the seven-year-old Joash enthroned as king (cf. 2 Kgs 11).

The growing power of Assyria manifested itself in campaigns by the Assyrian king, Tiglath-pileser III, in Galilee, down the Mediterranean coast, and in Transjordan (c. 734–732), forming the Assyrian provinces of Dor, Megiddo, and Gilead. A decade or so later, King Shalmaneser V of Assyria invaded what was left of northern Israel and besieged the capital Samaria for three years before it was captured. Northern Israel ceased to be an independent kingdom; it was swallowed up into the Assyrian Empire. What might be called a prophetic experiment was at an end. A late Judean reflection on the failure of the north put it down to apostasy (although reasonably the demand for worship in Jerusalem is not made); interestingly, however, among the crimes alleged were some that the biblical record notes exclusively for Judah (2 Kgs 17:7–20; cf. Campbell and O'Brien 2000, 442 n. 60).

A further Assyrian sweep into Palestine ended up with King Hezekiah of Judah besieged in Jerusalem by the forces of the Assyrians—in Sennacherib's words, "Himself [Hezekiah] I made a prisoner in Jerusalem, his royal residence, like a bird in a cage" (*ANET*, 288). Then all of a sudden the Assyrians melted away. The episode generated multiple traditions and a legend of the inviolability of Zion. Among the traditions is the intercession of the prophet Isaiah, assuring Hezekiah that his prayer for Jerusalem had been heard and Sennacherib would not prevail (2 Kgs 19).

Hezekiah had the reputation of a reformer. His son Manasseh enjoyed a fifty-five-year reign and the reputation (in the Deuteronomistic History at least) of being a thoroughly bad king. Amon, his son, reigned for two years. Another coup installed King Josiah on the throne of Judah, for a reign of thirty-three years. The Deuteronomistic History sets enormous hopes on a major reform under Josiah, but it is threatened by his unexpected death and is not carried on by the four kings who followed him. Jerusalem is sacked by the Babylonians, who have become the dominant imperial power in place of the Assyrians, and the history of an independent ancient Israel is at an end.

A characteristic of this presentation of Israel's kings after the division of the kingdom (therefore not expressed for David and Solomon within their regnal formulas) is the judgment passed on each as to whether he did right or wrong in the sight of YHWH. Two kings and only two kings—Hezekiah and Josiah—are declared unreservedly to have done "what was right in the sight of YHWH." David is sometimes used as a model for Judean kings, those who are judged to have acted or not acted "as David his father had done" (cf. Campbell and O'Brien 2000, 479–80). All of the kings of northern Israel without exception are judged to have done "what was evil in the sight of YHWH." A minority of the Judean kings (eight out of nineteen after David and Solomon) are judged to have done "what was right in the sight of YHWH," with the reserve expressed for six of them that "the high places were not taken away."

On this evidence, the elimination of the high places, mandated in Deuteronomy, was important but not decisive in the judgment of a king. Decisive appears to have been the observance of the law—for example, in the words given David for Solomon: "Keep the charge of the LORD your God, walking in his ways and keeping his statutes, his commandments, his ordinances, and his testimonies, as it is written in the law of Moses" (1 Kgs 2:3). The evil of the northern kings was associated with "the sins of Jeroboam"—apparently apostasy and religious impropriety (especially the indiscriminate consecration of priests) rather than the failure to sacrifice exclusively in Jerusalem. It is against this background of universal infidelity among the northern kings and partial infidelity in the south that the reforming zeal of Hezekiah and Josiah has to be measured and the high hopes they inspired in the text have to be understood.

This overview is represented sketchily in the outline below. For the sake of brevity, the middle section (i.e., part II)—the kingdoms of north and south: Israel and Judah—is divided into three for schematic reasons rather than on textual grounds. The prophetic cycles have also been indicated within this middle section. The inauguration of the northern kingdom under Jeroboam, and his dismissal, can mark the beginning, part A. Part B can end with the conclusion of the four generations of Jehu's dynasty. There is a trace of support for this with 2 Kgs 14:27 and a further trace with 15:12. For part C, opening with 15:13, the absence of a conjunction before Shallum facilitates a beginning. A tiny bit convenient—certainly not compelling—the division is almost solely schematic.

THE MONARCHY AFTER DAVID IN
ANCIENT ISRAEL   1–2 KINGS

I.	The kingdom of Solomon	1 Kgs 1–11
	A. Solomon's accession to the throne	
	of David	1–2
	B. Solomon's reign	3–11
II.	The kingdoms of north and south: Israel	
	and Judah	1 Kgs 12:1—2 Kgs 17:41
	A. At the beginning	1 Kgs 12:1–14:20
	Including the Ahijah cycle (Jeroboam)	*11:26–40; 14:1–20*
	B. In the middle	1 Kgs 14:21—2 Kgs 15:12
	Including the Elijah cycle (Ahab)	*1 Kgs 17:1–19:21; 21:1–29;*
		2 Kgs 1:1–2:14
	Including the Elisha cycle (Jehu)	*2 Kgs 2:15–9:13*
	C. At the end	2 Kgs 15:13–17:41
	Including comment (prophetic warnings)	*2 Kgs 17:7–23*
III.	The kingdom of Judah alone	2 Kgs 18–25
	A. Hezekiah to Amon	18–21
	B. Josiah	22:1–23:30
	C. The end	23:31–25:30

THE BOOK OF CHRONICLES
AN OVERVIEW CONTINUED

At the start of 1 Chr 23 David, old and full of days, makes Solomon king over Israel. For almost the next seven chapters, Chronicles tells its own story, without parallels elsewhere. David assembles the Levites, and the descendants of Aaron are singled out. David and the army officers set people apart for the service of the temple; the names follow. Divisional officers and tribal officers are listed (27:1–22). Given the problems of the census back in 1 Chr 21, two verses are of interest: "David did not count those below twenty years" (27:23) and "Joab son of Zeruiah began to count them, but did not finish" (27:24). An extended list of David's royal officials follows (27:25–34).

The importance given to David in Chronicles in relation to the future temple comes to the fore in 1 Chr 28–29, which concludes David's life. According to the text, David has assembled at Jerusalem all the officials and worthies of the kingdom (28:1). Before them all, he announces God's choice of Solomon to build the temple and gives

Solomon the plan for the building and the specifics of its service and its vessels. All the plans were given Solomon in writing, at the LORD's direction (28:19).

Finally, in chapter 29, David speaks to the assembled gathering of the provisions he has made to assist the "young and inexperienced" Solomon in this construction project of such magnitude (vv. 1–5), the leaders themselves give freely and generously (vv. 6–9), prayer of thanks is offered to God (vv. 10–19), and lavish sacrifices are offered with great joy (vv. 20–22). The handover to Solomon is confirmed, and David dies "in a good old age, full of days, riches, and honor" (29:28).

The story of Solomon's reign in his own right is begun by 2 Chronicles with the famous episode of the gift of wisdom at Gibeon. The next major block, some six chapters, is taken up with the construction and consecration of the temple and associated issues. No mention is made of David's plans and provisions for the temple. Solomon's reign is wrapped up with the capture of a city, extensive construction and the use of conscript labor, even a pious reason for the relocation of Pharaoh's daughter (and no mention of other foreign wives), further prescriptions for temple service, the visit from the Queen of Sheba, and the wealth of Solomon's kingdom.

From Solomon to Cyrus, the Persian king, Chronicles follows the succession of the Davidic dynasty in Jerusalem. A standard wisdom theology is present: The good prosper and become strong (e.g., 2 Chr 27:6); the wicked are oppressed and brought low (e.g. 2 Chr 28:19–20). The sequence is linear and largely uninterrupted by anything outside the southern kingdom. The schism of the northern kingdom is the story of Rehoboam. That it fulfills God's word to Ahijah is mentioned (2 Chr 10:15); that Jeroboam's death is God's doing is also noted (13:20). King Baasha of Israel pushes Judah into alliance with Aram-Damascus (2 Chr 16:1–6). Jehoshaphat, king of Judah, is given a mixed verdict: firmly located among the good kings (17:1–6), but not spared obloquy (19:1–3)—after all, he married into the house of Ahab. Four chapters are consecrated to his reign, including the Ahab-Micaiah story. A lengthy story about the deliverance from Moabites and Ammonites has echoes of Solomon's prayer at the consecration of the temple but nothing that might suggest dependence. Whereas at the beginning the high places are said to have been removed (17:6 and cf. 19:3), at the end it is said that they were not (20:33); as with the house of Ahab, Jehoshaphat's trade alliance with Ahaziah, king of Israel, gets him in trouble. It is remarked that "it was ordained by God" that Ahaziah, king of Judah, is killed in Jehu's revolt, while visiting the north; he is succeeded by Queen Athaliah. Joash, the beneficiary of the coup against her, does well under Jehoiada, the priest, but lapses dramatically when Jehoiada dies (chap. 24). Amaziah's failure against King Joash ben Jehoahaz ben Jehu of Israel is chronicled (cf. 2 Kgs 14) and anticipates the eventual end of the temple—apostasy begets punishment. His son, Uzziah, is said to have done "what was right in the sight of the LORD, just as his father Amaziah had done" (26:4); yet the verdict on Amaziah is far from a happy one. As it turns out, neither is Uzziah's; strength turns to pride, to destruction and leprosy.

The theology is explicit: Jotham, Uzziah's son, became strong "because he ordered his ways before the LORD his God" (27:6). Ahaz, on the other hand, "did not do what was right in the sight of the LORD" (28:1) and paid for it with defeats at the hand of the king of Aram and the king of Israel. The fall of northern Israel does not rate a mention, except for almost an aside in the message by Hezekiah to Israel and Judah (30:6–9; cf. ". . . so that he may turn again to the remnant of you who have escaped from the hand of the kings of Assyria. Do not be like your ancestors and your kindred, who were faithless to the LORD God of their ancestors, so that he made them a desolation, as you see" [vv. 6–7]). The appeal reflects the concern of Chronicles: "Yield yourselves to the LORD and come to his sanctuary, which he has sanctified forever" (30:8). Exile is assumed; the echo of 1 Kgs 8:46–50 is there, but faint: "your kindred and your children will find compassion with their captors, and return to this land" (30:9). A reformer like Jehoshaphat, Hezekiah receives four chapters; in contrast to Kings, a much-needed conversion is reported for Manasseh, after a spell in captivity in Babylon (allegedly brought there by "the commanders of the army of the king of Assyria," 33:11). Josiah's passover is described in detail; none like it had been held "since the days of the prophet Samuel" (35:18). Pharaoh Neco's words to Josiah are described as "from the mouth of God" (35:22); Josiah does not listen and dies. The next four kings do not sustain Josiah's reforms. The people mock God's messengers (36:15–16). So the Lord brings the Babylonians against Judah and Jerusalem, the temple is pillaged and burned, and the survivors of the devastation are taken into exile.

But after seventy years of sabbath, in the first year of King Cyrus of Persia, a written edict authorizes the building of a temple in Jerusalem and encourages the return there of the exiled people. With this, Chronicles ends.

MAJOR TEXT SIGNALS IN 1–2 KINGS

1. David's dominance: for two chapters, the text is David's.

2. Solomon's supremacy: Solomon occupies seven triumphant chapters and then crashes without a safety net.

3. A nation newly born is torn apart, and prophets are at the center of three out of the four chapters.

4. Kings are left to themselves for a couple of chapters, and Israel ends up with Ahab ben Omri.

5. Prophets almost take over for some fourteen chapters, especially the cycles of Elijah and Elisha.

6. The storyline returns to kings alone; first one kingdom is swallowed up, then the other.

7. Beyond David, two kings are fully approved: Hezekiah and Josiah. Hezekiah behaves foolishly (2 Kgs 20:12–19). He is granted an extra fifteen years of life and does nothing noteworthy with them; he dies in his bed. Josiah does something foolish too (2 Kgs 23:29–30): He dies in a battle he should not have been fighting.

Reading the Sections

THE KINGDOM OF SOLOMON
1 KINGS 1:1–11:43

(The diachronic dimension of the text in Kings is too complex for adequate discussion in a book of this scope. Interested readers may consult Campbell and O'Brien 2000.)

1 Kings 1–2   Solomon's accession to the throne of David

It is important to recognize that 1 Kgs 1 and 2 are dominated by the figure of David; they begin with his age and they end with his kingdom, following his instructions, secure in the hand of Solomon. The chapters have often been regarded as part of the Succession Narrative or Court History (2 Sam 9–20; cf. Gray, comm., 14–15; Jones, comm., 1:48–49; Nelson, comm., 15). A revised understanding of 2 Sam 11–20, however, allows the two chapters an independence of their own, legitimating Solomon as David's heir (see Campbell and O'Brien 2000, 329).

The little episode with Abishag (1:1–4) signals "David's senility and its accompanying impotency" (Jones, comm., 1:88). It is time for a successor (at first, at least, a coregent). David's senility need not extend to being taken in by Nathan and Bathsheba; the vow appealed to by Bathsheba is unknown to us (1 Kgs 1:17), but, for example, so is the LORD's promise to David quoted in 2 Sam 5:2. David's political acumen is evident in the narrative; it is unlikely that he is being portrayed as fooled at the beginning. We cannot evaluate the political weight of the forces arrayed behind Adonijah and Solomon (cf. Jones, comm., 1:91–92); it is possible that David's precipitate move to action tips the scales in Solomon's favor. According to the text, it puts a sudden end to Adonijah's celebration (vv. 41–50).

Two elements need to be recognized before reading chapter 2. One is the possible portrayal of David's ruthlessness. We know he has been shown as ruthless in having Uriah murdered; we are not sure of his role in the fates of Tamar, Amnon, and Absalom (not mentioned with Abner and Amasa). The other element concerns the correlation of David's instructions with Solomon's actions. It is not surprising that the sentences for Adonijah and Abiathar are not put on David's lips (cf. 1:6 and 2:26b). We are certainly unsure whether Adonijah was foolish enough to make the request for Abishag on his own behalf, whether Bathsheba was deceitful enough to make it for him, or whether the pretext originated with Solomon. Loyalty shown the sons of Barzillai needed no telling; they were not a threat to Solomon's security. Joab had backed Adonijah; he had to die. Shimei was of the house of Saul; he was an influential danger.

So finally "the kingdom was established in the hand of Solomon" (2:46b). The repetition (2:12, 46b; cf. also vv. 24, 45) is witness to the density and complexity underlying the tradition in these chapters. There is also an ominous note of conditionality in 2:4; it will recur as condition at 6:12–13; 8:25; 9:4–5 and—because of Solomon's apostasy—become a matter of imminent punishment in 11:1–13.

1 Kings 3–11   Solomon's reign

The story of Solomon is perplexing; uncannily, it anticipates the end of the book of Kings. Solomon had wealth, power, and undreamed-of wisdom—and still he failed royally. For all that David sinned, the text has him remain faithful to his God. For all that Solomon succeeded, the text has him abandon his God. Ultimate fidelity appears to be the touchstone of the book of Kings.

According to the text, Solomon was given a gift accorded few humans, "understanding to discern what is right" (3:11). He was given a reminder that, appropriately adjusted, applies to all humans: Live with integrity and what has been promised will be yours (9:4–5). He was also given a threat. The use of the plural suggests hindsight, but hindsight does not take the edge off reality—often it clarifies: "If you [plural] turn aside from following me, you or your children, . . . Israel will become a proverb and a taunt . . . [:] 'the LORD has brought this disaster upon them'" (9:6–9). According to the text, Solomon fell victim to the threat: "For when Solomon was old, his wives turned away his heart after other gods; and his heart was not true to the LORD his God" (11:4; cf. vv. 1–13). The first man blamed his wife; the text blames Solomon's wives. Plus ça change, plus ça reste la même chose (the more it changes, the more it stays the same). Such is the experience of human life!

1 Kings 3:1–5:14 (NRSV, 4:34)   Solomon: the wise administrator

Solomon's marriage to Pharaoh's daughter is listed first in the account of his reign; she crops up again near its end (9:24). Flights of fancy apart, we know nothing about her. The next episode takes us to the "principal high place" at Gibeon; we know about it, but it escapes our imaginations. What was the role of this "great high place" in ancient Israel? We are not told.

At that high place, at Gibeon, Solomon asks for and is gifted with "understanding to discern what is right" to govern God's people. Beyond that, God gives him wealth and honor; he will be incomparable among kings (3:13). The parable of two women and one baby reflects this capacity to govern. The text lists his immediate officials (4:2–6), then the twelve officials and their districts, each responsible for palace supplies for a month (4:7–19). The remaining verses hymn Solomon's wealth and wisdom (4:20–5:14; NRSV, 4:20–34).

1 Kings 5:15 (NRSV, 5:1)–9:28   Solomon: the builder

Solomon's public works program is portrayed as immense. Popular legend associates him with the temple, on which he spent seven years. But he spent thirteen years on his own palace and invested vast resources in buildings and other public works around Jerusalem and elsewhere. He had a minister in charge of forced labor (*mas*; Adoniram ben Abda, 3:6); Jeroboam, his man in charge of the forced labor (*sēbel*) of the house of Joseph, was after his death to be king of northern Israel. The exact significance of the two terms for forced labor escapes us. Undoubtedly, Solomon is portrayed as one of the great builders.

In the biblical text, detailed attention is given to the construction of the Jerusalem temple and its consecration. Initially (Heb., 5:15–32;

NRSV, 5:1–18), there is an account of the transactions between Solomon and the Phoenician, King Hiram of Tyre, that preceded the Phoenician contribution to the temple building. First Kings 6–7 provides details of the construction and associated buildings, while chapter 8 describes the ceremony of consecration of the temple, including Solomon's prayer. Chapter 9 begins with YHWH's response to Solomon's prayer.

It is not possible here to go into detail on the finer points of Solomonic temple design or on the contribution of Phoenician technology. Some of the biblical text bears clear marks of post-Solomonic composition. Concerning the substantial points of the temple, its fittings, and the Phoenician contribution to its construction, William Dever deserves to be heard: "The fact is that we now have direct Bronze and Iron Age parallels for every single feature of the 'Solomonic temple' as described in the Hebrew Bible; and the best parallels come from, and only from, the Canaanite-Phoenician world of the 15th–9th centuries" (Dever 2001, 145; cf. 144–57). Details may be followed up in specialist studies; here our task is to look to significance.

In 1 Kgs 5, verses 3–7 are replete with deuteronomistic expressions, with the exception of verses 4b and 6. It is probable that the speech given Solomon has been thoroughly rewritten by deuteronomistic editors, while what precedes and follows has been left pretty much alone. This kind of rewriting by deuteronomistic editors is probable at the start of chapters 3 (vv. 6–15) and 9 (vv. 3–5), and also possible in chapter 8 (vv. 14–25). The Jerusalem temple is of central importance in the Deuteronomistic History (cf. Deut 12:10–11); in these chapters, skilled highlighting can be expected from deuteronomistic editors and other interested parties. Here the theological reason is given why David could not build the temple, and Solomon's undertaking is situated within God's promise.

First Kings 6 is concerned with the temple proper, the structure itself and its fittings. Notice of the completion of the core structure is given at verse 9a and repeated in verse 14. In verses 11–13, a speech of the LORD is reported (to be discussed shortly). In 7:1–12, the construction of the other buildings in the palace complex is succinctly noted. The rest of the chapter is substantially devoted to the furnishings of the temple proper.

The divine speech in 6:11–13 is remarkable. It comes at the completion of the core structure, and anticipates something of God's speech in 9:3–9. Three points need highlighting. First, the king's conduct, not the temple he is building, is determinative of the future. Second, depending on Solomon's behavior, the promise made to David (cf. 2 Sam 7:12–15) will be established; what was unconditional has become conditional (cf. 1 Kgs 2:4; 8:25; 9:4–5). Third, the consequences of Solomon's (good) conduct impact primarily on the people ("I will dwell among the children of Israel, and will not forsake my people Israel," 6:13). Here, at the moment when the structure of the temple is completed, a speech is attributed to God in which the temple is downgraded in comparison with the conduct of the king. It is possible to understand the specification of Solomon's conduct as an example of deuteronomistic legalism, although the expression is highly abstract. It is also possible to understand it as a globalizing reference to good conduct—to those values that embody life (cf. Deut 30:15–20). The achievement of the building that is so central to deuteronomistic ideology is subordinated to the embodiment of life values in the person of the king. The temple Solomon builds matters less than the life he leads. Solomon's conduct is not correlated with the division of the kingdom or the survival of the Davidic dynasty; his leadership is correlated with God's relationship to Israel ("dwell with"; "not forsake"). This divine speech, as the core of the temple has been built, foreshadows what will be said in more detail after the temple's consecration (cf. 9:1–9). Solomon's conduct is to be the touchstone of Israel's fate. These two demanding divine speeches (6:11–13 and 9:1–9) bracket the establishment of Israel's most significant religious building, the Jerusalem temple. A people's identity and destiny are determined by its faith—in this case, embodied in its political leadership—rather than by its fabric. The ultimate achievement of our lives is ourselves and those we touch.

It is likely that 6:11–13 is a late addition. Read as present text, it functions as above, with the whole narrative a meditation on the correlation between the conduct of the king and the fate of the people. If emphasis is given to the status of both 6:11–13 and 9:6–9 as additions, there is the remarkable claim—made with clarifying hindsight—that the people's destiny was determined almost from the beginning by the behavior of Solomon, the builder of the temple.

Temples not only have to be built; they have to be consecrated. The ark of the covenant that had played a key role in the narrative, moving from Shiloh to Jerusalem via Philistine cities and Kiriath-jearim, had to be installed in the new temple. Everybody who was anybody had to be there; those left out were put in later. With the transfer of the ark completed, it was Solomon's job as king to name the moment and pronounce the prayer. Note that after this chapter, the ark is not mentioned again in the books of Kings; in the prophets, it is mentioned only at Jer 3:16, in the Psalms at Ps 132:8. Note also the considerable divergence between the accounts of the making of the ark by Moses for the two tablets (Deut 10:1–5) and by Bezalel at Moses' command for the tent sanctuary (Exod 25:10–22; 37:1–9).

According to Exodus, when "Moses finished the work" (Exod 40:33) the cloud covered the tent and even Moses was not able to enter it because of the cloud. Here, when the ark has been set in place, "a cloud filled the house of the LORD, so that the priests could not stand to minister because of the cloud" (8:10–11). The work was finished; an exalted house had been built for God "to dwell in forever" (8:13).

The king, presiding over all the assembly, situates the celebration broadly within the context of God's words to David (cf. 2 Sam 7:1–17). From the time Israel was brought out of Egypt, YHWH had not chosen a city to build a temple for his name, but had chosen David to lead Israel. And now, according to God's word, in Jerusalem the temple has been built by Solomon for God's name and for the ark (8:20–21). Having blessed YHWH in this recital of the past, Solomon turns to prayer. God's promise has been fulfilled in part and in part lies in the future. Verse 24 must refer to the temple David's son would build; the promise has been fulfilled. Verse 25 picks up a second aspect, necessarily as yet unfulfilled: the secure dynasty and the "throne that shall be established forever" (2 Sam 7:16). Unconditional in 2 Sam 7, it has here been made conditional: "if only your children look to their way, to walk before me as you have walked before me" (1 Kgs 8:25). Verse 26 takes up a third aspect, the house "for my name" (2 Sam 7:13; cf. 1 Kgs 8:29: "the place of which you said, 'My name shall be there'"). Solomon's plea is made in verses 29–30 and very skillfully so. The text has reached a safe distance from 1 Kgs 8:13 and the building of an exalted house, a place for God "to dwell in forever." The caution has been voiced in verse 27. YHWH's own words to David are quoted about "a house for my name" (2 Sam 7:13) and "the place of which you said, 'My name shall be there.'" (1 Kgs 8:29). Solomon's plea is magnificent but modest: "that your eyes may be open night and day toward this house" (8:29). YHWH's answer to this prayer is given in 9:3, adding the element of God's heart: "I have heard your prayer and your plea, which you made before me: I have consecrated this house that you have built, and put my name there forever; my eyes and my heart will be there for all time" (9:3). Among other signals, the concern for God's "name" betrays the presence of deuteronomistic editing in this material.

Before this, however, the text turns to the future. There is a distinct shift of focus. It is about prayer "toward this place," and it is the prayer "of your servant and of your people Israel" (8:29b–30). In all, there are seven prayers—ranging from sin against another, involving an oath within the temple, to defeat and captivity, as a result of sin, and prayed in exile—asking that God in heaven might heed and forgive. At the end, the text modulates back into the present celebration (vv. 52–53), includes an inauspicious prayer that God may not "leave us or abandon us" (v. 57; it does not bode well), and ends with the appropriate celebratory sacrifices and a seven-day festival (8:54–66).

What is couched as the LORD's response to Solomon's prayer is set within a second appearance, similar to the earlier one at Gibeon (3:4–14). The repeated theophanic setting is indicative of the great importance placed on the words given God in this response. Chronicles has its equivalent to 1 Kgs 9:1–9 (cf. 2 Chr 7:15–22), but there is no similar equivalent to 1 Kgs 6:11–13 and nothing to parallel 1 Kgs 11:1–13.

As in the cases already mentioned (3:6–15; 5:3–7; and possibly 8:14–25), in 9:3–5 a speech with marked Deuteronomistic characteristics follows an apparently unaltered introduction (vv. 1–2). In the text, first, God responds to Solomon's prayer; the temple is guaranteed "for all time"—unconditionally (v. 3). Second, the Davidic dynasty's rule over the united kingdom ("the throne of Israel") is guaranteed, but is conditional on the behavior of Solomon: "if you [singular] walk before me . . . with integrity of heart and uprightness . . ." (v. 4). When Solomon fails, this is spelled out: The kingdom will be torn away in the next generation; one tribe will remain under Davidic rule, for the sake of David and Jerusalem (cf. 11:9–13).

The text goes on after 9:5, however. Signals in verses 6–9 point to a late addition, therefore with the considerable benefit of hindsight. First Kings 9:6–9 is a remarkable statement that picks up something of 6:11–13; already in Solomon, this dispensation of the people of Israel is doomed. The condition for this, which extends beyond Solomon ("you and your children," etc.), is expressed in verse 6; the consequences, first for the people and second for the temple, are expressed in verse 7a. The unconditional commitment to the temple is here reversed: "The house that I have consecrated for my name I will cast out of my sight" (v. 7a). Verse 7b is unfolded in verses 8–9 to picture total disaster for Israel. While 11:13 leaves a hope and a base for a reforming king like Josiah, 9:6–9 leaves no hope at all. As pointers to the future, at the crowning moment of the consecration of the Jerusalem temple, 6:11–13 and 9:6–9 cast an ominous shadow over Israel's future.

Two elements are involved in these chapters but need to be kept separate. First, there is God's long-term commitment to the temple, while Davidic rule over the united kingdom is threatened and will be definitely short-term (basically, 1 Kgs 2:4; 8:25; 9:4–5). Second, there is the picture of overwhelming disaster for the people of Israel in the long term (1 Kgs 6:11–13 and 9:6–9). First Kings 11:1–13 does not permit even a faint glimmer of hope that Solomon's conduct might be marked by integrity and fidelity; it is not. First Kings 11:1–13 seals the fate of a united kingdom. It will take until the end of the book of Kings to assess Israel's story in the light of 6:11–13 and 9:6–9.

After this shadow has been cast, 9:10–25 is devoted to Solomon's settlement with Hiram, the forced labor he used for his building activities, and sundry other issues.

1 Kings 9:26–10:29   Solomon: the wise and wealthy

The temptation is to focus treatment on the visit of the Queen of Sheba, but there is more to the block than that. In addition to an account of her visit (10:1–10, 13), the text covers extensively issues of Solomon's sea trade and material wealth, as well as his wisdom and world renown. The figure of Solomon assumes legendary proportions (e.g., "Your wisdom and prosperity far surpass the report that I had heard," 10:7). Between the conclusion of his building activities and his lapse from grace, traditions are gathered here that reflect Solomon's wealth and wisdom. Dating this tradition is difficult; it is probable that some of the traditions are early and some late. Some are laudatory, exalting Solomon; others can be assessed more negatively, criticizing Solomon's excess. The interpretative moves available are of interest. As present text, any celebration of his wealth and wisdom is ironic immediately before his lapse into apostasy. As later additions, it is surprising that the critical aspect is not more explicit. What is read as laudatory or critical will largely reflect the stance of the reader; the text, despite what is to come, refrains from overt evaluation.

1 Kings 11:1–43   Solomon: the apostate

Gathered in chapter 11 are first a report of Solomon's active apostasy, involving "many foreign women" and their gods, followed by a report of God's anger and its consequences for the people after Solomon's death. Second, two traditions are noted of "adversaries" (*sāṭut\aṭun*) raised up by God against Solomon. Third, there is the prophetic tradition of Ahijah, the prophet from Shiloh, who proclaims God's word to Jeroboam in remarkable terms: "You shall reign over all that your soul desires; you shall be king over Israel. . . . I will be with you, and will build you an enduring house, as I built for David, and I will give Israel to you" (11:37–38).

As a response to Solomon's apostasy, this action and speech of Ahijah's has to be situated within an extensive context. Ahijah will shortly pronounce sentence of dismissal on Jeroboam (1 Kgs 14:1–16). Viewed within the longer term, three kings of Israel, and only three, were anointed by a prophet: Saul by Samuel (king-designate, *nāgîd*), David by Samuel (king-to-be), and Jehu by Elisha's disciple (king). Jeroboam was designated by Ahijah. Three kings were dismissed by prophets: Saul by Samuel, Jeroboam by Ahijah, and Ahab by Elijah. Setting Saul and David apart, the three remaining kings—Jeroboam, Ahab, and Jehu—all belong within the northern kingdom. It is probable that these traditions were given their present formulation in association with Jehu's coup that "wiped out Baal from Israel" (2 Kgs 10:28; for details, see Campbell 1986; Campbell and O'Brien 2000). With Saul and David, God is portrayed establishing Israel's monarchy, despite the preservation of traditions that regarded the move to monarchy as apostasy. The setting up of the northern kingdom under Jeroboam and its reform under Jehu are equally attributed to God. Precisely what theological moves were being pursued here is not yet clear. Noteworthy in these sections of Samuel–Kings is the interplay between the expression of God's will and its realization in history.

The exchange between Ahijah and Jeroboam is portrayed as private: "The two of them were alone in the open country" (11:29). Nevertheless, Solomon got to hear of something and Jeroboam fled to Egypt and remained there till Solomon's death. With the future laid out— Solomon's son to succeed him in Jerusalem and Jeroboam as king to take ten tribes into a new kingdom—the text can bring the account of Solomon's reign to an end (11:41–43).

THE KINGDOMS OF NORTH AND SOUTH:
ISRAEL AND JUDAH
1 KINGS 12:1—2 KINGS 17:41

As noted in the initial overview, the book of Kings is organized according to the sequence of kings. The narrative "achieves this by a certain synchronicity. Each king is dated in relation to his colleague in the other kingdom. The king in one kingdom is followed through until the end of his reign, at which point the narrative backtracks to deal with those who meantime have become king in the other kingdom. By switching back and forth, the narrative progresses simply enough. Prophetic stories are set within the reigns of kings" (above). This pattern of organization did not apply to Solomon's reign, before the division of the kingdom; of course, it does not apply after the fall of Samaria. The major prophetic interventions occur within the story of the northern kingdom: the Ahijah cycle, Elijah cycle, Elisha cycle, and the comment immediately following the fall of the north. To keep discussion here within bounds, the organization is more schematic than is the biblical text.

There is a substantial expansion in the LXX following 1 Kgs 12:24 (= 3 Reigns 12:24a–z). It is helpful to be aware of the content of such an expansion; it, and others like it, can offer alternative traditions, variant readings and alternative translations, or imaginative interpretations, and so on. In this case, a notice is given of Solomon's death and Rehoboam's accession (v. a), a notice about Jeroboam (vv. b–f), a prophecy from Ahijah of the death of Jeroboam's child (vv. g–n), a prophecy from Shemaiah concerning the formation of northern Israel (v. o), and an account of Rehoboam's consultation on taxes (vv. p–z). (For a brief notice, see Jones, comm.; 248–49; fuller discussion is available in Trebolle Barrera 1990 [and, for the earlier miscellanies at 1 Kgs 2:35a–k and 2:46a–l, see Gooding 1976; later there is also 1 Kgs 16:28a–h]). It would be unwise to underestimate the wide variety and wealth of ancient Israel's literary traditions and literary activity.

Before going into the text's account of the northern kingdom of Israel, it is worth recognizing a couple of factors that are not widely emphasized in biblical studies. First, according to the MT, the northern kingdom was given its start by prophets in God's name (Ahijah and Shemaiah), was seriously shaken up by prophets (Elijah and Elisha), and ended in oblivion, overrun by the Assyrians. It appears as a failure; it achieved nothing. A thorough condemnation at its end however (2 Kgs 17:7–20) is applied to both Israel and Judah (cf. vv. 13, 19). Second, while the Deuteronomists at the end of the process were convinced that Jeroboam's sin, the fatal sin of the north, was apostasy, the texts at the start of the process (i.e., 1 Kgs 12–13) do not appear to share that conviction and cannot be said to be clear about what Jeroboam's sin was. From a religious point of view, the period of the northern kingdom—a couple of centuries—is an enigma. Initiated by God, nothing came of it.

1 Kings 12:1–14:20   At the beginning

Something is brewing, but the text is coy about it. "All Israel" has come to Shechem, and Rehoboam, Solomon's son, has gone up there to be made king (12:1). In ordinary circumstances, these events should happen in Jerusalem; clearly these are not ordinary circumstances. Forewarning was given in chapter 11; Ahijah had given God's word to Jeroboam: "I will take the kingdom away from his son and give it to you—that is, the ten tribes" (11:35). As is usual in these texts, what God proposes through a prophet is brought about through the usual dynamics of secular life. For the text, the two are inextricably intertwined.

Kings do not normally hold elections. Rehoboam holds one and loses it, on the perennial issue of taxation. The text says it is God's will (12:15). The role Jeroboam may have played is uncertain. According to 12:3, he is there before the negotiations; according to 12:20, he appears to have been summoned late in the proceedings (for views in the LXX, see Gooding 1967). Preparations by Rehoboam to recover the north by force (cf. 2 Sam 20) are emphatically prohibited in God's name by the prophet Shemaiah (12:21–24: "This thing is from me").

Once he is made king over the north, Jeroboam has to organize his kingdom, including a capital and appropriate places of worship. He is quite right in thinking that for his people to worship in the southern capital of Jerusalem would be political suicide (12:27). Hence the famous episode of the golden calves and the statement, "Here are your gods [OR: is your God], O Israel, who brought you up out of the land of Egypt" (12:28). In Exod 32:5, the interpretation given by Aaron is clearly intended as orthodox (i.e., festival for YHWH). The calves can have been understood as pedestals for the divinity rather than as idols. "On Jeroboam's sin, the text is almost delphic, shrouding detail in obscurity and double meaning" (Campbell and O'Brien 2000, 325; cf. 325–26, 374–76; also Jones, comm., 1:257–59). There are two references to this thing/matter becoming sin; one at 12:30 referring to the calves and one at 13:34 referring to the indiscriminate consecration of priests for the high places: "This matter became sin to the house of Jeroboam, so as to cut it off and to destroy it from the face of the earth." We are left in the dark on details. The sin is not automatically to be identified with the worship of Baal; see, for example, 2 Kgs 3:3–4 and 10:28, 31, where Baal is rejected but the sin of Jeroboam ben Nebat remains.

In my judgment, it would be easy to associate this fundamental sin of Jeroboam's with the golden calves, if only 12:30 said that this became a sin *for Israel* (as the Lucianic recension of the LXX does). The indiscriminate consecration of priests for the high places would certainly qualify as the fundamental sin, but in that case "the house of Jeroboam" (13:34) needs to be understood as the kingdom of northern Israel—which runs strongly against the usage of the biblical text (cf. esp. 1 Kgs

14:14). If the charge against Jeroboam (1 Kgs 14:9) is taken as the paradigm—where the indiscriminate consecration of priests is not mentioned—it would appear that the fatal "sin of Jeroboam" by which he caused Israel to sin was the generalized worship of other gods. In specific instances, the worship of Baal might have been rejected (e.g., 2 Kgs 3:3–4 and 10:28, 31) while the worship of some other gods might have been retained. An attractive option is that "the sin of Jeroboam" by which he caused Israel to sin was specifically the making of images (the calves, understood as either pediment for YHWH or symbol for Baal) and also, possibly, the fragmenting of the single focus of YHWH worship, by the casting of two and their positioning at either extremity of the kingdom (i.e., Bethel and Dan)—with local priesthoods. This is neither simple nor clear.

The account of Jeroboam's measures for worship is followed by a prophetic story which begins with a man of God coming out of Judah and prophesying against the newly established altar and the truth of his word that leads to his death for disobedience (1 Kgs 13). As the text now stands, in a prophecy against the altar, Josiah is named some three hundred years before his time—unusual in prophecy. It is possible that later editing transformed the original prophecy into a sign validating the edited version. The weight for the present of the total story is that the prophecy is true and points to Josiah's future reform.

Jeroboam's punishment will not wait so long. The text's statement is emphatic: "You have not been like my servant David, . . . you have done evil above all those who were before you and have gone and made for yourself other gods, and cast images, provoking me to anger, and have thrust me behind your back; therefore, I will bring evil upon the house of Jeroboam" (14:8–9). "Above all those who were before you" suggests the stereotyped phrasing of editors centuries later. His son dies. His own death is reported immediately, despite a reign that lasted twenty-two years (14:20).

Prophetic traditions: Ahijah

The inauguration of a new kingdom, instigated by Ahijah and protected by Shemaiah, opens with a twenty-two-year reign. Beyond Rehoboam's folly that triggered it and Jeroboam's folly that will destroy it, the text focuses on matters prophetic.

Jeroboam's commission was given by Ahijah, with the symbolic action of the torn cloak (11:26–40). The dismissal was also given by Ahijah, along with the death sentence for Jeroboam's son (14:1–20). In between, two other prophetic traditions are included: Shemiah's and an anonymous prophecy. Shemaiah's prophecy (12:22–24) prevented military power being used to crush the nascent kingdom in the north. The anonymous prophecy announced the nascent kingdom's end. Prophetic power is on display, predominating in the text. For all of the annals and history to come, the prophets are never far away.

1 Kings 14:21–2 Kings 15:12   In the middle

With the death of Jeroboam, there is a rash of unguided kings. Except for Jehu ben Hanani's summary word condemning Baasha, prophets have no part to play. In the south, the dynasty unfolds, with father followed by son—four of them: Rehoboam, Abijam, Asa, and Jehoshaphat. In the north, on the other hand, no dynasty is dominant, with seven kings in the same period. Jeroboam's son, Nadab, succeeds him and is assassinated by Baasha, who promptly wipes out the house of Jeroboam. Baasha's son, Elah, succeeds him and is assassinated by Zimri, who in a short reign of seven days kills all the house of Baasha. Omri besieges Zimri, who commits suicide, burning the palace at Tirzah over himself. Omri then faces a rival, Tibni; their armies fight, Tibni is defeated and dies, and Omri becomes king. The text's judgment on Omri is: "He did more evil than all who were before him" (1 Kgs 16:25); history's judgment is: "His influence is attested by the use of his name by the Assyrians (bit Humri) to designate Israel long after his death" (McKenzie 1965, 627). Omri was succeeded by his son Ahab, who would marry Jezebel and give his endorsement to the worship of Baal.

The text signals selected events but does not provide a comprehensive picture. Shishak, pharaoh of Egypt, plunders Jerusalem in Rehoboam's fifth year. There had been war between Rehoboam and Jeroboam; it continues throughout Abijam's life and goes on under Asa and Baasha, with a note of Baasha's fortifying Ramah and Asa's alliance with Damascus. Omri buys the land and builds the capital Samaria. Ahab, Omri's son, marries a Sidonian princess, Jezebel, and establishes an altar and temple for Baal in the newly built city of Samaria, as well as a symbol for the goddess Asherah (cf. 1 Kgs 14:15, 23; 15:13; 16:33; 18:19). A crisis is coming to a head.

Prophetic traditions: Elijah

Although the crisis is not spelled out in detail, it is there between the lines of the narrative. At stake is the survival or at least the dominance of Yahwism in the kingdom of northern Israel (cf. 2 Kgs 17:10, 16; important for the background behind the far-from-objective text is

Miller and Hayes 1986, 271–74). The three previously long-reigning kings—Jeroboam, 22 years; Baasha, 24 years; Ahab, 22 years—all are given bad reputations religiously. Despite slaughtering 450 prophets of Baal (with 400 prophets of Asherah mentioned eating at Jezebel's table, 1 Kgs 18:19), Elijah describes himself as the sole surviving prophet of YHWH: "I alone am left" (19:10, 14; cf. 18:22).

Into the portrayal of this conflict the narrative pitches the Elijah cycle and a couple of associated prophetic traditions. The Elijah traditions of 1 Kgs 17 legitimate the great prophet and set up the drought story, within which the confrontation on Mount Carmel will be enacted. The confrontation orchestrated by Elijah faces one stark question: Who is indeed God (cf. 18:24)? The people's answer in the narrative, after the confrontation: YHWH indeed is God; YHWH indeed is God (18:39).

This success might have seemed enough but, according to the text, the figure of Elijah is to cast a long shadow. His achievement on Mount Carmel incites Jezebel's mortal enmity and he flees for his life (19:1–3). The text takes him to Sinai (Horeb), the place of Israel's encounter with God. There three names are brought under his authority: Hazael, as king of Aram-Damascus; Jehu, as king of northern Israel; Elisha, as his successor (19:15–17). The association with Elisha is cemented immediately (19:19–21); the other two will be delayed. The conflict between Elijah and Ahab over Ahab's judicial murder of Naboth and seizure of Naboth's vineyard—"Have you killed and also taken possession?" (21:19)—leads to the most fearful condemnation of Ahab (vv. 20–24) and prepares the way for Jehu's anointing as king of northern Israel.

On either side of this chapter (in the MT) are traditions involving prophets in wars between Israel and Aram-Damascus (southern region of modern Syria). In their present context, they facilitate an association of Elijah with Hazael, future king of Aram-Damascus, and they provide supportive evidence of the reality of prophetic power and authority. Like 1 Kgs 13, 1 Kgs 22 is also an insightful reflection of the tension between prophet and prophet. As to the origins of the traditions, Jones comments:

> Nevertheless the reliability of the biblical tradition is suspect for several reasons. References to Ahab are surprisingly few, and in several of its occurrences the king's name is unnecessary because of the presence of the title 'the king of Israel'; this may suggest that the proper name was added to suit the present context. Moreover, because the phrase 'the king of Israel' is so characteristic of the Elisha cycle, a link is established between these narratives and the Elisha tradition. . . . Conse-

quently, the three battle-accounts in 1 Kg. 20:1–43; 22:1–38 are dated
in the dynasty of Jehu rather than at the end of the Omride dynasty.
(Jones, comm., 2:337–38; see also Miller and Hayes 1986, 252–55)

Jehoshaphat came to the throne in Jerusalem in the fourth year of
Ahab. His reign is signaled at the end of 1 Kgs 22; in contrast with
Chronicles, almost nothing is said of it beyond the standard formulas.
In Jehoshaphat's seventeenth year, Ahab's son Ahaziah succeeded him.
Ahaziah's accession leads into the end of the Elijah cycle and the tran-
sition to Elisha.

Second Kings opens with a reference to Moab's rebellion against
Israel after the death of Ahab (2 Kgs 1:1). The text does not pick this
up until chapter 3, when the transition to Elisha is complete. Ahab has
been condemned (1 Kgs 21:17–24); the disaster has been delayed a generation (21:27–29). It will be actualized in Jehu's coup against Joram,
son of Ahab, king of Israel (2 Kgs 9). In the narrative, Jehu's coup is
legitimated by the action of Elisha's disciple, who anointed Jehu king
(2 Kgs 9:1–10). The question users of the text have to face is why almost
eight chapters are taken up with traditions about Elijah and Elisha.

One element of an answer is the need for continuity; what Elijah has
begun with the confrontation on Mount Carmel and the condemnation of Ahab has to be brought to conclusion with the installation of
Jehu as Ahab's replacement. This process was signaled in 1 Kgs
19:15–16 and immediately begun in the case of Elisha (19:19–21).
What has been begun must be completed. Second is the need to establish Elisha's legitimacy as the successor to Elijah. Third is the need to
demonstrate Elisha's power and authority as prophet. In the course of
these major moves, some traditions of less immediate relevance may
also have been included.

The tradition of Elijah's involvement in Ahaziah's death is told in
two versions (vv. 2–8 and 9–16). Both make the same point: Ahaziah
shall surely die (vv. 4 and 16). The first version (vv. 2–8) is a particularly
good example of the density of a story text that has great potential for
unfolding by a storyteller. What the messengers tell the king in verse 6
is not reported between verses 4 and 5. It is implied; it can be easily
imagined. A good storyteller would be unlikely to pass over its possibilities. The second version (vv. 9–16) has structural similarities with
the story of Saul's experience with Samuel (1 Sam 19:18–24).

Two points are made in both versions of the story and are relevant
to the surroundings. (1) After the episode on Mount Carmel, the les-
son should have been learned: seek YHWH and not Baal (cf. vv. 3 and

16). (2) Across the two versions, the message is clear: The prophet has the power of life and death over kings and captains, the monarchy and the military. This has been the case for Elijah; it will be the case for Elisha.

Prophetic traditions: Elisha

The transition will take Elijah off the scene and leave Elisha—a very different figure—as his successor. This highly stylized formulation reflects on what it means to be prophet: someone with utter commitment and independence, with knowledge and authority, with insight to see what few can see. Elisha qualified to carry on the work of Elijah (2 Kgs 2).

The bulk of the stories of Elisha provide substance for the figure whose disciple will be responsible for the singularly significant prophetic endorsement of Jehu. According to the text, a disciple of Elisha's anointed Jehu king. As we have seen, only two other kings were anointed by prophets (Saul by Samuel as king-designate; David by Samuel as king-to-be). Other kings may have been anointed, but not by prophets. Elisha's disciple and Jehu were in private for the anointing; a similar concern for privacy is visible in the cases of Saul and David. Speeches of designation and/or dismissal were addressed to Jeroboam and Ahab; a similar speech of designation is addressed to Jehu by Elisha's disciple. It has been argued that a core structure involving the prophets within Samuel–Kings can be attributed in its final form to the group associated with Elisha (as noted earlier, see Campbell 1986; Campbell and O'Brien 2000, esp. 24–32). If this is the case, it is not surprising that stories of Elisha are included in the text here.

The stories may not be what we expect of Israel's prophets. Elisha is not Elijah; he seems, especially at first sight, more wonder-worker than awe-inspiring prophet. But both men multiplied oil and restored children to life (Elijah: 1 Kgs 17:8–16 and 17:17–24; Elisha: 2 Kgs 4:1–7 and 4:11–37); the stories are different and worth comparing—not to Elisha's detriment. Allowing for some adjustment, the Elisha traditions are for the most part not inappropriate to their context.

In 2 Kgs 3, the presence of Jehoshaphat, treated with respect, associates this story with the story of Micaiah in 1 Kgs 22. In the latter, the two kings send for the prophet to come to them; in the former, the three kings when they need rescue have to go to the prophet (v. 12). In chapter 5, the king of Israel tears his clothes in fear, but the apparently impossible demand does not trouble Elisha, who brings healing and faith to Naaman, the senior Syrian general; there is indeed a prophet in Israel (v. 8). In chapters 6–7, Elisha totally outwits the king of Aram (vv. 8–23) and, in the following story, Elisha rightly predicts to a despairing king of Israel the immediate deliverance of Samaria and the abundance of food in the starving city (cf. 6:24–7:20). Finally, in chapter 8, at home the mention of Elisha is enough to move a king to action (vv. 1–6), and abroad Elisha's reputation is such that, when he visits Damascus, King Ben-hadad of Aram sends Hazael to him with forty camel loads of "all kinds of goods of Damascus" (v. 8), and Elisha predicts Hazael will be king. The prophet is right—Hazael murders Ben-Hadad the next day (vv. 7–15). Not infrequently, the stories reveal the prophet doing what the king had proved unable to do.

On the domestic front, Elisha's actions seem more homely, more in keeping with what is expected of the local wonder-worker. They do more, however, than align Elisha with Elijah; they represent the prophet caring about health and welfare in the community—the care for the common good that is the responsibility of kings. So, as noted above, two stories parallel two of the traditions of Elijah (2 Kgs 4:1–7, 8–37); two of them have the prophet provide for the needs of the community, by sanitizing stew and multiplying food (4:38–41, 42–44). Elijah may have been a lone outsider and Elisha, his successor, a leader of a prophetic group; nevertheless, both men have the spirit of God and dismiss and designate kings for the good of their people.

The text moves to set the scene for Jehu's coup, to be authorized by Elisha. King Ahaziah of Judah (whose mother was Athaliah, granddaughter of King Omri of Israel) and King Joram of Israel waged war together against Hazael of Aram-Damascus. Joram was wounded and returned to recover in Jezreel; Ahaziah paid a royal visit to the convalescent king. The scene is set; both kings are in the same town.

According to the text, Jehu is in conference with the army commanders when a disciple of Elisha's announces himself with a message for Jehu. The two withdraw into privacy inside, and Elisha's disciple anoints Jehu king and commissions him to strike down the house of Ahab. Elijah's threat is to be realized. The result: the army commanders acclaim Jehu king, and in a vicious military coup both Joram and Ahaziah are killed; in the words of the text, "Jehu wiped out Baal from Israel" (2 Kgs 10:28). The coup was a bloody affair. It cost the lives of the kings of Israel and Judah; Jezebel, Ahab's queen; the seventy sons of Ahab being schooled in Samaria; the relatives of the royal family of Judah on a visit; and the priests, prophets, and worshipers of Baal. A hundred years later, Hosea did not approve (cf. Hos 1:4); for all the blood shed, the measures against Baal worship were, in the long term, ineffectual. At the time, it must have seemed a good idea. The prophets around Elisha gave the coup their approval; God is reported to have given Jehu a four-generation dynasty as a reward (10:30). In the light of passages such as 2 Kgs 9:25–26, 36–37; 10:10, 17, it seems clear that variant traditions as well as subsequent editing impacted on the account of Jehu's coup itself, the prophetic preparation for it (Elijah), and approval of it (Elisha); conclusions are contested (cf. Gray, 537–39; Jones, comm., 2:450–54; Nelson, comm., 199–206; in detail, Schmitt 1972; Barré 1988; White 1997). The precise configuration of text, event, and the flow of influence between prophets and plotters is complex and details remain uncertain.

The text underscores another area of uncertainty. "Jehu wiped out Baal from Israel. But Jehu did not turn aside from the sins of Jeroboam son of Nebat, which he caused Israel to commit—the golden calves that were in Bethel and Dan" (10:28–29). In some eyes at least, the sin of Jeroboam was not identical with the worship of Baal; we are left uncertain as to what precisely that sin was (cf. Jones, comm., 2:472–73).

Jehu occupied the throne of northern Israel and was followed by a four-generation dynasty. Jehu reigned for twenty-eight years, and the three who followed him for seventeen, sixteen, and forty-one years respectively; the dynasty petered out with the six-month reign of Zechariah. The throne in Judah was vacant, thanks to Jehu's assassination of Ahaziah. The vacancy was filled by Israel's first and only queen, Athaliah, who reigned over Judah for six years. She was the daughter of King Ahab of Israel, married King Jehoram of Judah, and was the mother of Jehoram's son, King Ahaziah (cf. 8:18, 25–27). According to Chronicles, when Jehoram became king "he put all his brothers to the sword" (2 Chr 21:2–4). Athaliah took the same path her husband had trodden, as well as Jehu; when she heard of the death of her son, Ahaziah, she promptly assassinated his children and then took the throne in their place. Jehosheba, Ahaziah's sister, saved one of his sons from the massacre. After six years, a coup organized by the priest Jehoiada, in conjunction with the palace guard and the temple guard, placed this son, Joash, who was seven years old, on the throne of Judah.

As readers will have realized, the historical narrative unrolling after Solomon in the book of Kings is circumscribed, with an unsystematic and often narrow focus. Israel and Judah are two small states, along with half a dozen others competing for space in the Levant, the Fertile Crescent that stretches between the big powerbrokers: Egypt in the southwest and Assyria, later Babylonia, later still Persia, in the northeast. Babylon took over the Assyrian Empire in the west around 612–605

B.C.E.; the Persian emperor, Cyrus, occupied Babylon in 539. Among the smaller fry were Phoenicia and Philistia, on the eastern coast of the Mediterranean, respectively north and south of Israel and Judah. Further to the south, and inland, were the nomadic Amalekites. Beyond the Jordan, from south of the Dead Sea moving northward, were Edom, Moab, and Ammon. Further north was Aram-Damascus (in the south of modern Syria) with its capital at Damascus. Other small states occupied the interstices, especially to Israel's north and northeast.

The text of Kings touches on incidents in relation to these neighboring states, incidents within or between Israel and Judah, and provides specific information on the kings of Israel and Judah. That information includes such details as age at accession, length of reign, often the manner of death and place of burial, with a final reference to the annals of the kings of Israel or Judah for further details. There is almost invariably a religious judgment, whether the king did or did not do what was right in the eyes of the LORD. This judgment was negative for all the kings of northern Israel, positive for two of the kings of Judah (Hezekiah and Josiah), partially positive for half a dozen others (Asa, Jehoshaphat, Jehoash, Amaziah, Azariah, Jotham—but the high places were not taken away), and negative for the rest (Abijam, Jehoram, Ahaziah, Ahaz, Manasseh, Amon, and the final four). Looming over both kingdoms was the increasingly ominous shadow of the great powers, above all Assyria, also Egypt, later Babylonia.

The Bible's "historical" material does not provide an economic history of the relative well-being of the two states. Military and political details are given, but scarcely systematically. Even the religious picture is often left vague. Whether the restricted focus of the text is due to the lack of information or the lack of interest among those responsible we do not know. Apart from the major prophetic interventions we have discussed, there are other notes of prophetic utterance or reports of limited divine intervention. A strong religious viewpoint was expressed in the early chapters under Solomon and again in 2 Kgs 17:7–23, but overall the record is largely left to speak for itself. Moral lessons are seldom drawn.

In the northern kingdom, even under Jehu, "the LORD began to trim off parts of Israel" (2 Kgs 10:32). Hazael of Aram-Damascus annexed much of the territory northeast of the Jordan. Under Jehoahaz, Jehu's son, the aggression was continued by Hazael and his son, Ben-hadad (13:3). This is one of the places where a theology of divine anger and compassion is expressed, alleging these to be at the back of the historical sequence: "The anger of the LORD was kindled against Israel, so that he gave them repeatedly into the hand of . . ." (13:3). "Therefore the LORD gave Israel a savior, so that they escaped . . ." (13:5; cf. 17:18–23; 24:2–4, 20). Nothing is noted for the reign of the son of Jehoahaz, beyond the observation that "he also did what was evil in the sight of the LORD; he did not depart from all the sins of Jeroboam son of Nebat" (13:11). Having reported the death of Jehoash/Joash (son of Jehoahaz), the text goes on to have him meet with the dying Elisha, make war on Ben-hadad of Aram, the Edomites, and Amaziah of Judah—which includes sacking the temple and breaking down a substantial section of the wall of Jerusalem (cf. 14:11–14). Jehoash's death is then reported again (14:15–16). A fully satisfactory explanation for this state of affairs in the text is yet to be advanced.

The third of Jehu's dynasty was Jeroboam II, who reigns for forty-one years and was probably one of northern Israel's great kings. In his time, Israel's borders are substantially expanded (cf. 14:25a). According to the biblical text, apart from this "he did what was evil in the sight of the LORD." With King Zechariah, who reigns in Samaria for six months, Jehu's dynasty came to an end (cf. 15:12).

In the southern kingdom, meanwhile, Queen Athaliah is followed by another King Jehoash, who had been educated by the priest Jehoiada and who is to enjoy a forty-year reign. The main item reported from his reign is how he bypasses clerical peculation to assure funds for the maintenance of the temple (12:4–16). How Jehoash buys off Hazael of Aram-Damascus is also mentioned. Jehoash is assassinated by two of his court; his son Amaziah succeeds him. Amaziah instigates a civil war with Jehoash of Israel, which he loses, with the result that Jehoash sacks the Jerusalem temple and destroys some two hundred yards of the city wall. Some fifteen years later, Amaziah is killed by conspirators and his son put on the throne. Leprosy keeps him out of public life, and his son, Jotham, runs the kingdom (15:5).

2 Kings 15:13–17:41   At the end

With the end of Jehu's dynasty, the northern kingdom of Israel petered out ingloriously, victim of the westward expansion of Assyrian power. Five kings were left. Shallum, who assassinated Zechariah, reigned for a month. Menahem killed him, took his throne, and reigned for ten years. His son, Pekahiah, reigned for two years; he was assassinated and replaced by Pekah, one of his military. Pekah held sway over Israel for twenty years before he fell victim to a conspiracy under Hoshea (15:30). Hoshea ruled for nine years; for the last three, his capital Samaria was besieged by the king of Assyria and captured in 722. As a result of the

Assyrian campaigns of 734–732 and 724–722, the northern kingdom of Israel was dissolved into the Assyrian provinces of Dor, Megiddo, and Gilead.

Pekah's conflict with Ahaz of Judah is noted below. The ominous shadow of Assyrian power needs to be briefly sketched first. Pul of Assyria (Tiglath-pileser III) moved against Menahem and was bought off with a thousand shekels of silver (15:19). The same Tiglath-pileser mounted a devastating campaign against Pekah (15:29), probably in association with the Syro-Ephraimite war against Ahaz of Judah (cf. 16:5–9). Finally, Shalmaneser V (726–722 B.C.E.) moved against King Hoshea and his capital of Samaria. Hoshea's appeal to the Egyptian pharaoh is noted as the treachery that triggered the Assyrian assault (17:4); it is an indicator of the political tension between the two great powers. Samaria withstood the siege for three years; then it fell and its inhabitants were deported. The northern kingdom of Israel was at an end.

In the south, King Azariah/Uzziah is said to have reigned for fifty-two years (15:2). He was succeeded by his son Jotham, who had been running the kingdom during his father's isolation with leprosy (15:5). According to the text, Jotham's own reign began in the second year of King Pekah of Israel and lasted sixteen years (15:32–33). His son Ahaz succeeded him and promptly came under attack from Pekah and Rezin, king of Aram-Damascus, who were strengthening their coalition against Tiglath-pileser III of Assyria. Ahaz appealed to the Assyrian for help, an appeal funded by the temple and royal treasures. Ahaz went to Damascus for an audience with Tiglath-pileser III and was sufficiently impressed with the altar there that he had a copy installed in Jerusalem. Ahaz is regarded in the biblical text as one of the thoroughly bad kings of Judah (cf. 16:1–4); shortly before the fall of Samaria, he was succeeded by his son Hezekiah, regarded as one of the thoroughly good kings of Judah (18:1–6).

After the fall of Samaria in 722 (2 Kgs 17:5–6), the text has a lengthy reflection on why it occurred, an interesting pointer to the complications of the text of Kings. It begins, "This occurred because . . ." (17:7), following directly on the fall of Samaria and exile of its population. It ends with a note that only Judah remains (17:18) but then notes that Judah also failed (17:19), before concluding with a summary reflection on northern Israel, "exiled from their own land to Assyria until this day" (17:23; cf. vv. 21–23). While the body of the reflection is aimed at northern Israel (cf. the two calves, v. 16), the prophets were sent to "Israel and Judah" (v. 13). Among the crimes alleged in the body of the reflection, some are exclusively reported against Judah:

> For example only Judah is accused of setting up pillars and asherim on
> the high places and burning incense there (1 Kgs 14:23; 22:43; 2 Kgs
> 12:4 [NRSV, 12:3]; 14:4; 15:4, 35a); only Davidic kings and Judah are
> accused of worshiping the host of heaven, of passing children through
> fire, and of using divination and sorcery (2 Kg 16:3; 21:6; 23:10).
> (Campbell and O'Brien 2000, 442 n. 60)

Blame for what has happened is placed on the people and not on
their God. They were warned. Why such an experiment should have
been undertaken in God's name is neither addressed nor explained.

THE KINGDOM OF JUDAH ALONE
2 KINGS 18–25

2 Kings 18–21   Hezekiah to Amon

Hezekiah was one of the two great reforming kings in the deuteronomistic record. His achievements are summed up in 2 Kgs 18:1–8, which
encapsulates something of what those responsible for these texts
expected of their kings. Hezekiah did what was right in the sight of the
LORD: he removed the high places, broke down the pillars, and cut
down the sacred pole; he broke the bronze serpent; he trusted in the
LORD the God of Israel; he held fast to the LORD and did not depart
from following him. The LORD was with him; wherever he went he
prospered. His encomium is pitched in the highest terms: "There was
no one like him among all the kings of Judah after him, or among those
who were before him" (18:5b—quite puzzling in the light of Josiah
after him and David before). It is highly likely that the energies of
Hezekiah's reign translated into intense literary activity; unfortunately,
practically speaking, we are unable to identify anything substantial with
any certainty.

It says something for the inclusive quality of the text of Kings that,
despite the encomium, two passages are strongly negative toward
Hezekiah: 18:14–16 and 20:12–19. Differing traditions find their way
into the Scriptures. Note that 18:14–16 is not found in the corresponding material in Isa 36; on the other hand, 20:12–19 is in Isa 39.
Sweeney observes that "the Isaiah version of the narrative appears to
have been produced in relation to the late-6th-century edition of the
book of Isaiah" (Sweeney 1996, 509).

The major single event of Hezekiah's twenty-nine-year reign is the
sudden abandonment of the Assyrian siege of Jerusalem in 701. The

complex of texts associated with this event is substantially shared with Isaiah (Isa 36–39). The classical analysis reveals two legendary accounts with a prayer and response (see Childs 1967; Clements 1980; for a visually helpful layout, see Campbell and O'Brien 2000, 448–54); an integrated view is given by Sweeney (1996, esp. 465–87). This is one of the cases in the biblical record where there is significant confirmation from Assyrian sources (for Sennacherib's annals, see *ANET*, 287–88); Sennacherib, naturally, does not mention the sudden withdrawal from Jerusalem which, understandably, is the high point of the biblical tradition.

Immediately following Hezekiah, the great reforming king, the text turns to his son, Manasseh. He had a fifty-five-year reign and plenty of time in which to reverse the reforms of his father and introduce evils of his own. Among other charges, he rebuilt the high places, erected altars for Baal, made a sacred pole, worshiped all the host of heaven and built altars for them in the temple, and installed a carved image of Asherah in the temple. The text gives him a thoroughly bad name: "Manasseh misled them [the people] to do more evil than the nations had done that the LORD destroyed before the people of Israel" (21:9; note the development in 2 Chr 33:10–13, radically different from 2 Kgs 21:10–16). Manasseh is accused of causing Judah to sin (21:11); only Jeroboam I is accused regularly of a similar sin regarding Israel. Beyond cultic issues ("besides the sin that he caused Judah to sin"), Manasseh is charged with social crime, the only king of Judah so accused: He filled Jerusalem with blood (21:16). The fact that, despite a fifty-five-year reign, so little is said about Manasseh in a near-contemporary document is a pointer to the specific focus of those responsible for the book of Kings—or the risks they ran (cf. 21:1–18, with more than half of the passage likely to reflect exilic or later additions).

Manasseh was succeeded by his son Amon, who followed in his father's footsteps. A conspiracy at his court saw him assassinated after two years (21:23). The text goes on that "the people of the land" killed all the conspirators and established Amon's son Josiah as king in his place (21:24). It is unexplained that the group which punished Amon's killers should then install his son on the throne—a son who would pursue policies diametrically opposed to those of his father. We may make suggestions; the text does not. The identity of the group known as "the people of the land" is almost impossible to pin down (cf. Oded 1977, 456–58; Jones, comm., 483–84, 602). The phrase occurs some fifty times in the Hebrew Scriptures and, with broad variations in time and context, has a wide variety of applications, from Genesis to Chronicles, and even within Kings from poor to wealthy, and so forth. "The people of the land" were involved in the succession of Jehoash, Josiah, and Jehoahaz (2 Kgs 11:14, 18–20; 21:24; 23:30); they may have been committed to the Davidic dynasty or to political stability or both. In the case of Amon's killers, they may have moved to protect the Davidic dynasty or to oppose an anti-Assyrian coup by Egyptian sympathizers, or again both. As so often in the biblical text, the intense political background remains background.

2 Kings 22:1–23:30   Josiah

Josiah's reign began when he was eight and lasted thirty-one years. Three chapters were devoted to Hezekiah; their core issue is the negotiations with the Assyrians. Almost two chapters are devoted to Josiah; their core issue is religious reform. Josiah's summary encomium is almost as idiosyncratic as Hezekiah's: "Before him there was no king like him, who turned to the LORD with all his heart, with all his soul, and with all his might, according to all the law of Moses; nor did any like him arise after him" (23:25).

The story of Josiah's reign begins with the story of his confrontation with the book of Deuteronomy (2 Kgs 22:3–23:3 [and 23:21–23]; cf. Lohfink 1978, esp. 320–22). The "book of the law" found during temple repairs in Josiah's eighteenth year is widely agreed to be substantially the lawcode of Deuteronomy. As Lohfink has ably argued, the topic is not how the book came to be found but how the king came to comply with the demands of the book. The complexity of the text is evident in Huldah's endorsement of the book and her condemnation in 22:16–17 of the people who are about "to perform the words of this covenant that were written in this book" (23:3). Some rewriting is evident here.

It is worth noting that here, as in the rest of Kings, the basic thrust of the narrative is report: this is what the king did. Exhortation, the appeal to what ought to be done, is largely left to the book of Deuteronomy. If the book of Kings is to be seen as basically composed in support of the Josianic reform, it can hardly function adequately in this way in isolation from the book of Deuteronomy (assuming, incidentally, that the deuteronomic regime for the king, Deut 17:14–20, is a later addition to the book). The book of Kings can provide evidence of the understanding and theology that supported the Josianic reform. The exhortations that advocated the stuff of this reform are restricted to the book of Deuteronomy.

The religious reforms carried out by Josiah are not summarized at the start, as they were for Hezekiah (18:3–6), but are sandwiched between the account of the conclusion of the covenant (23:1–3) and the proper observance of the Passover (23:21–23). Jones speaks of "two strands of tradition" of which the second is 23:4–20 (Jones, comm., 604–5); having established the unit, he then speaks of "different strands of tradition" within it (616; more recently, see Campbell and O'Brien 2000, 461–63).

However legitimate it may be to struggle to reconstruct the historical background in all of this, a primary task has to be the interpretation of the text rather than the history. Within the text, the focus on religious reform is evident. No attention is given to the international situation, significant as it was. The centralizing of so much on Jerusalem and the temple there would have had immense ramifications that go unmentioned. Patterns of worship in the country would have been disrupted; unemployment among the clergy would have been high. Considerable social disruption could be expected. The financial consequences would have been extensive (cf. Claburn 1973). About such matters, the text is silent.

What has to be said, painfully, is that although Josiah and his generation are portrayed fulfilling the law to the letter—despite the absence of reference to the lawbook in 23:4–20 (cf. Jones, comm., 616)—far from being rewarded with life and length of days (Deut 30:20), Josiah dies unexpectedly in battle (23:29). The text accounts for this by appeal to the provocations of Manasseh (23:26–27). This is a strange change of heart on the part of God (23:27). The historical understanding for Josiah's motivation in opposing Neco is well put by Jones: "Josiah was not unaware of the consequence for Judah in the event of Egyptian success against Babylon. In taking action against Neco in 609 B.C.E., he was throwing his dice for Babylon against Egypt and Assyria, and may have hoped for control over Palestine after their defeat by Babylon" (Jones, comm., 629). The theological dilemma is indicated by Sweeney: "The DtrH leaves the reader to wonder why this righteous monarch [Josiah] had to die. The DtrH provides no clear answer to this question" (Sweeney 2001, 4).

2 Kings 23:31–25:30 The end

The final four kings are all of Josiah's family: three sons and a grandson. All abandon his reform; perhaps they had no choice. Jehoahaz had a three-month reign. Egyptian power is evident: when Pharaoh Neco, responsible for Josiah's death, installed Eliakim on Josiah's throne, he changed his name to Jehoiakim and removed Jehoahaz to Egypt.

Babylonian hegemony began to replace Egyptian power. Guerrilla attacks against Judah were attributed to the extensive evil perpetrated by Manasseh (24:2–4). Jehoiachin followed his father Jehoiakim; he had a three-month reign before Nebuchadnezzar of Babylon took him prisoner. Nebuchadnezzar put Mattaniah on the throne, changing his name to Zedekiah. Zedekiah held power for eleven years. Toward the end, he risked rebellion against the king of Babylon, and this cost him dearly. Jerusalem was besieged by Nebuchadnezzar; Zedekiah tried to escape and was caught. He was brought before the king of Babylon, at Riblah far to the north, where his two sons were killed before his eyes and then his eyes put out. The ancients were as skilled as we are in the practice of inhuman cruelty. Zedekiah was taken in fetters to Babylon; no more is heard of him in the book of Kings (cf. Jer 52:11). The Babylonians installed Gedaliah as governor at Mizpah over the remnant of Judah. A final note concerns Jehoiachin, under house arrest in Babylon, and the recipient of favorable treatment—but it is left open whether this is a sign of hope or the signal of the end (as with Mephibosheth, 2 Sam 9). Jerusalem was sacked, Judah had lost its independence, and as a result the remaining kingdom of Israel was at an end.

READING THE WHOLE

1–2 Kings can come as a complete surprise to us—if we let them. They concern two nations and their kings, yet more than a third is about prophets (some seventeen chapters out of forty-seven). The books of Kings are about kings and there is not an unsullied hero among them all. Hezekiah dies in bed after showing his all to Babylonian envoys; Josiah dies in a battle where he had no place to be. David had God's favor, but a more undeserving hero is hard to imagine. Whatever else it is, 1–2 Kings tell a story of failure—divine failure. (Of course it is human failure too, but God might be expected to have known better, especially after Saul.) All this may sound a tad cynical, but it is not far from the reality depicted in the text.

According to the text, God had David anointed king-to-be by Samuel, God favored Solomon, God gave ten parts of the kingdom to Jeroboam; yet, according to the text, "the LORD was very angry with Israel . . . rejected all the descendants of Israel" (2 Kgs 17:18, 20) and "the LORD sent bands . . . against Judah to destroy it" (2 Kgs 24:2). Two books, Samuel and Kings, but they have the same outcome as two chapters did earlier, Gen 2 and 3—dismal failure. Thank God the story of the flood had been told, evoking wonderment at God's commitment to the impossible (cf. Gen 8:21–22). To the fate of history, there is the answer of faith:

> Just as I swore that the waters of Noah
> would never again go over the earth,
> so I have sworn that I will not be angry with you
> and will not rebuke you.
> For the mountains may depart
> and the hills be removed,
> but my steadfast love [*ḥesed*] shall not depart from you
> and my covenant of peace shall not be removed.
> (Isa 54:9–10)

Postscript

The Bible Unearthed (see chapter 1, 15–16) provides a helpful corrective to an uneducated and pious view of biblical history, but itself offers too many loose and sweeping statements; a couple of comments are in order with regard to David and Solomon. Finkelstein and Silberman occasionally exaggerate the Bible's claims the better to shoot them down. In our case, it is worth noting that the biblical record has David's forces fighting a long civil war with the house of Saul in the north. The "house of Saul" was no big deal; the "kingdom" of David need not have been either. The Philistines, defeated in a couple of battles (2 Sam 5:17–25), seem to have left David alone. Sure, the ark came to Jerusalem, Nathan's prophecy was articulated, 2 Sam 8 made the kind of claim that many a proudful ruler might have made. What I have here called the Stories of David's Middle Years make no claim for a vast Davidic empire; they could well be termed the Stories of David's Fragility.

For the text on Solomon, the situation is different. Solomon's kingdom may not have been as grand and as administratively brilliant as the text claims. Many reports about the achievements of statesmen suffer a similar defect. Jehoash, king of Israel, certainly did not think much of Judah's status (2 Kgs 14:8–14). Some biblical texts can be read grandiloquently or minimally; minimally may often be closer to the truth. Similarly, what archaeology finds is often immensely significant and enlightening; what archaeology fails to find may not always have the same significance.

What is most troubling—and Finkelstein and Silberman are of no help in regard to it—is the presence of a significant Jerusalem temple in Hezekiah and Josiah's times, to be the focus of the deuteronomistic demand for the centralization of worship. According to the biblical text, it was there to be pillaged by Pharaoh Shishak at the beginning of Judah's independent existence (1 Kgs 14:25–26). According to Finkelstein and Silberman, archaeologically there is virtually no trace of it, "since its site was obliterated in later building operations" (Finkelstein and Silberman 2001, 241); archaeologically, the context for its construction cannot be accounted for. Yet in the seventh century apparently it was there. According to Dever, "the *only* life-setting for 'Solomon's temple' [as described in the biblical text], whether there was a biblical Solomon or not, is to be found in the Iron Age, and in the 10th–8th centuries at *latest*" (Dever 2001, 157). That the south was significantly inferior to the north over much of Israel's history should not surprise anyone. To claim that the context from which the Jerusalem temple emerged—a temple that was surely a cut above the rural and miserable—should have been a Jerusalem for which "the most optimistic assessment" was "perhaps not more than a typical hill country village" (Finkelstein and Silberman 2001, 133) points to inadequate theorizing. Something is amiss. Something better is needed than near-silence.

REVIEW ISSUES

1. How is the impact of Solomon's reign on the history of Israel portrayed?

2. What is the role given the northern prophets in the story of the northern kingdom of Israel?

3. Does the failure of Josiah's reform leave a theological problem unresolved?

THE BOOK OF CHRONICLES:
A COMPARISON CONTINUED

At the start of 1 Chr 23, David hands over the monarchy to Solomon: "He made his son Solomon king over Israel" (23:1). The power struggle with Adonijah goes unmentioned (by contrast, see 1 Kgs 1–2). Instead, a census of the Levites is reported, with details on the sons of Gershon, Kohath, and Merari. In the middle of a summary of the Levite census, the following is quoted from David: "The LORD, the God of Israel, has given rest to his people; and he resides in Jerusalem forever" (23:25).

David organized the details of priestly service, according to the divisions of the descendants of Aaron, coming down to Zadok of the sons of Eleazar and Ahimelech of the sons of Ithamar. Lots were cast in the presence of King David (chap. 24). Further lots were likewise cast in the presence of David and the officers of the army for a variety of temple services, from the provision of music to the gatekeepers and other duties (chaps. 25–26). With the temple duties accounted for, the text turns to the royal needs. There is a list of those responsible for serving the king for each of twelve months, as well as those responsible for the tribes. Those over the king's treasuries are also listed, along with the stewards responsible for the various aspects of production on the royal estates (chap. 27). There is also a brief list of David's officials (27:32–34). Noth's comment is important in regard to these chapters: "It is generally recognized that 23.(2b), 3–27.34 is a massive insertion; it clearly interrupts the original connection between 23.1, 2a and 28.1ff" (Noth 1987, 31; cf. Rudolph, comm., viii).

Far from the murderous last counsels that David gives Solomon in 1 Kings, the last two chapters of 1 Chronicles have David convene a vast assembly at Jerusalem of all those with some authority in the kingdom (28:1). Before he dies, "in a good old age, full of days, riches, and honor" (29:28), David is given a series of speeches, to the people, to Solomon, and to the people again, first as an appeal for a freewill offering and second as a blessing (chaps. 28–29). The first speech to the people rehearses why Solomon and not David should build the temple (28:2–8). The second, to Solomon, encapsulates the plans for the temple precinct, the divisions of service, and the vessels with which the temple was equipped. An apparent quotation from Solomon ("he made clear to me"; LXX, to Solomon) completes the handover of these documents: "All this, in writing at the LORD's direction, he made clear to me—the plan of all the works" (28:19). The two passages of address (vv. 9–10, 20–21) call Solomon to fidelity and courage.

The appeal for freewill offerings is prefaced by an account of all that David was able to provide for the building of the temple; in addition, there is a report of what was freely given (29:1–9). David then blesses the LORD (vv. 10–19) and has the whole assembly bless the LORD, with a sacrifice the next day at which "they ate and drank before the LORD . . . with great joy" (vv. 20–22a). Finally, Solomon is crowned a second time, sits on David's throne, and all the leaders and warriors pledge their allegiance (vv. 22b–25). David's death is reported and the records of his reign noted (vv. 26–30).

These eight chapters take the place of 1 Kgs 1–2. Instead of scheming and bloodshed around the issue of succession to David, they are concerned with the proper organization and planning for the temple. Despite the probability of later expansion here, which—if it is the case—has to be accounted for, we need to be aware of the enormous emphasis given to the temple as David's achievement, even if Solomon is soon to be portrayed doing the actual building.

2 Chronicles

Second Chronicles opens with Solomon summoning all Israel to the high place at Gibeon. There Solomon asks for wisdom and is given wealth and honor as well. Solomon's horses and his wealth are mentioned succinctly (2 Chr 1:14–17). Next comes the building of the temple and Solomon's palace. The massive preparations of the previous eight chapters are passed over unmentioned. Solomon's building activity occupies 2 Chr 2–5, with the transfer to the new building reported in chapter 5. Solomon's blessing and prayer at the consecration of the temple occupy chapter 6. At the end of Solomon's prayer, "the glory of the LORD filled the temple" (7:1). More sacrifices are offered, and the completion of Solomon's building program (temple and palace) is reported (7:11).

An appearance of the LORD to Solomon is reported with an acceptance of Solomon's prayer at the consecration of the temple. The temple is chosen by God "as a house of sacrifice" (7:12). Three elements are picked up from Solomon's prayer—drought, locust plague, and pestilence—and a response to humble prayer guaranteed. The lovely words from Kings are repeated almost verbatim: "For now I have chosen and consecrated this house so that my name may be there forever; my eyes and my heart will be there for all time" (7:16). The divine speech goes on with a conditional promise of a successor and also with a grave threat to the future of the temple (7:17–22, with vv. 19–22 in the plural, as in Kings). References to "Israel" are omitted or adjusted. Solomon's later apostasy will not be reported.

Solomon's broader building program, his use of forced labor, his moving Pharaoh's daughter away from where the ark of the LORD had been, his provision for the temple, and his trade with Ophir are all retailed in chapter 8. Chapter 9 recounts the visit of the Queen of Sheba and the great wealth and wisdom of King Solomon in almost identical terms with 1 Kgs 10.

Solomon's apostasy is passed over. The division of the kingdom is reported, much as in 1 Kgs 12:1–24 (v. 20, however, is omitted). Jeroboam's activities in the north and his condemnation by the prophet Ahijah are passed over, as is the prophetic story of 1 Kgs 13. Chronicles will not show an interest in the northern kingdom. The temple, after all, was in Jerusalem. One sentence dismisses northern Israel: "So Israel has been in rebellion against the house of David to this day" (10:19; identical with 1 Kgs 12:19).

At this point the text follows the story of Judah, the southern kingdom, until the decree of Cyrus authorizing the rebuilding of the temple. A brief mention is made of Jeroboam's innovations in the north (2 Chr 11:14–15), not surprising given their impact on Jerusalem. A few northern kings or their actions will be mentioned where they impact on the south. In one case, the year of accession of a southern king, Abijah, is given as occurring in the eighteenth year of King Jeroboam, the northern king—but only once (2 Chr 13:1).

Rehoboam, Judah's first king, is given more attention in Chronicles than in Kings. The early years of Rehoboam's reign are regarded benignly (chap. 11). That changes: "When the rule of Rehoboam was established and he grew strong, he abandoned the law of the LORD, he and all Israel with him" (12:1). Pharaoh Shishak's campaign and his plundering the temple is carefully accounted for as divine punishment and instruction (chap. 12). Rehoboam's son Abijah succeeds him, noted as being in the eighteenth year of Jeroboam (13:1). Abijah's war with Jeroboam, which may account for the reference in 13:1, is given much more extensive treatment than in Kings. Abijah's speech (vv. 4–12) provides a theological underpinning for much that is to come and pillories Jeroboam for his innovations in the north (vv. 8–9). The theology is clear: Jerusalem has YHWH their God with them and therefore they will triumph. Despite being trapped in an ambush and facing an enemy army twice their number, Abijah's troops prevail (chap. 13). We will meet this position frequently in what is to come: The south, faithful to YHWH, will overwhelmingly defeat vastly superior enemy forces.

Asa, Abijah's son, succeeds him and again receives much fuller treatment than in Kings. Asa's report card is extensive and favorable. Through trust in the LORD, he defeats an Ethiopian army of a million men and three hundred chariots (14:9–13). A prophet, Azariah ben Oded, articulates the Chronicler's theology: "The LORD is with you, while you are with him. If you seek him, he will be found by you, but if you abandon him, he will abandon you" (15:2). Thus encouraged, Asa undertakes a religious cleanup in Judah. In the thirty-sixth year of his reign, King Baasha of northern Israel fortifies Ramah, just over his southern border, with a view to bottling up Judah. Asa takes money from the temple and royal treasuries and appeals for help to Ben-hadad of Aram-Damascus. Ben-hadad moves against Israel and Baasha retreats from Ramah. However, the theologians get to Asa; the seer Hanani charges him with trusting in Ben-hadad rather than YHWH. Asa turns cruel; he also gets a disease in his feet, and seeks help from doctors rather than YHWH. His son Jehoshaphat succeeds him.

Jehoshaphat gets the Micaiah story and ten verses in Kings (1 Kgs 22:1–38 and 41–50); in Chronicles, he gets the Micaiah story and three chapters (2 Chr 18:1–34 and chaps. 17, 19, 20). The differences are significant. The Micaiah story is in both Kings and Chronicles. The Elijah and Elisha traditions are in Kings but not Chronicles; Ahab and Jehu, of course, being northern kings, remain basically untreated. Elijah has one reference (2 Chr 21:12); Elisha none; Ahab a few through the Micaiah story, marriages into the royal house of Judah, and his campaign with Jehoram; and Jehu a few through his killing of King Ahaziah of Judah and his relatives. The story of the man of God at Bethel (1 Kgs 13) is not in Chronicles either. Not that Chronicles is opposed to the prophets; brief traditions of the prophets abound in Chronicles: Samuel (1 Chr 9:22; 11:3; 2 Chr 35:18), Nathan (1 Chr 17), Gad (1 Chr 21:9–13), Shemaiah (2 Chr 11:2–4; 12:5–8), Azariah ben Oded (2 Chr 15:1–7), Hanani (2 Chr 16:7–9), Micaiah ben Imlah (2 Chr 18), Jehu ben Hanani (2 Chr 19:2–3), Jahaziel ben Zechariah (2 Chr 20:14–17), Elijah (2 Chr 21:12–15), anonymous man of God (2 Chr 25:7–9), anonymous prophet (2 Chr 25:15–16), Oded (2 Chr 28:9–11), Isaiah ben Amoz (2 Chr 32:20), Huldah (2 Chr 34:22–28), Jeremiah (2 Chr 36:12). The northern prophets are of minimal interest in Chronicles unless they impinge on the southern kingdom.

Second Chronicles 17 speaks highly of Jehoshaphat and his campaign of teaching in the cities of Judah (vv. 7–9); the chapter's content might be summed up, "Jehoshaphat grew steadily greater" (2 Chr 17:12). It is followed by the Micaiah story (chap. 18; cf. 1 Kgs 22). On his return to Jerusalem, Jehoshaphat sets up judges and other adjudicators, exhorting them to good judgment and fear of the LORD (chap. 19). The final chapter given to Jehoshaphat recounts a theological set piece (chap. 20). A vast army—listed as Ammonites, Moabites, and Edomites—is reported threatening Judah. Great trust in YHWH is expressed in prayer and prophecy. Singers precede the army, and a great victory is given Judah, thanks to the internecine errors of the enemy (v. 23). Again, the theological position is succinctly put: "This battle is not for you to fight; take your position, stand still, and see the victory of the LORD on your behalf, O Judah and Jerusalem" (v. 17). Treatment of Jehoshaphat's cultic reforms is confused (cf. 17:6; 19:3; 20:33).

Jehoshaphat's son Jehoram succeeds him. Once on the throne, he puts his half-dozen brothers to the sword; he also marries Ahab's daughter. Edom and Libnah break free from his rule. A letter from Elijah threatens him with a severe sickness and, after a couple of painful years, he dies of it (chap. 21). His son Ahaziah succeeds him, and gets a bad press. He campaigns with King Jehoram of northern Israel against King Hazael of Aram-Damascus. Jehoram is recovering from his wounds and is being visited by Ahaziah when Jehu, "whom the LORD had anointed to destroy the house of Ahab" (22:7), catches up with both of them and kills them both, along with others from Judah. These events lead to Queen Athaliah's coup in Jerusalem (chap. 22).

Queen Athaliah reigns for six years, during which time Joash, son of King Ahaziah, is hidden by his aunt in the temple (22:11–12). The account of Athaliah's assassination is focused on Jehoiada. For a chapter, Joash is not named (chap. 23). Joash is reported to have kept on the straight and narrow while Jehoiada was alive, who was "one hundred thirty years old at his death" (24:15). The report of his temple repairs is a little less hard on the priests than that in Kings. When Jehoiada dies, Joash is reported to go off the right path, and a small army from Aram, aided by the LORD, "executed judgment on Joash" (24:24).

Joash is succeeded by his son Amaziah, who kills his father's assassins. The civil war with King Joash (ben Jehoahaz ben Jehu) of northern Israel (cf. 2 Kgs 14:8–14) is reported (25:17–24), but it is preceded by the report of strange military behavior on the part of Amaziah, illustrating the view that "God has power to help or to overthrow" (25:8). Uzziah succeeds his father Amaziah, installed by "the people of Judah" ('am yĕhûdâ; 26:1). He starts remarkably well, with successful campaigns, multiple fortifications, and extensive farming, "for he was marvelously helped until he became strong. But when he had become strong he grew proud, to his destruction" (26:15–16). He clashes with the priests over service in the temple and ends up with leprosy (vv. 16–21).

Uzziah's son Jotham succeeds him (chap. 27). The brief report on him typifies the theology of Chronicles: "Jotham became strong because he ordered his ways before the LORD his God" (27:6). He is succeeded by his son Ahaz (chap. 28). Ahaz is given a thoroughly bad report, being likened to the kings of Israel. His military expeditions meet with the failures that might be expected. In one, "the people of

Israel took captive two hundred thousand of their kin" (v. 8). The prophet Oded rebukes them, demanding the return of the captives (vv. 9–11), and is effectively backed up by "certain chiefs of the Ephraimites" (vv. 12–13). The Chronicles account of Ahaz's reign can be summed up in a verse: "The LORD brought Judah low because of King Ahaz of Israel [sic], for he had behaved without restraint in Judah and had been faithless to the LORD" (28:19).

Hezekiah is the subject of the next four chapters (chaps. 29–32). The confrontation with Sennacherib occupies two chapters in Kings (chaps. 18–19) and Isaiah (chaps. 36–37) and in Chronicles it takes up no more than a single chapter (chap. 32). The first activity credited to Hezekiah is a major cleansing of the temple (chap. 29). Hezekiah's address ordering it is given, followed by a report of the Levites' compliance, with names and details, and finally the sacrificial celebration when the cleansing is complete. The second activity credited to Hezekiah is the celebration of a passover in Jerusalem in the second month (chap. 30). Messengers are sent through all Israel, inviting people to the passover. There are different responses: They are laughed to scorn in the north (30:10); some come from Asher, Manasseh, and Zebulun (30:11); many come from Judah (30:13). A multitude eat the Passover who had not cleansed themselves; for them Hezekiah prays and is heard (30:18–20). "There was great joy in Jerusalem, for since the time of Solomon son of King David of Israel there had been nothing like this in Jerusalem" (30:26). Finally, a great upsurge of religious well-being is portrayed (chap. 31). First, pillars, poles, high places, and altars are pulled down wholesale throughout much of the country. Second, the tithes contributed for the support of the priests and Levites are so generous that store-chambers have to be prepared to hold the surplus. The verdict on Hezekiah is that "he did what was good and right and faithful before the LORD his God . . . and he prospered" (31:20–21). Nevertheless, King Sennacherib of Assyria invades Judah (32:1), besieges fortified cities and heads for Jerusalem. The text recounts Hezekiah's preparations to defend the capital. Then he and the prophet Isaiah pray to God, and the LORD sends an angel; Sennacherib returns in disgrace to his own land. "So the LORD saved Hezekiah and the inhabitants of Jerusalem from the hand of King Sennacherib of Assyria" (32:22). This is followed by a strange little note: Hezekiah becomes ill, prays, is answered, becomes proud, incurs divine wrath, then humbles himself, and so "the wrath of the LORD did not come upon them in the days of Hezekiah" (32:26). Verses 27–31 summarize Hezekiah's great wealth, his cutting of the Gihon tunnel, and his dealings with the envoys of

Sennacherib. In this latter situation he is left to himself by God, "in order to test him and to know all that was in his heart" (32:31).

The comparison with Kings needs to be pondered. Roughly speaking, Kings has two chapters on Hezekiah's negotiations with Sennacherib's officials, a chapter on Hezekiah's illness, and a few verses on Hezekiah's reforms. Chronicles, on the other hand, has three chapters on Hezekiah's reforms and a chapter that is shared between his negotiations with Sennacherib's officials and his illness. Different interests generate different texts.

Manasseh comes next, with a fifty-five-year reign. The report of it in Chronicles begins in much the same vein as in Kings. What his father Hezekiah reformed, Manasseh dutifully deformed—"Manasseh misled Judah and the inhabitants of Jerusalem, so that they did more evil than the nations whom the LORD had destroyed before the people of Israel" (33:9, cf. vv. 1–9). Suddenly Chronicles parts company with Kings. The Assyrians swoop, and Manasseh is taken to Babylon in chains. There he prays and is restored to his kingdom. "Then Manasseh knew that the LORD indeed was God" (33:13). In my judgment, the historicity here is less important than the theology. The theology of Chronicles is almost mechanistic. God's favor generates prosperity; wickedness brings disaster. The rest of Manasseh's reign is consecrated to good. The people only meet him halfway; "the people, however, still sacrificed at the high places, but only to the LORD their God" (33:17).

Amon succeeds Manasseh; he follows his father's evil practices and pays no heed to his conversion. Assassination terminates his reign after two years, and the people of the land install his eight-year-old son Josiah as king. Josiah has a thirty-one-year reign, and two chapters are given to his reform (chaps. 34–35). Josiah's reforming activities are noted in three stages. First, in the eighth year of his reign, "while he was still a boy" (34:3), he begins to seek the God of his ancestor David. In the twelfth year, he begins a religious purge of Judah and Jerusalem, as well as areas to the north. Second, in the eighteenth year of his reign, "the book" is found in the temple and confirmed by Huldah; king and people take part in a formal covenant ceremony. Third, Josiah keeps a passover to the LORD in Jerusalem (35:1). Much detail is given, but no reference is made to the Passover of Hezekiah. Instead, it is said that "no passover like it had been kept in Israel since the days of the prophet Samuel; none of the kings of Israel had kept such a Passover as was kept by Josiah" (35:18). It echoes something of 2 Kgs 23:22; in its silence over Hezekiah, despite 2 Chr 30, it is as odd as the comparative encomiums of Hezekiah (18:5) and Josiah (23:25) in Kings.

Finally, Josiah goes to his death in battle with Pharaoh Neco. It is consonant with the theology of Chronicles that Josiah should be converted into a sinner before he dies. Neco delivers an extraordinary message: "God has commanded me to hurry. Cease opposing God, who is with me, so that he will not destroy you" (35:21). Alas for Josiah, he opposes Neco and God and dies for his pains. The reform dies with him.

The enigma of Chronicles is remarkably clear at this point. Chronicles agrees with Kings regarding Huldah's prophecy, quoting the reported prophecy almost verbatim, with the condemnation of Josiah's generation (2 Kgs 22:17 = 2 Chr 34:25) and the reward of an early death given Josiah (22:19–20 = 34:27–28)—words that are historically inappropriate and almost certainly late additions in Kings (cf. Campbell and O'Brien 2000, 458–61). On the other hand, Chronicles disagrees with Kings regarding Josiah's death. Chronicles has three verses that are absent from Kings (2 Chr 35:21–23). In them, Neco claims to have God with him and casts Josiah in the role of opposing God. Effectively, then, Josiah is placed in the sinner role and is punished for it with his death. The enigma: Chronicles follows Kings almost verbatim regarding Huldah and Josiah; Chronicles departs from Kings significantly regarding Neco and Josiah. We must ask, is history here shaped to accommodate theology?

The final chapter takes up the tale of the next four kings, none of whom show any stomach for reform. The Jerusalem temple is going to be destroyed (36:17–21); strong reasons are needed for such a disaster. Chronicles provides them:

> The LORD, the God of their ancestors, sent persistently to them by his messengers, because he had compassion on his people and on his dwelling place; but they kept mocking the messengers of God, despising his words, and scoffing at his prophets, until the wrath of the LORD against his people became so great that there was no remedy. (36:15–16)

The books of Kings are driven toward a similar hard place and end on a miserably ambiguous note. Perhaps their solace might be found in the faith of Isa 54:9–10. Perhaps the solace of Chronicles is found in the decree of King Cyrus of Persia, who declares in a written edict: "The LORD, the God of heaven, . . . has charged me to build him a house at Jerusalem, which is in Judah" (36:23). Chronicles goes no further.

Conclusion

Chronicles is a document in its own right with its own theology and its own goals. Modern interpreters may not always like the theology, frequently finding it demeaning of God, and may often rightly suspect exaggeration. The historical reliability of the conflicting traditions in Samuel–Kings on the one hand and Chronicles on the other needs to be carefully assessed in each case. No informed reader of Samuel–Kings would believe that text to be free of bias. The theological acceptability of the various theologies will involve the different criteria of different interpreters. The sources available to the Chronicler and the value of Chronicles for text-critical study also needs careful assessment in each case. Any dependence of both the Deuteronomistic History and Chronicles on a prior "common text" (a conservative thesis from the late-eighteenth century, recently revived by A. G. Auld) appears most unlikely. Even in substantially common passages, there are constant differences that are not easily accounted for. Beyond this, there are huge differences in the coverage provided.

REVIEW ISSUES

1. What meaning can be made from the fact that the book of Chronicles begins with the beginning of the human race?

2. What meaning can be made from the fact that the book of Chronicles gives so much attention to David's contribution toward the preparation for building the temple?

3. What meaning can be made from the fact that the book of Chronicles ends with the decree of Cyrus for the rebuilding of the temple?

EZRA AND NEHEMIAH

In a work such as this it is probably unwise to attempt a treatment of the books of Ezra and Nehemiah. Anything brief would be inadequate, and there is no space for anything long. Both books are short enough that they can be easily read. Both books are problematic enough that any brief treatment would be inappropriate. There is no consensus to summarize.

The following comments from Robert Carroll in a recent handbook highlight something of the difficulty involved:

As an example of the problematical nature of the biblical material consider the vexed question of the Ezra–Nehemiah texts. Did Ezra's visit to Jerusalem precede Nehemiah's or come after it, or did Ezra visit Jerusalem twice with Nehemiah's visit taking place in-between those two visits? . . . What about the Ezra–Nehemiah literature? Does it have a common author (the Chronicler?) or are they two independent pieces of writing, with different authors? So many questions must be debated and resolved before the texts can be brought into play in the discussion about the Persian colony in Jerusalem. . . . In my judgment we are currently in a period when there are many competing points of view jostling for territorial gain in this area and wise readers will allow for diversity of opinion, uncertainty and agnosticism, and will therefore recognize the lack of any consensus in the treatment of this topic. (Carroll 2001, 110–11)

We will take the liberty of counting ourselves wise.

Bibliography other than commentaries

Auld, A. Graeme. 1994. *Kings without Privilege: David and Moses in the Story of the Bible's Kings*. Edinburgh: T. & T. Clark

Barré, Lloyd M. 1988. *The Rhetoric of Political Persuasion: The Narrative Artistry and Political Intentions of 2 Kings 9–11*. CBQMS 20. Washington, D.C.: Catholic Biblical Association of America.

Campbell, Antony F. 1986. *Of Prophets and Kings: A Late Ninth-Century Document (1 Samuel 1–2 Kings 10)*. CBQMS 17. Washington, D.C.: Catholic Biblical Association of America.

Campbell, Antony F. and Mark A. O'Brien. 2000. *Unfolding the Deuteronomistic History: Origins, Upgrades, Present Text*. Minneapolis: Fortress.

Carroll, Robert P. 2001. "Exile, Restoration, and Colony: Judah in the Persian Empire." Pages 102–16 in *The Blackwell Companion to the Hebrew Bible*. Edited by Leo G. Perdue. Oxford: Basil Blackwell.

Childs, Brevard S. 1967. *Isaiah and the Assyrian Crisis*. SBT 2/3. London: SCM Press.

Claburn, W. Eugene. 1973. "The Fiscal Basis of Josiah's Reforms." *JBL* 92:11–22.

Clements, Ronald E. 1980. *Isaiah and the Deliverance of Jerusalem: A Study of the Interpretation of Prophecy in the Old Testament*. JSOTSup 13. Sheffield: JSOT Press.

Dever, William G. 2001. *What Did the Biblical Writers Know and When Did They Know It? What Archaelogy Can Tell Us about the Reality of Ancient Israel*. Grand Rapids: Eerdmans.

Finkelstein, Israel, and Neil Asher Silberman. 2001. *The Bible Unearthed: Archaeology's New Vision of Ancient Israel and the Origin of Sacred Texts*. Touchstone. New York: Simon & Schuster.

Gooding, D. W. 1967. "The Septuagint's Rival Versions of Jeroboam's Rise to Power." *VT* 17:173–89.

———. 1976. *Relics of Ancient Exegesis: A Study of the Miscellanies in 3 Reigns 2*. SOTSMS 4. Cambridge: Cambridge University Press.

Lohfink, Norbert, SJ. 1978. "Die Gattung der 'Historischen Kurzgeschichte' in den letzten Jahren von Juda und in der Zeit des Babylonischen Exils." *ZAW* 90:319–47.

McKenzie, John L. 1965. *Dictionary of the Bible*. New York: Macmillan.

Miller, J. Maxwell, and John H. Hayes. 1986. *A History of Ancient Israel and Judah*. London: SCM Press.

Noth, Martin. 1987. *The Chronicler's History*. JSOTSup 50. Sheffield: JSOT Press. German original, 1943.

Oded, Bustenay. 1977. "Judah and the Exile." Pages 435–88 in *Israelite and Judaean History*. Edited by J. H. Hayes and J. M. Miller. Philadelphia: Westminster.

Schmitt, Hans-Christoph. 1972. *Elisa: Traditionsgeschichtliche Untersuchungen zur vorklassischen nordisraelitischen Prophetie*. Gütersloh: Mohn.

Sweeney, Marvin A. 1996. *Isaiah 1–39 with an Introduction to Prophetic Literature*. FOTL 16. Grand Rapids: Eerdmans.

———. 2001. *King Josiah of Judah: The Lost Messiah of Israel*. New York: Oxford Univ. Press.

Trebolle Barrera, Julio C. 1980. *Salomon y Jeroboan: Historia de la recensión de I Reyes 2–12, 14*. Salamanca: Universidad Pontificia.

White, Marsha C. 1997. *The Elijah Legends and Jehu's Coup*. BJS 113. Atlanta: Scholars Press.

Conclusion

Experiences and Ingredients

Great literature is distilled from experience, but at times the originating experience can be elusive. The biblical texts are best understood as the outcome of the struggle to give expression to experience. The challenge we often face is identifying the experience and then reflecting on its transformation into literature. When, as in the Bible, we look at a wide sweep of literature, reflecting some six or seven centuries, we can be reasonably sure that multiple experiences are involved. American history incorporates a mass of experiences in fewer centuries. Similarly, the experience of England that fired Dickens or Shakespeare is not what is felt by the English of today's European Union. In this, the Bible is no different; its experiences are many and varied.

At this point, it may be appropriate to lay some personal cards on the page. I am theologically comfortable with the reinterpretation of experience; in life we do it all the time, so why not in the sources of theology? I am theologically uncomfortable, however, with the invention of experience. In life we may do it occasionally; if it is serious and if we are caught, we go to jail (or the equivalent). In form-critical categories, I think of experience mainly in terms of account or report; I think of interpretation mainly in terms of story. While stories are usually grounded in experience, it is often not the experience in which they are grounded that is the experience told in the story. Often the grounding experience is related to identity (who am I?); the story is likely to be related to activity (what happened?). At a public level, it is often in the exploration of what happened that we discover who we are. I might also mention that I seldom expect God to do what I would not expect or ask of a good friend (see Campbell 2000, x, 60). I do not always expect ancient Israel to share that theology; I am comfortable with the reinterpretation and reformulation of experience.

For W. Dever, who is as solidly conservative a well-informed archaeologist as any in the United States today, "the traditional account contained in Genesis through Joshua simply cannot be reconciled with the picture derived . . . from archaeological investigation" (Dever 2001, 121). Archaeological investigation does not have the field to itself; the evidence of the Bible is just as compelling. There is enough emphasis in Genesis on the origins of groups and peoples to raise the question whether the sequence of Abraham to Isaac to Jacob is a relationship that is familial (father, son, and grandson) or political (bringing related groups into unity). It has long been accepted that all Israel was not present at the exodus. It is clear that the biblical texts regarding Israel's entry into Canaan are complex and do not offer a simple picture of conquest. So the question demands to be asked: What can we say about the experiences that may have generated this biblical literature?

We can refine the question. It is widely recognized that in the formulation of traditions, "all Israel" is portrayed as present where all Israel certainly could not have been. This pan-Israelite perspective has its implications for the time of formulation (see Noth 1981, 42–62, esp. 42–45 but for an assumed preliterary stage). For Noth, the preliterary stage is premonarchic. For others, the period of Saul-David-Solomon is possible; in the light of the occurrences, it is unlikely (i.e., significant references [personal names, theological claims] do not appear in Samuel and the early traditions of Kings). The time of the divided monarchy (roughly 922–722) cannot be ruled out, but formulations would need to be located in one or the other kingdom, claiming to articulate an identity that applied to the whole. After the absorption of the northern kingdom into the Assyrian Empire, and accepting a Josianic Deuteronomistic History, there is roughly a century (722–622) before the formulations found now in Genesis–Joshua are firmly in place elsewhere. Two questions need to be answered: What dates suit these traditions? What dates suit these formulations? A date after the composition of the Deuteronomistic History is theoretically possible, whether exilic and post–Deuteronomistic History but pre–Priestly source (cf. Van Seters 1994, 458) or later, responding to the Persian concern for the formulation of national identity (cf. Blenkinsopp 1992, 239–42). Assessment of the references to Moses in 1–2 Kings—and other factors—suggest that a date before the composition of the Deuteronomistic History is more likely.

In a nutshell, as a whole the present formulations within Genesis–Joshua are likely to be relatively late. On the other hand, the experiences in which they are grounded may have been preserved as traditions in familial or tribal circles for we do not know how long. The reinterpretation of such traditions in varying circumstances to cope with differing needs probably has a long history. The precise nature of the originating experiences almost certainly escapes us.

My tendency in this book has been to deal with the text as we have it in the Bible, that is, the final or present text. I have looked at the past development of the text where this development has affected the meaning of the final text. As a matter of policy, I have not set out to explore the development and growth of the text in its movement toward its final form. At this point, however, it will be worthwhile to outline briefly the earlier texts that to some degree have become components of the books treated here.

JOSHUA

Of the books we have dealt with, the one most affected by the comments above and the one where it is hardest to pin down the experiences that have generated its text is undoubtedly the book of Joshua. Two stages of text are easy to identify: first, the sacral focus of the three stories of the Jordan crossing, the Jericho capture, and the Achan fiasco; second, the soldierly focus of the narrative of a military campaign, extending from Josh 2:1 to 10:27, 42–43. This military campaign narrative evidently existed. Its first traces are in Josh 2; there may have been some account of a Jordan crossing. Later references indicate that it included the treatment of Jericho, Ai, and Gibeon (cf. Josh 10:1). It concludes with an account of the defeat of a coalition of five kings under Adoni-zedek of Jerusalem (10:1–27, 42–43).

Textually, the territory involved in this narrative is minimal; Jericho, Ai, and Gibeon are all within a thin strip of Benjamin. Archaeologically, we are aware that the nature of Israel's entry into Canaan does not correspond with the narrative's military portrayal. So we have to ask about the experience that may have generated the text. Dever has written of the period's "large-scale socio-economic disruption [and] major demographic shifts to the hill-country frontiers" revealed by intense archaeological investigation; he notes the "life-and-death struggles between competing ethnic and cultural groups that lasted anywhere from one to two centuries" (Dever 2001, 122). It is evident also that the inhabitants of the small agricultural villages in the central hill country, stretching from lower Galilee to around Beer-sheba, at some time moved to occupy larger towns in the mainstream of economic life. It is unlikely that this happened without some military activity. Either of these moments, or others like them, might have provided the experience in which the military campaign narrative was grounded. The "sacral stories," if correctly understood here, emerge from the faith claim that the newcomers' success in their undertakings was owed entirely to their God. The close geographical association with the sanctuary at Gilgal may well have played its role.

The periods when these experiences were transformed into literary text are unknown to us. The references to Moses and Joshua, discussed earlier, suggest that the bulk of the final text might be no earlier than the end of the eighth century or later. Dating is less important to us than meaning. Alongside these are the passages in Josh 10:28–12:24, which I characterized earlier as list-like or summarizing style. Above all, the extermination in Josh 10:27–41 is of a density and intensity unparalleled elsewhere in Hebrew Scripture. Even by the standards of the times (cf. Amos 1:3, 6, 11, 13), they are abhorrent. Historically, they are aberrant. That such extermination never took place is evident from passages such as Josh 23:7, 12 and Judg 2:2–3, 21, 22–23; 3:1–3, 4–6, and we do not know what experiences or fanatical theology, apparently in late deuteronomistic circles, may have triggered such texts. The dating of the extensive texts on the allocation of lands within Israel is best left to specialists. A period particularly appropriate to the concern about the east-of-Jordan tribes is also unknown to us.

JUDGES

We would be hard-pressed to be specific about a time of composition for the three major stories that are at the core of the carefully organized series of stories early in the book of Judges (Judg 3:12–8:35). The stories themselves bring experience to expression; their organization takes experience a step further. The preface (2:11–19*)—emphasizing the cyclic aspect, confirming the evil as apostasy, and naming the deliverers as judges—can be dated to the Josianic Deuteronomistic History (late seventh century B.C.E.). The paradigm associated with Othniel is not likely to be much earlier; the framing of the three stories is more difficult to date. By the time of the Josianic Deuteronomistic History, a narrative text from 2:11–8:35 can be assumed.

To attempt to be specific about the experiences or the dating of much of the rest would be an act of supreme imprudence. Most would agree that the opening section on the conquest and the final chapters following Samson (the "texts of terror") have come into the final text later than the completion of the Deuteronomistic History (there are exceptions to this view, e.g., Boling). The date of incorporation into the final text says nothing about the date of composition, not to mention later editing. It would be widely believed that the conquest traditions of chapter 1 are, in the main, likely to be early. Stories of Abimelech and Jephthah and the traditions of the minor judges may well be early. The stories of Samson are an enigma. The final stories, the "texts of terror," are set within a premonarchic refrain—"there was no king in Israel"—but, as has just been noted, they are generally believed to have come into the final text later than the completion of the Deuteronomistic History. Their dates of composition, on the other hand, are most uncertain. Editing is seen as likely.

SAMUEL

Four major sources have been discussed in relation to the composition of the books of Samuel: the Ark Narrative, the Story of David's Rise, the Story of David's Middle Years (traditionally, the Succession Narrative or the Court History), and the Prophetic Record. At this point, the multiplicity of influences makes it unhelpful in a brief space to reflect on the experiences that undergird the literary expression.

The hypothesis of a four-chapter Ark Narrative (1 Sam 4–6; 2 Sam 6) was proposed in 1926 by Leonhard Rost (1982). The text focuses exclusively on the ark of the covenant and its function as a symbol of God's presence and God's power and purpose for Israel. There have been two thoroughgoing studies relatively recently in English, by Campbell (1975) and by Miller and Roberts (1977). This issue has been revisited more recently by Campbell (comm. [2003], see esp. the chapter "Diachronic Dimension"). For Campbell, the narrative comprised basically 1 Sam 4–6, with 2 Sam 6 either an original part of the narrative or composed with 1 Sam 4–6 in view so that the two blocks constitute virtually a single text (the latter option adapting Miller and Roberts 1977, 23–24). Campbell considers the most probable period for the composition to be prior to the consecration of Solomon's temple and the transfer of the ark

there. Miller and Roberts argue for the inclusion of the anti-Elide material in the narrative (i.e., 1 Sam 2:12–17, 22–25, and 27–36) and for
bringing it to a close with 1 Sam 7:1. In their judgment, the composition lay essentially in the period before David's major victories.

A "Story of David's Rise" is not so much a source document within
Samuel but a source for various stories and other traditions concerned
with David's rise to power in Israel. The majority of these stories are
either independent or nearly so. We do not have evidence for a single
version or document; we have evidence for stories and traditions that
might have been variously selected as the components of a number of
versions. Its beginnings could range from early levels of text around
1 Sam 9:1 to 1 Sam 16:14; its conclusion has often been put at 2 Sam
5:10 or 12, but could be extended to early levels of text as far as 2 Sam
8:15. What it offers are traditions about David's emergence from the
court of Saul until his establishment on the throne of both Israel and
Judah. As might be expected from a collection of quasi-independent stories, there is a variety of versions and repetitions. From the point of view
of historian or theologian, one must reckon with an evident bias in favor
of David. Saul's supporters might have told a very different tale. The
date for much of the material is controverted, but evidence pointing to
something like our modern "oral history," with minor details recorded
that would not have been remembered except as part of a larger project,
suggests an originating time not far from the events. (For further detail,
see Campbell, comm. [2003], esp. the chapter, "Diachronic Dimension.")

What is here termed neutrally "Stories of David's Middle Years" has
been traditionally known as the Succession Narrative (cf. Rost 1982)
or, more recently, as the Court History (cf. Flanagan 1972). In my judgment, it should be restricted to 2 Sam 11–20 and is not about succession or a court history. Its concerns reflect the ambiguity of human
motivation that every political leader needs to be aware of. "An affair,
a death in battle, and two pregnancies [2 Sam 11–12] are not the stuff
of courtly chronicles. A princely rape might precipitate fratricide [chap.
13]; it would not make the chronicles in detail. A major rebellion
[chaps. 15–19] might well be a matter for a chronicler, but scarcely the
details of David's flight and return. Sheba's revolt might be of interest
[chap. 20], but not Joab's recovery of power, without appropriate follow-
up" (Campbell, comm. [in press], 318). A potential purpose for such
stories can be suggested:

> Might these stories have been told for royal courtiers to explore the
> boundaries of counsel given the king? At what points in the stories

would counsel have been desirable? What options might have been proposed and what consequences might have followed from them? Such a function would account for this peculiar capacity of the stories to leave space for questions that could be asked and to close off almost none. Such is the wisdom of a counselor: to open unthought-of options for reflection and to choose wisely. (Campbell, comm. [in press], 319)

A setting too close to David or too far from David's time is unlikely. The traditions are too unfavorable to David to be close, too favorable to be too far away. The court of Jeroboam I, in the newly established kingdom of northern Israel, would have needed royal counselors; it offers a setting from which such stories might have emerged. (As noted earlier, fuller discussion of recent research in this area is available in the final chapter, "Diachronic Dimension," of Campbell, comm. [in press].)

The Prophetic Record is a hypothetical document, proposed by Antony Campbell (1986) to account for the stereotyped prophetic anointings of Saul, David, and Jehu and the equally stereotyped pre-deuteronomistic core of prophetic addresses to Jeroboam, Ahab, and Jehu; its extent is reckoned from 1 Sam 1:1 to 2 Kgs 10:28. It was first proposed by Campbell in 1986. It has been presented more briefly in two recent works (Campbell and O'Brien 2000; Campbell, comm. [2003]). It has been described as an extended version of a Story of David's Rise, with expansions fore and more particularly aft. As such, it is at the core of much of 1 Samuel, the first part of 2 Samuel, then 1 Kings and the first part of 2 Kings. (It would be unhelpful to provide chapter and verse for the text here; such details can be found in Campbell 1986 or Campbell and O'Brien 2000). It is assumed to have been concerned with the legitimacy of Jehu's revolt (c. 845–841) and to have been composed probably in the late ninth century.

KINGS

Within the narrative of the books of Kings there is, of course, the "Book of the Acts of Solomon" (1 Kgs 11:41) and the latter part of the Prophetic Record. Beyond these there are a variety of references in the text to sources from which information is said to have been excerpted (e.g., the Book of the Annals of the Kings of Israel/Judah). A Prophetic Record is not listed among such sources, presumably because, in the hypothesis, it is not excerpted but adopted in its entirety and expanded.

It is widely accepted that some sort of record, some Book of the Acts of Solomon, was used in the composition of 1 Kgs 3–11; it is probably to be dated "not far removed from Solomon's own time" (Jones, comm., 1:60; cf. Liver 1967). It is one thing to agree on the likelihood that a source was exploited and even to reach a consensus on its probable date; it is a different task to identify the material that is believed to have been taken from such a source and the degree to which it has been modified.

In this regard, the hypothesis of a Prophetic Record (see above) claims to identify material that is used rather differently. Instead of being a source from which information is drawn, the Prophetic Record is postulated as a written text found within 1 Sam 1:1 to 2 Kgs 10:28, providing the foundation on which the text of 1–2 Kgs was built. As noted, the Prophetic Record is assumed to have been concerned with the legitimacy of Jehu's revolt (c. 845–841) and to have been composed probably in the late ninth century. The text attributed to the Prophetic Record in Kings is identified in Campbell and O'Brien (2000, 336–427). Two other sources tentatively noted there are what are called the Prophetic Record Extension and the Hezekian King List. Both are based on lists of kings. For the first, "it is suggested that reflection on the fate of the northern kingdom led to a list of its kings, from Jehu to the end, who were infected by the sin of Jeroboam"; the grounds for this identification is the tight pattern of judgment applied to these kings, from Jehu to Hoshea (Campbell and O'Brien 2000, 33, 478). For the second, a minimal stance suggests that the distinctive feature of concern for the high places noted with regard to a series of the kings of Judah—characterized as doing good in the eyes of YHWH except that "the high places were not taken away"—may reflect literary activity from Hezekiah's time (Campbell and O'Brien 2000, 33–34, 479–80).

CHRONICLES

Chronicles is a postexilic work. While it begins with Adam, Seth, and Enosh, it ends with Cyrus, King of Persia, and his decree for the restoration of the temple at Jerusalem. It is evident that the work is not a unitary piece. For example, the extensive preparations made by David for the building of the temple, dealt with at length toward the end of 1 Chronicles, scarcely figure within the account of the building of the temple at the beginning of 2 Chronicles. The judgment may be endorsed: "Chronicles contains a variety of material which is not to be found in Gen.–Kings, but which cannot be due to the Chronicler's own invention. . . . He must have derived this from an earlier source" (Eissfeldt 1965, 532). The Chronicles text takes a certain liberty with its sources. It is generally agreed that some edifyingly pious parts may be theologically motivated inventions of the Chronicler's own. As a rule, however, the traditions preserved in Chronicles need to be assessed on a critical basis equally with those in Samuel–Kings. We need to be aware of our uncertainty about the nature and extent of the Chronicler's sources and take into account the characterization of some passages as "to a large extent trustworthy" and containing "concealed valuable ancient material" (Eissfeldt 1965, 535) or "undoubtedly early and reliable" (Fohrer 1968, 241).

Aspects of the theology present in Chronicles sit uncomfortably with the modern interpreter, but this should not invite arrogance to go beyond evidence—as, for example, Eissfeldt does in his unsupported "*no doubt* historical but *clearly* improperly interpreted by the Chronicler" (Eissfeldt 1965, 536 [emphasis mine]). Once this has been recognized, we are also free to admit to total ignorance regarding the antiquity of the Chronicler's sources. Generous space needs to be made for later editing. Caution can be brought to bear on parts believed to be unduly under the influence of the Chronicler's pietistic theology. But on possible early sources in Chronicles, we may end with Eissfeldt: "It is not possible to give a more exact dating in terms of century or decade" (1965, 538).

DEUTERONOMISTIC HISTORY

The hypothesis of a Deuteronomistic History (DH), a single literary work extending within the biblical books from Deuteronomy to 2 Kings, was elaborated by Martin Noth in 1943. In 1968, Frank Cross proposed in an article that there was an original Josianic DH, revised by an exilic edition; in 1973 this was made more widely available in Cross's *Canaanite Myth and Hebrew Epic*. Also in 1973, Cross's position was supported by a Th.D. dissertation from Richard Nelson (1981) who, originally, had set out to dispute Cross. In 1971, Rudolf Smend, in article form, maintained an exilic date for the DH, but pointed to secondary features in Joshua–Judges, attributed to a DtrN (N for nomistic); his work was supported by two pupils at Göttingen: Walter Dietrich, focusing on later contributions in Kings emphasizing prophetic concerns, attributed to a DtrP (P for prophetic), and Timo Veijola, focusing in two monographs on later contributions in Samuel, attributed to DtrP and DtrN (Dietrich 1972; Veijola 1975 and 1977). In 1989, Mark O'Brien brought together insights from both approaches, identifying a Josianic DH later revised with a couple of focuses visible—antiroyal and antipeople. Finally, in 2000, Campbell and O'Brien combined to identify and lay out in visually accessible form the major sources or traditions that had been drawn on to constitute a Josianic DH and the subsequent editorial revisions.

Exhortation for reform bulks large in Deuteronomy, in the sections surrounding the lawcode. Also prominent in these sections is the evidence for failure of the reform and the subsequent disaster of exile (e.g., Deut 4, esp. the tone-setting vv. 25–31; Deut 29:1–30:10, esp. 29:21–27 [NRSV, vv. 22–28]). The differences between the optimism of a Josianic DH and the darker sentiments within the subsequent revision can be seen in the following pairs, with the optimism first followed by the darker sentiment: Deut 30:11–20 and 30:1–10; Josh 1:1–6 and 23:1–16; Judg 2:11, 14–16, 18–19 and 10:10–16; 1 Sam 16:1–13 and 8:4–22; 1 Kgs 9:3–5 and 11:9–13. Within the complete final text, one view of the specific contributions of the Deuteronomists, the origins, the DH itself, and subsequent editing and additional material is identified and rendered readily accessible in Campbell and O'Brien (2000).

Overall, the experiences reflected in the Deuteronomistic History are clearly multiple, extending from those reminiscences on experience close to the events down to experiences of the postexilic community. The wealth of these many ingredients contributes to the richness of the final text.

Bibliography of works cited above, other than commentaries

Blenkinsopp, Joseph. 1992. *The Pentateuch: An Introduction to the First Five Books of the Bible*. London: SCM Press.

Campbell, Antony F. 1975. *The Ark Narrative (1 Sam 4–6; 2 Sam 6): A Form-Critical and Traditio-Historical Study*. SBLDS 16. Missoula, Mont.: Scholars Press.

———. 1986. *Of Prophets and Kings: A Late Ninth-Century Document (1 Samuel 1–2 Kings 10)*. CBQMS 17. Washington, D.C.: Catholic Biblical Association of America.

———. 2000. *God First Loved Us: The Challenge of Accepting Unconditional Love*. New York: Paulist.

Campbell, Antony F., and Mark A. O'Brien. 2003. *Unfolding the Deuteronomistic History: Origins, Upgrades, Present Text*. Minneapolis: Fortress.

Cross, F. M. 1968. "The Structure of the Deuteronomic History." Pages 9–24 in *Perspectives in Jewish Learning*. Annual of the College of Jewish Studies 3. Chicago: College of Jewish Studies. Republished as "The Themes of the Book of Kings and the Structure of the Deuteronomistic History." Pages 274–89 in *Canaanite Myth and Hebrew Epic: Essays in the History of the Religion of Israel.* Cambridge, Mass.: Harvard Univ. Press, 1973.

Dever, William G. 2001. *What Did the Biblical Writers Know and When Did They Know It? What Archaeology Can Tell Us about the Reality of Ancient Israel.* Grand Rapids: Eerdmans.

Dietrich, Walter. 1972. *Prophetie und Gechichte: Eine redaktionsgeschichtliche Untersuchung zum deuteronomistichen Geschichtswerk.* FRLANT 108. Göttingen: Vandenhoeck & Ruprecht.

Eissfeldt, Otto. 1965. *The Old Testament: An Introduction.* Translated by P. Ackroyd. Oxford: Basil Blackwell.

Flanagan, James W. 1972. "Court History or Succession Document? A Study of 2 Samuel 9–20 and 1 Kings 1–2." *JBL* 91:172–81.

Fohrer, Georg. 1968. *Introduction to the Old Testament.* Initiated by E. Sellin. Completely rev. and rewritten by G. Fohrer. Trans. D. Green. Nashville: Abingdon.

Liver, J. 1967. "The Book of the Acts of Solomon." *Bib* 48:75–101.

Miller, Patrick D., Jr. and J. J. M. Roberts. 1977. *The Hand of the Lord: A Reassessment of the "Ark Narrative" of 1 Samuel.* Baltimore: Johns Hopkins Univ. Press.

Nelson, Richard D. 1981. *The Double Redaction of the Deuteronomistic History.* JSOTSup 18. Sheffield: JSOT Press.

Noth, Martin. 1981. *A History of Pentateuchal Traditions.* Translated with an introduction by B. W. Anderson. Chico, Calif.: Scholars Press. German original, 1948.

———. 1991. *The Deuteronomistic History.* JSOTSup 15. 2d ed. Sheffield: JSOT Press. German original, 1943.

O'Brien, Mark. 1989. *The Deuteronomistic History Hypothesis: A Reassessment.* OBO 92. Freiburg: Universitätsverlag.

Rost, Leonhard. 1982. *The Succession to the Throne of David.* Historic Texts and Interpreters in Biblical Scholarship 1. Sheffield: Almond. German original, 1926.

Smend, Rudolf. 1971. "Das Gesetz und die Völker: Ein Beitrag zur deuteronomistischen Redaktionsgeschichte." Pages 494–509 in *Probleme biblischer Theologie: Gerhard von Rad zum 70. Geburtstag.* Edited by H. W. Wolff. Munich: Kaiser.

Van Seters, John. 1994. *The Life of Moses: The Yahwist as Historian in Exodus–Numbers.* Louisville. Ky.: Westminster John Knox.

Veijola, Timo. 1975. *Die ewige Dynastie: David und die Entstehung seiner Dynastie nach der deuteronomistischen Darstellung.* AASF B 193. Helsinki: Suomalainen Tiedeakatemia.

———. 1977. *Das Königtum in der Beurteilung der deuteronomistischen Historiographie: Eine redaktionsgeschichtliche Untersuchung.* AASF B 198. Helsinki: Suomalainen Tiedeakatemia.

Commentaries

A bibliography of selected current commentaries

Bibliographical details provided here are not repeated within the relevant chapters. Other works by these scholars cited in the treatment of each book are listed in the bibliographies at the end of each chapter.

Joshua

Boling, Robert G. 1982. *Joshua*. AB 6. Garden City, N.Y.: Doubleday.
Butler, Trent C. 1983. *Joshua*. WBC 7. Waco, Tex: Word.
Fritz, Volkmar. 1994. *Das Buch Josua*. HAT 1/7. Tübingen: Mohr (Siebeck).
Gray, John. 1967. *Joshua, Judges, and Ruth*. NCB. London: Thomas Nelson & Sons.
Hawk, L. Daniel. 2000. *Joshua*. Berit Olam. Collegeville. Minn.: Liturgical Press.
Nelson, Richard D. 1997. *Joshua*. OTL. Louisville, Ky.: Westminster John Knox.
Noth, Martin. 1971. *Das Buch Josua*. HAT 1/7. 3d ed. Tübingen: Mohr (Siebeck). First edition, 1938.
Pressler, Carolyn. 2002. *Joshua, Judges, and Ruth*. Louisville, Ky.: Westminster John Knox.
Soggin, J. Alberto. 1972. *Joshua*. OTL. London: SCM Press.

Judges

Amerding, Carl E. 1999. *Judges*. WBC 8. Waco, Tex: Word.
Boling, Robert G. 1975. *Judges*. AB 6A. Garden City, N.Y.: Doubleday.
Gray, John. 1967. *Joshua, Judges and Ruth*. NCB. London: Thomas Nelson & Sons.
Martin, James D. 1975. *The Book of Judges*. CBC. Cambridge: Cambridge Univ. Press.
Moore, George F. 1898. *Judges*. ICC. Edinburgh: T. & T. Clark.
Pressler, Carolyn. 2002. *Joshua, Judges, and Ruth*. Louisville, Ky.: Westminster John Knox.

Schneider, Tammi. 1999. *Judges*. Berit Olam. Collegeville, Minn.: Liturgical Press.
Soggin, J. Alberto. 1987. *Judges*. 2d ed. London: SCM Press.

Brenner, Athalya, ed. 1993. *A Feminist Companion to Judges*. Sheffield: Sheffield Academic Press.
———. 1999. *Judges: A Feminist Companion to the Bible*. Second series. Sheffield: Sheffield Academic Press, 1999.

Ruth

Bush, Frederic. 1996. *Ruth, Esther*. WBC 9. Dallas: Word.
Campbell, Edward F. 1975. *Ruth*. AB 7. Garden City, N.Y.: Doubleday.
Gray, John. 1967. *Joshua, Judges and Ruth*. NCB. London: Thomas Nelson & Sons.
Linafelt, Tod. 1999. *Ruth*. Berit Olam. Collegeville: Liturgical Press.
Nielsen, Kirsten. 1997. *Ruth*. OTL. London: SCM Press.
Pressler, Carolyn. 2002. *Joshua, Judges, and Ruth*. Louisville, Ky.: Westminster John Knox.
Sasson, Jack M. 1979. *Ruth*. JHNES. Baltimore: Johns Hopkins Univ. Press.
Wolde, Ellen van. 1997. *Ruth and Naomi*. London: SCM Press.

Brenner, Athalya, ed. 1993. *A Feminist Companion to Ruth*. Sheffield: Sheffield Academic Press.
———. 1999. *Ruth and Esther: A Feminist Companion to the Bible*. Second series. Sheffield: Sheffield Academic Press.

Samuel

Anderson, A. A. 1989. *2 Samuel*. WBC 11. Waco, Tex: Word.
Brueggemann, Walter. 1990. *First and Second Samuel*. Interpretation. Louisville, Ky.: John Knox.
Campbell, Antony F. 2003. *1 Samuel*. FOTL 7. Grand Rapids: Eerdmans.
———. In press. *2 Samuel*. FOTL 8. Grand Rapids: Eerdmans.
Hertzberg, Hans Wilhelm. 1964. *I and II Samuel*. OTL. London: SCM Press.
Klein, Ralph W. 1983. *1 Samuel*. WBC 10. Waco, Tex: Word.
Mauchline, John. 1971. *1 and 2 Samuel*. NCB. London: Oliphants.
McCarter, P. Kyle, Jr. 1980–84. *I–II Samuel*. AB 8–9. Garden City, N.Y.: Doubleday.
Smith, Henry Preserved. 1992. *The Books of Samuel*. ICC. Edinburgh: T. & T. Clark.
Stoebe, Hans Joachim. 1973–94. *Das erste und das zweite Buch Samuelis*. KAT VIII/1–2. Gütersloh: Mohn.

Brenner, Athalya, ed. 1994. *A Feminist Companion to Samuel and Kings*. Sheffield: Sheffield Academic Press.
———. 2000. *Samuel and Kings: A Feminist Companion to the Bible*. Second series. Sheffield: Sheffield Academic Press, 2000.

Kings

Cogan, Mordechai. 2001. *1 Kings*. AB 10. Garden City: Doubleday.

Cogan, Mordechai, and Hayim Tadmor. 1988. *II Kings*. AB 11. Garden City: Doubleday.

Cohn, Robert L. 2000. *2 Kings*. Berit Olam. Collegeville, Minn.: Liturgical Press.

DeVries, Simon J. 1985. *1 Kings*. WBC 12. Waco, Tex.: Word.

Gray, John. 1964/70. *I and II Kings*. OTL. 2d ed. Philadelphia: Westminster.

Hobbes, T. R. 1985. *2 Kings*. WBC 13. Waco, Tex.: Word.

Jones, Gwilym H. 1984. *1 and 2 Kings*. 2 vols. NCB 7. Grand Rapids: Eerdmans.

Long, Burke O. 1984. *1 Kings*. FOTL 9. Grand Rapids: Eerdmans.

———. 1991. *2 Kings*. FOTL 10. Grand Rapids: Eerdmans.

Montgomery, James A. 1951. *The Books of Kings*. Edited by H. S. Gehman. ICC. Edinburgh: T. & T. Clark.

Nelson, Richard. 1987. *First and Second Kings*. Interpretation. Louisville, Ky.: John Knox.

Noth, Martin. 1968/1983. *Könige*. Vol. 1, *I. Könige 1–16*. BKAT 9/1. Neukirchen-Vluyn: Neukirchener Verlag.

Walsh, Jerome T. 1996. *I Kings*. Berit Olam. Collegeville, Minn.: Liturgical Press.

Chronicles

Braun, Roddy. 1986. *1 Chronicles*. WBC 14. Waco, Tex.: Word.

Curtis, Edward Lewis, and Albert Alonzo Madsen. 1910. *The Books of Chronicles*. ICC. Edinburgh: T. & T. Clark.

De Vries, Simon J. 1989. *1 and 2 Chronicles*. FOTL 11. Grand Rapids: Eerdmans.

Dillard, Raymond B. 1987. *2 Chronicles*. WBC 15. Waco, Tex.: Word.

Hooker, Paul K. 2001. *First and Second Chronicles*. Louisville, Ky.: Westminster John Knox.

Japhet, Sara. 1993. *I and II Chronicles*. OTL. Louisville, Ky.: Westminster John Knox.

Johnstone, William. 1997. *1 and 2 Chronicles*. 2 vols. JSOTSup 253–54. Sheffield: Sheffield Academic Press.

Myers, Jacob M. 1965. *I–II Chronicles*. AB 12–13. Garden City, N.Y.: Doubleday.

Rudolph, Wilhelm. 1955. *Chronikbücher*. HAT 21. Tübingen: Mohr (Siebeck).

Tuell, Steven S. 2001. *First and Second Chronicles*. Interpretation. Louisville, Ky.: John Knox.

Williamson, H. G. M. 1982. *1 and 2 Chronicles*. NCB. Grand Rapids: Eerdmans.

Synoptic Parallels

Bendavid, Abba. 1972. *Parallels in the Bible*. Jerusalem: Carta.

Endres, John, William R. Millar, and John Barclay Burns (with contributors). 1998. *Chronicles and Its Synoptic Parallels in Samuel, Kings, and Related Biblical Texts*. A Michael Glazier Book. Collegeville, Minn.: Liturgical Press.

Vannutelli, Primus. 1931. *Libri Synoptici Veteris Testamenti seu Librorum Regum et Chronicorum Loci Paralleli, Quos Hebraice Graece et Latine Critice Edidit Primus Vannutelli*. Rome: Pontifical Biblical Institute.

Selected Studies

Graham, M. P., and S. L. McKenzie, eds. 1999. *The Chronicler as Author: Studies in Text and Texture*. JSOTSup 263. Sheffield: Sheffield Academic Press.

Graham, M. P., K. G. Hoglund and S. L. McKenzie, eds. 1997. *The Chronicler as Historian*. JSOTSup 238. Sheffield: Sheffield Academic Press.

Jones, Gwilym H. 1993. *1 and 2 Chronicles*. OTG. Sheffield: JSOT Press.

Kalimi, Isaac. 1990. *The Books of Chronicles: A Classified Bibliography*. Simor Bible Bibliographies. Jerusalem: Simor.

McKenzie, Steven L. 1985. *The Chronicler's Use of the Deuteronomistic History*. HSM 33. Atlanta: Scholars Press.

Noth, Martin. 1987. *The Chronicler's History*. JSOTSup 50. Sheffield: JSOT Press. German original, 1943.

Scripture Index

(Biblical citations correspond to NRSV versification. Parenthetical references are to the Hebrew text.)

Subject Index